I0879876

Blues, How Do You Do?

Blues, How Do You Do?

Paul Oliver and the Transatlantic Story of the Blues

Christian O'Connell

University of Michigan Press • Ann Arbor

Copyright © by Christian O'Connell 2015
All rights reserved

This book may not be reproduced, in whole or in part, including illustrations, in any form (beyond that copying permitted by Sections 107 and 108 of the U.S. Copyright Law and except by reviewers for the public press), without written permission from the publisher.

Published in the United States of America by
the University of Michigan Press
Manufactured in the United States of America
♾ Printed on acid-free paper

2018 2017 2016 2015 4 3 2 1

A CIP catalog record for this book is available from the British Library.

ISBN 978–0-472–07267-5 (hardcover)
ISBN 978-0-472-05267-7 (paper)
ISBN 978–0-472–12112-0 (e-book)

Contents

Acknowledgments

This book is the product of a long-standing fascination for African American music, and a continuing investigation into the reasons why the music of black Americans in the first half of the twentieth century has had such an impact on people across the world. While my personal interest in this music, in American and African American history, and in the processes of "Americanization" have led me to this study, I have been privileged by the level of support I have received. First and foremost I would like to thank Neil Wynn for his role in my development as a researcher and historian. His historical expertise and genuine interest, combined with his direct and sometimes uncompromising words of wisdom, have been invaluable. A special debt of gratitude goes to Brian Ward, whose work has provided inspiration, and whose support and advice have been hugely beneficial. I would also like to thank my fellow historians at University of Gloucestershire: Iain Robertson, Melanie Ilic, Anna French, and Vicky Morrisroe, who were very supportive of this project, helping to obtaining research funding and providing valuable feedback in research seminars. My sincerest thanks also goes to Lorna Scott at the Archives at the University of Gloucestershire, who had to endure many of my queries and tolerate my presence on many occasions when I was making use of the Paul Oliver Collection of African American Music and Related Traditions. Other past and present colleagues at the University of Gloucestershire also deserving of thanks are Joe Wilson, Shelley Saguaro, Debby Thacker, Kate Page, John Hockey, Rachel Reid, Ros Jennings, and many others. My fellow postgraduates, Nikki Rivers, Rowan Middleton, Nigel Harrison, and Shelley Campbell among others, provided warm audiences and constructive criticism in our guerilla-style postgraduate research seminars.

This book was supported by a number of organizations that gave me the opportunities to conduct the necessary research: the British Association of

American Studies (BAAS) provided funds to visit the Blues Archive at the University of Mississippi, and to make my first visit to the Mississippi Delta region; the Eccles Centre provided a fellowship that allowed time to consult the wealth of resources held at the British Library; and finally the Royal Historical Society, whose support allowed me to present and confront my research at various conferences. Thanks also to Helen Kirby at Devon Transcription for her speedy services and infinite patience. On the subject of patience, I want to thank my wife, Raquel, and my family, who have needed it in abundance to tolerate me over the many years this project has been in making. I would not have been able to begin or finish this project had it not been for their words of encouragement, their moral support, their occasional (and justified) frustration and reprimands.

Over the course of this project, I have been very fortunate to meet and speak to a number of musicians and writers that have provided invaluable insights into their experiences of discovering the blues and experiencing the blues revival. Tom McGuiness and Bob Groom deserve special thanks for agreeing to be interviewed and providing some fascinating information used in this book. I would also like to thank Elijah Wald, Duck Baker, Denny Ilett, Will Kaufman, Robert Riesman, David Evans, Adam Gussow, and William Ferris, for their advice and encouragement. Michael Roach of the European Blues Association was kind to provide his support for this project, and provide time for the occasional jam; Marcel Vellinga was on hand to tolerate me on the issue of permissions. Overall, however, my greatest thanks and deepest debt is owed to Paul Oliver, who I interviewed over three years in his Oxfordshire home. These conversations, which provided fascinating, revealing, and sometimes moving insights into the long and wide-ranging history of the blues, will live long in my memory, and I sincerely hope that this book helps to place him firmly at the center of scholarship on the blues.

Introduction

In the 1950s and 1960s African American music emerged as one of the major influences in white popular music on both sides of the Atlantic. A remarkable aspect of this movement was the significance of the blues in providing inspiration for groups and individuals such as the Rolling Stones, Alexis Korner, The Animals, The Yardbirds, Eric Clapton, Peter Green's Fleetwood Mac, and John Mayall. However, while popular narratives about how the Brits discovered the blues and took it back to America have, unsurprisingly, played a central role in histories of pop music in the 1960s, there is another significant story that has been blurred from view. The "blues revival" was accompanied, but also preceded, by a significant body of research and writing on the blues. One of the most prominent and influential writers is the Englishman Paul Oliver, who over a period of sixty years has written some of the best-known and widely referenced books on the subject, including *Blues Fell This Morning: The Meaning of the Blues* (1960), *Conversation with the Blues* (1965), and *The Story of the Blues* (1969). Such is Oliver's reputation among blues historians that leading American ethnomusicologist David Evans argued, "it would hardly be an exaggeration to state that most of our present understanding of the blues is based on the work of Paul Oliver." Other notable blues writers have supported Evans's claims. William Ferris argues that Oliver "pioneered the study of blues"; and Paul Garon believes that the British author "is surely the most important commentator on the blues in the world today." The ethnomusicologist and author of *Early Downhome Blues* (1977), Jeff Titon, affirmed that Oliver's first major book on the subject, *Blues Fell This Morning,* became the model for young academics who began to make the blues the subject of their research. So deep has Oliver's influence been in the field that some writers have even referred to an "Oliverian" tradition of blues scholarship.[1]

With this in mind, one would imagine that any reconsideration of the nature of blues writing throughout the twentieth century would spend a considerable amount of time scrutinizing the British scholar's contribution. However, Oliver barely features at all in either Elijah Wald's *Escaping the Delta: Robert Johnson and the Invention of the Blues* (2004), or Marybeth Hamilton's *In Search of the Blues: Black Voices, White Visions* (2007). These writers have convincingly argued that blues scholarship during the fifties, sixties, and beyond has been as much about "invention" as it has been about discovery.[2] They suggest that, since the revival, the blues has been repeatedly represented as an authentic African American folk culture at odds with popular music and the commercialism of the music industry. Blues singers, such as Robert Johnson, have been idolized as noble rebels that renounced the worldly benefits of commercial success in favor of their art. By contrast, Wald and Hamilton have emphasized that the blues was the popular music of its time, and part of the music industry, and therefore much more *modern* in character. Revivalist blues writers of the 1960s, however, caught up in the heightened romanticism following the discovery of this seemingly forgotten and mysterious music, reframed the blues based on what they *wanted* to see: a "folk" form that was opposed aesthetically and philosophically to commercialism or any notion of "pop" music.

So far Wald and Hamilton have only told an American story, and focused on the role of notable American folklorists, collectors, and scholars involved in defining representations of the blues, such as Alan Lomax, Frederic Ramsey, Samuel Charters, and James McKune. There is no doubt that the blues is American music with origins firmly rooted in the African American experience of the late nineteenth and early twentieth centuries, but the story of its journey through the public consciousness and its reverberations within popular memory since World War II has not been limited by the same physical and cultural boundaries. Therefore, this book will attempt to move away from nationally or ethnocentrically based discourses of blues historiography by acknowledging the transatlantic character of blues appreciation and writing in the postwar era. Oliver's seminal scholarship demonstrates that the music existed within a much more fluid context of cultural intermixture, permitted by the increasing availability of music through mass media and transatlantic interactions during the fifties and sixties. Therefore, through a close examination of the manner in which Oliver researched and wrote about the blues, we can gain an insight into the ways in which the music was interpreted and reconstituted through a range of methods, from the analysis of lyrics, field trips to the United States, oral history, photography, to the writing of blues history. This introduction will begin by placing a study of Oliver's work within the context of the current revisionist emphasis on the "invention" of the blues, and demonstrate the need for a detailed consideration his contribution to "our present understanding of the blues."

The "Invention" of the Blues: Origins and Debates

Traditionally, written interpretations of the blues and blues history have been victims of what George Lipsitz has defined as one of the main problems of popular culture studies: the subjective aesthetic criteria driving the analysis of cultural texts.[3] In other words, the writers themselves have arbitrarily decided what is blues and what is not, what is authentic and what is inauthentic, and who the *real* blues musicians are, and who are not. As a consequence, the music has all too often been framed within the context of a binary opposition between white popular (and thus commercial) culture and black folk culture. Obviously, there are clear cultural distinctions that can be made between the music of African American musicians during the 1920s and 1930s, and the white Anglo-American blues aficionados of the 1950s and 1960s. However, in terms of the manner in which the history of the blues has been interpreted and written, and as Wald and Hamilton have convincingly argued, the opposition of black folk versus white pop has often led to an idealization of blues singers as folk heroes, outsiders and rebels against the consumerism of the fickle entertainment industry. The fact that the blues emerged amid the harsh realities of racial segregation and social deprivation augmented the sense that the music represented distinct human qualities of heroic dignity and resilience. This is best exemplified by the music journalist Robert Palmer in his famous history *Deep Blues* (1981): "It's the story of a small and deprived group of people who created, against tremendous odds, something that has enriched us all."[4] The tendency has been to envision the most deprived and those most distant from mainstream culture as the most representative of the blues idiom, giving rise to the popular conception of the "bluesman":

> The men and women who played and sang the blues were mostly poor, propertyless, disreputable itinerants, many of them illiterate, many of them loners, many of them living on the edge. Rejecting the static lives of their parents, almost always on the move, they felt freer than most, and prided themselves on being masterless, on being able to enjoy a

> freedom of movement and expression denied many of their people, on being free from a labor system that tied others (including their families) to the land through violence, coercion, and the law.[5]

The rebels described here have most often been identified with the Mississippi Delta, creating an almost supernatural link between blues singers and their environment. The Delta, the heart of the Deep South and plantation slavery in the nineteenth century, has been frequently viewed as the heartland of the blues, as it was also the home of singers such as Charley Patton, Robert Johnson, Skip James, and Muddy Waters. This is a legacy that lives on strongly today, as thousands of tourists from around the world follow the Mississippi Blues Trail each year.[6] Terms such as the "poorest" and "blackest" region of the South frequently characterize descriptions of the area in blues histories, and while these terms accurately describe the region, the emphasis blues scholars place on the Delta reveals the significance they placed on the relationship between the experience of ordinary African Americans, and the Deep South.[7] This is accompanied by a distinctive sense of awe and fascination for the music, built around the thematic narrative of beauty arising from tragedy, of humanity surviving, as Litwack put it, "against tremendous odds." Ted Gioia likened the Delta to "a Third World country [that] had been abandoned in the heart of the United States."[8] These visions have most frequently been personified by the legendary singer Robert Johnson, who was represented as the "King of the Delta" blues during the revival, and for many blues scholars has since then personified "the African American voice as it sounded before the record companies got to it."[9] Many of these blues tropes still persist today. An example can be seen in the question directed to the musician Seasick Steve (who was promoting his new album, *Man From Another Time*) on BBC Breakfast on British television in 2009:

> PRESENTER: It's blues music that evokes a kind of hobo lifestyle, and people talk about your background in that way. Tell us a bit about where you were before you got to where you are.

Steve's response was telling:

> SEASICK S.: Well, you know, that's like another problem I have. People think they found me under a bridge a few years ago, but I raised five boys, you know, I had normal jobs, I had thirty-five years. . . . But when I was a young fella, I had to leave home when I was thirteen, and I did some pretty rough living and wandering around. We used

> to ride trains or hitchhike, and follow migrant work around the farmwork. But, you know, that ended many years ago, and I just sort of had to be, tried to be a regular fella.[10]

The interview on the morning show echoes the events of the sixties blues revival, when ageng and forgotten African American blues singers such as Son House, Skip James, and Bukka White were "rediscovered" and presented to mainstream white audiences. Indeed, Seasick Steve's aptly titled album also supports the idea of a past in the process of being rediscovered. As the singer demonstrates in his answer to the stereotype that he was not discovered "under a bridge" and was more of a family man, this imagined perception of blues musicians needs to be constantly challenged with the reality.

The problematic processes of discovery and rediscovery were addressed by the American ethnomusicologist Jeff Titon, who recalled the activities of blues enthusiasts during the 1960s revival:

> The governing metaphor at the time for what we were doing was "discovery" and "rediscovery," as if what we were doing was finding something that was unknown or had been lost. But the notion of discovery is complex, as anyone knows who has thought about the grade-school "fact" that Columbus discovered America. Our discoveries, like those of the European explorers, were mixtures of invention and interpretation, and in a way instead of finding our object, blues, we constituted it.

In recent years blues enthusiasts of the sixties blues revival have been able to—borrowing an expression from Titon—"turn a reflexive eye" on their own early experiences with the music.[11] Titon, Wald, Hamilton, and Karl Hagstrom Miller have sought to deconstruct some of the major assumptions about the blues, blues singers, and black and white music, following the trend of revising popular music history such as in Scott DeVeaux's analysis of jazz histories and Richard Peterson's of country music.[12] The reconsideration of blues scholarship seems to have been motivated in no small part by a personal sense of self-reflection. Wald recalls being captivated by the romantic vision of the music as an early blues fan, prior to a moment of clarity in which he began to realize that the music he had imagined bore little resemblance to the historical reality.[13] Similarly, the photographs Hamilton took of the landscape in her visit to the Mississippi Delta at first seemed to mark the entrance into "'a mythic, primordial world,' and it would take several months "for the spell to be broken," allowing a more considered interpretation of the images.[14] In these confrontations with prevalent attitudes, these writers have aimed to challenge depictions that saw the blues represented as an authentic folk music with roots firmly within working-class African American culture, and of bluesmen as anticonformist heroes.

The revisionist emphasis has been on the social and cultural distance separating the music and the blues enthusiasts of the revival. Wald, for instance, argues that blues writing has been dominated by white middle-class enthusiasts whose remoteness from the context of the music has created a tendency for blues research "to be permeated with a romanticism that obscures at least as much as it illuminates." For Wald, the neglect of empirical evidence in favor of romanticized interpretations resulted in figures such as Robert Johnson, who sold relatively little and was largely unknown even to African American audiences in his own time, becoming idolized and revered as a fundamental musician in the history of African American music. This was at the expense of singers who were more widely known among black audiences, more successful commercially, and therefore more culturally significant, such as Leroy Carr or the Mississippi Sheiks.[15] Marybeth Hamilton, on the other hand, focused her study on the manner in which folklorists, writers, and enthusiasts from Alan Lomax to the enigmatic collector James McKune (spearhead of the "blues mafia") "felt imaginatively tied to the South" and in their quests for "authentic black voices . . . remade the blues itself."[16]

While the revision of blues scholarship would seem to be a recent phenomenon, the prevalent representations of the blues from the time of the revival have always been under scrutiny. Even amid the blues boom of the sixties, Charles Keil was highly critical of writing that marginalized more urban blues forms in favor of what those of the "moldy fig mentality" saw as the *real* blues:

> The criteria for a real blues singer, implicit or explicit, are the following. Old age: the performer should preferably be more than sixty years old, blind, arthritic, and toothless (as Lonnie Johnson put it, when first approached for an interview, "Are you another one of those guys who wants to put crutches under my ass?"). Obscurity: the blues singer should not have performed in public or have made a recording in at least twenty years; among deceased bluesmen, the best seem to be those who appeared in a big city one day in the 1920's, made from four to six recordings, and then disappeared into the countryside forever. Correct tutelage: the singer should have played with or been taught by some legendary figure. Agrarian milieu: the bluesman should have lived the bulk of his life as a sharecropper, coaxing mules and picking cotton, uncontaminated by city influences.[17]

Keil drew attention to the divergence between blues writers and musicians, implying that certain representations were being imposed on musicians. Albert Murray followed suit and, like Keil, criticized the widespread conceptions of the folk blues musicians as "fallacious," arguing that what was interpreted as traditional, self-taught, and instinctive in blues from the race records era of the 1920s and 1930s was actually closer to being derivative and conventional in reality. Essentially, Murray was highlighting the constructed nature of "folk" as a category upon which many revivalist interpretations of the blues rested: "There are those who assume that folk simplicity represents a deliberate, down-to-earth, self-confident rejection of over-refinement and decadence. . . . It is no such thing."[18] Both Keil and Murray were unconvinced by the motives of the "moldy figs" that associated the more authentic forms of blues with a folk ideal at odds with the commercialism of the mainstream. They therefore felt that the folk/urban divide was not an accurate reflection of African American reality. The segregation of music into arbitrary folk and commercial categories failed to acknowledge that what was regarded as commercial was also culturally significant for black audiences.

Probably the most important characteristic of music scholarship that has conditioned the written interpretations of the blues is what Karl Hagstrom Miller refers to as the "folkloric paradigm." This approach to the study of the blues developed out of the late nineteenth-century emergence of folklore studies, and Miller demonstrates that the paradigm has come to pervade most studies of music seen as rooted within rural cultures. In essence, the folkloric paradigm relied on an often exaggerated ideal of a pure folk culture and identity as a way of reacting to the oppressive forces of modernity. As a consequence, in the work of major blues scholars such as Alan Lomax, Samuel Charters, and Robert Palmer, black folk cultures are imagined as pure, unchanging, untouched by the modern ideals of progress or consumerism, and representative of real folk voices. It is in this approach that the classical divisions between folk and pop emerge in popular histories of the blues.[19] During the blues revival, the folkloric paradigm found many adherents considering the frequency of counterhegemonic social upheavals and movements. As Titon suggests, the postwar Beat movement and folk revival both played a large part in paving the way for the identification of white rebels and nonconformists with the music of a segregated minority such as the blues.[20] Importantly, the emphasis here on the constructed nature of the folk category is not an attempt to deny the existence of a blues tradition, or that certain "folk" characteristics of the blues, such a local styles (Delta, Piedmont, Texas, etc.) are invalid. There has been considerable musicological scholarship in this area to argue otherwise. For instance, Evans's comparison of four different recorded versions of Tommy Johnson's "Big Road Blues" in the area of Drew, Mississippi, revealed the persistence of compositional elements consistent with a folk blues tradition, traits that did not disappear with the onset of records or radio.[21] Nonetheless, drawing attention to the malleability of the folk as a theoretical concept allows us to examine and question the romantic nature of blues scholarship during the revival.

The trend of reconsidering blues scholarship seems to share an affinity with the deconstruction of the "folk" category in cultural studies. Robin Kelley began to question the very nature of the concept by arguing that terms such as "folk" and "traditional" can only really be understood if considered alongside the terms "modern" and "commercial." Definitions are always developed in opposition, based on contemporary attitudes toward issues such as race, gender, hierarchy, and class.[22] Kelley effectively made the case that what was considered folk could never quite be the stable and unchanging entity it was imagined to be. Benjamin Filene applied this to the history of American vernacular music more generally by demonstrating that folk categorizations are constantly in flux and never stable, thus resisting simple definitions. The notion of folk authenticity in music has repeatedly been redefined to cope with the changing nature of whatever has been considered "commercial." In one effective example, he demonstrates how the categorization of Muddy Waters—firstly as a down-home blues singer, then a "down-home" commercial blues singer, followed by commercial pop star, and finally as an old-time roots musician later in his career—exemplifies the unstable and constructed nature of folk authenticity.[23] It therefore seems that the idea of the folk rested on an arbitrary definition of something that was rooted in the past, but the instability of its conceptualization meant that the folk category was in a constant process of redefinition. Being rooted in the past also meant that the folk concept had what David Nicholls refers to as an "hallucinatory effect." While referring to African American literature, he argued that its use as an "organizing trope" for racial heritage and cultural pride was as much the product of a reaction and resistance to modernity, as it was an actual discovery of an African American past.[24] Thus, interpretations and representations of folk cultures such as the blues have always been determined by a dialogue between an imagined past and a seeming dissatisfaction with the present.

In seeking to counter the biased and exaggerated depictions of the folk, revisionist writers have focused their efforts on uncovering historical events that have either been forgotten or deliberately ignored. Miller's study aims to uncover a more realistic history that challenges the simplistic view of wholly "segregated" white and black musical cultures. He thus seeks a story more faithful to historical events than the whims of "folkie" revivalists. The attempt to reveal a more objective past is the first of the two main approaches employed in revisionist blues writing. Wald's investigation into the white representations of Robert Johnson seeks to reveal events that have been blurred from view. Evidence of the singer's poor record sales and relative anonymity among African American audiences indicate that rather than being a "folk hero," Johnson was much more similar to a present day "wannabe" who was trying to "make it." Similarly, Hamilton demonstrates how revivalists and historians have persistently adopted romanticized visions of history at the expense of more reliable historical sources. An example is provided by the recurrent use of W. C. Handy's first encounter with the blues as the marker for the genesis of the genre in blues histories. Blues scholars, she argues, have repeatedly fallen for the romantic image of Handy hearing a musician playing the guitar on a lonely Delta railway platform in 1903, neglecting the more reliable evidence provided in the research of Howard B. Odum that had pointed to the existence of the blues much earlier than Handy's autobiography.[25]

The recent focus on the "invention" of the blues has also been influenced by an appreciation of the role of historical analysis in popular culture. Wald states that much of the writing on the blues during the revival was produced retrospectively. The historical gap between the context of the 1960s revival and pre–World War II blues favored a lack of considered appreciation for the historical realities of the music, as well as the indulgence of personal fantasies on the part of revivalist writers.[26] For Wald, therefore, invention is synonymous with bad historical practice and an overpersonalized involvement of the blues writer with the music. Hamilton takes this approach further by examining the work of what she calls "mediators and shapers of taste," such as the Lomaxes, Frederic Ramsey Jr., and James McKune, arguing that their work is more revealing of their "fears and obsessions" than of the blues itself. Echoing the thoughts of Titon, she argued that the work of revivalists was indicative of the influence of the Beat movement's notion of a "male flight from commitment," manifested in the idealization of bluesmen.[27] This was an approach also adopted by Filene, who concentrated on the role of "middlemen," those protagonists who rather than simply presenting the music to audiences, reconstituted and reconditioned it to conform to their own ideals of "America's true musical traditions" and standards of authenticity.[28] He argues that folklorists, musicians, and scholars such as Lomax, Charters, and Willie Dixon actively participated in the advancement of "visions of America's musical past" and acted as "memory workers."[29] These protagonists, he argues, were constantly redefining and reconstructing this past by opposing it to an ever-changing modern musical landscape.

The Neglect of the "Transatlantic" and the Role of Paul Oliver

Phrases such as "America's musical traditions" and "America's musical past" indicate that writers such as Wald, Hamilton, and Filene have remained firmly within the borders of the United States when reconsidering the historiography of music scholarship. Consequently, "inventing the blues" is overwhelmingly depicted as an American story. This means that while the matter of the "British invasion" receives considerable attention in musical terms, the contribution of transatlantic scholarship in the "invention of the blues" has been underplayed, making light of the fact that Europeans (as well as others around the world) have been listening to and writing about the blues since World War II. This gap in current writing on the nature of blues scholarship outside the American narrative has begun to be addressed in recent years in Roberta Schwartz's survey of the reception of the blues in Britain, in Ulrich Adelt's consideration of representations of the blues and race in Germany, and in edited collections focusing on the influence of African American music in Europe.[30] Perhaps there still exists an element of resentment toward non-American interpretations of American music that lingers from Michael Bane's claim in the early eighties: "despite all the research, I think the English have a sort of very basic misunderstanding of what the music is all about . . . somewhere right at the beginning they missed a basic connection."[31] More recently these sentiments of cultural nationalism were echoed by Wald when he argued that Chicago-born harmonica player Paul Butterfield made "all the Brits sound like the foreigners they were." He also ascribes the misinterpretations of the blues to these "foreigners," by arguing that the blues as it exists today is "the image presented by Keith Richards and Mick Jagger."[32] The present author has experienced these sentiments first hand. Following a paper I gave on the subject of British blues scholarship at an international conference in Manchester, I was asked the following question in a somewhat cynical tone: "What makes the British the cultural custodians of this *American* music?"

Another strand extends this division to include racial discourses. Hamilton's subtitle, "black voices, white visions," is representative of this idea of not only a cultural disconnection, but one based on race. In many cases, however, it has been much more explicit. Voicing a deeply entrenched ambivalence toward cultural and critical miscegenation, Jon Michael Spencer makes the case that "white blues scholars do not fully understand the blues because they do not understand the threat and experience of getting their heads beaten." He, by contrast, knows "what it means to be black and currently living on the underside of history." He thus argues that the racial and cultural distance of white critics has been the primary reason behind a series of misinterpretations of African American culture and music, such as the "Anglo-Victorian" fascination for the blues as an erotically charged idiom at the expense of its spiritual side.[33] Spencer's vision of blues scholarship stems from a long line of ethnocentric writing that emanates from the Black Arts movement of the middle and late sixties, keen to stress that the blues belongs firmly within a hermetic culture separate from and alien to the white world.[34] For instance, in his definition of blues as "secular spirituals," James H. Cone applied the model of segregation from the race records era to blues scholarship. He argued that the music would only be decipherable from an African American perspective, as the black music communicated the "*feeling* and *thinking* of African people, and the kinds of mental adjustments they had to make in order to survive in an alien land." For Albert Murray, the misinterpretation of the function and meaning of black folk music would be elusive to "self-styled liberal jazz critics" who were not "native to the idiom." Similarly, Samuel Floyd Jr. argues that the "blues spoke a musical code decipherable by knowers of culture but inaccessible to those outside it."[35]

While these nationalistic and ethnocentric undercurrents seem counterproductive in the study of a music that has persistently crossed national and cultural borders, it must be said that popular portrayals of the British blues boom and the role of British musicians in getting the blues an audience in America, as portrayed in the BBC4 documentary *Blues Britannia*, tend to maintain rather than challenge an awkward sense of cultural nationalism.[36] It may be that too much has been made of popular narratives such as that of the British invasion, exemplified in Peter Hall's *Cities in Civilization*: "When The Beatles first came to America they told everyone they wanted to see Muddy Waters and Bo Diddley; one reporter asked: 'Muddy Waters . . . where's that?' Paul McCartney laughed and said, 'Don't you know who your own famous people are here?'"[37] Although there were inherent differences in the reception and appreciation of the blues between mainstream American and British audiences, scholarship on the subject was characterized by numerous transatlantic links that had existed since the early days of transatlantic jazz appreciation. The neglect of these links in the formation of blues scholarship means that there are still many more questions to be answered regarding interpretations of the blues during the 1950s and 1960s. Indeed, blues records had been available in Britain since the 1920s, and blues musicians began to visit the UK from the early fifties. Also, the early days of blues writing in the music press were characterized by frequent transatlantic correspondence and exchange of information. Importantly however, to include the transatlantic element in the examination of blues historiography does not equate to asserting the importance of the "British connection." In the same way that Miller sees a much more intertwined black and white musical landscape in the American South, in the postwar years the blues proliferated at a time of increasing mass media, which permitted fluidity of exchange across physical and cultural borders. And it was in this postwar transatlantic context that ideas about the blues and African American culture were constructed. As the availability of blues music increased through mass media, critics, collectors, and enthusiasts became fixated by origins and definitions at a time when these were becoming ever more elusive. One of the ways to examine blues scholarship within this expanded Western context is through the work of the British blues writer Paul Oliver.

For all the focus on "memory workers" and the "shapers of taste" that have influenced popular representations of the blues and blues musicians, it is remarkable that revisionist writers have so far neglected the British scholar's role. This is even more surprising given Oliver's vast influence in both Europe and the United States for more than half a century, as evidenced in the praise of other blues scholars for Oliver's contribution to the field. What is interesting about Oliver's scholarship is that it provides an example very different from that of other notable blues writers who have been seen to "invent" the subject of their studies. For instance, Oliver's interpretation of the blues did not always privilege the Mississippi Delta as the unquestionable heartland of the music, unlike the protagonists of Wald's and Hamilton's studies. His main point of interest was always centred on the relationship between the music and the social environment in which it emerged. This included African American society from the rural to the urban South, as well as other cities that had received an influx of black migrants throughout the early twentieth century. [38] Oliver also acknowledged the artistry and contribution of female singers in the development of the blues far more than many of his contemporaries, as his first book, the biographical *Bessie Smith* (1958), demonstrates. He is also very different from individuals such as Alan Lomax, who may have regarded himself "as spokesperson for the Other America, the common people, the forgotten and excluded [and] the ethnic."[39] Consequently, many commentators regard Oliver's scholarship as more carefully considered and objective than typical revivalist visions. Evans, for instance, admires "the fact that he is led to his conclusions by facts and evidence and not by preconceived notions, sweeping theories, or passing intellectual fads."[40] Perhaps for this reason he has not been a straightforward candidate for revisionist analysis. However, Oliver not only wrote some of the most well-known books on the subject, but he was also an avid record collector, conducted numerous interviews with blues singers in Britain and on his field trips to the United

States, became friends with a number of musicians, including Big Bill Broonzy and Brother John Sellers, and provided visual representations of the blues through his own illustrations and iconic photographs (many of which went on to be used as album covers for blues musicians). Thus, Oliver's vast scholarship in the postwar era provides an invaluable opportunity to examine the manner in which the music and African American culture were represented during the revival.

Blues and History

The research of blues scholars like Oliver during in the post–World War II era, or "blues evangelists" as Schwartz names them, was in many ways historical in nature. Searching for the origins of the blues, tracing the lives and recording histories of blues musicians, and analyzing the music's relationship to the lives of black Americans in the late nineteenth and early twentieth centuries were endeavors that entailed required methods of historical enquiry. However, very little was under the formal academic discipline heading of history. Indeed, as Wald suggests, the very notion of history became blurred with nostalgia as blues scholars aimed to revive a music that had been, they thought, forgotten by history and consumed by modernity. Similarly, Hamilton is mystified by the ease with which prominent historians such as Leon Litwack fall back on romanticized descriptions when talking about the blues. Perhaps the malleable nature of the past in the eyes and ears of blues writers was most evident in Robert Palmer's famous quote: "How much history can be transmitted by pressure on a guitar string? The thoughts of generations, the history of every human being who's ever felt the blues come down like showers of rain."[41] In reviving the history of the music, however, these evangelists, enthusiasts, and historians were reconstructing the blues' past into a series of narratives that became "history." While Oliver's scholarship was more focused on the relationship between the music and African American society, and provided an unrivalled amount of historical, biographical, and analytical information, it also presents many examples of this reconstruction process through a reinterpretation of the past.

Given the emphasis placed on the constructed—or at its extreme—"invented" nature of representing the past, the examination of blues scholarship here has adopted some elements of deconstructionist thought. But instead of applying Derridean or Foucaldian notions of deconstructionism to their apocalyptic levels, and rather than attempting to use empiricism to highlight the inaccuracies of blues scholars, I am more concerned with what Alun Munslow describes as "the de-layering of . . . constructed meanings and interpretations."[42] Correcting factual errors has been the focus of recent studies that have attempted to reveal that historically the blues was very different from how it was imagined by revivalists of the mid-twentieth century (this is not to say that it is futile or impossible to uncover historical truths, as in the recent studies by David Evans and Peter Muir), but that to understand the invention of the blues, it is necessary to focus on the way in which the blues was interpreted in the context in which it was experienced.[43] Blues scholars such as Oliver were working with and negotiating their understandings of the past: they were collecting records from the interwar years; they "(re)discovered" singers and interviewed them, focusing on their memories of the past; and they repeatedly visited the American South on what Hamilton refers to as a "cliché-ridden trail."[44] Importantly, this accumulated knowledge of the past was shaped by the transatlantic cultural context of the fifties and sixties.

The focus of this study is to examine the manner in which Oliver engaged with the blues, through listening to and transcribing records, befriending musicians, reviewing performances, interviewing and photographing them, and organizing huge amounts of historical information to produce a historical narrative. This follows Hayden White's argument that all historical evidence is "value neutral," requiring the writer to organize and impose significance upon these elements, thus "emplotting" them into a narrative.[45] As the historian Munslow argues, written history presents a plausible history rather than a definitive historical truth. This is not to say that historical events did not occur or that historical truths do not exist, but that *knowing* them fully and accurately is not possible in the ontological sense. Instead, knowledge of the past is more "provisional, relative and constructed." History is known through the negotiation of the historical narrative, produced by the author's "emplotment" of documents that exist in a "pre-jigsawed state." In Oliver's case, and as in that of many other blues historians, the use of historical documents can be examined in the reliance on rare recordings from the interwar era. The historical details these records carried in terms of both sound and lyrics represented historical fragments, a few parts of the jigsaw that helped to produce representations of the music and of African American culture. This approach gives an insight into the peculiarities of blues scholarship during the 1950s and 1960s, allowing us to comprehend the reasons why the blues and blues musicians were represented as they were. It may also allow us to understand the creation of romantic interpretations of the blues, rather than reject them wholeheartedly.

Adopting White's view of the historian-author also entails an appreciation of the writer's contemporary contextual circumstances, the social, political, and cultural forces that characterize his "here and now," his existence in the present that shapes the narrative of the past. As Richard Middleton states, the postwar era was characterized by the rise of "pop culture" within a context of an increasingly globalized mass market culture.[46] It saw the increasing diffusion and reach of mass media, the rise of youth culture, the boom of genres such as skiffle, rock'n'roll, and rhythm and blues. Importantly however, it was also the period of great social and political upheaval, with the growing momentum of the civil rights movement, the culture of the Beat generation, and the folk revivals. It was in these arenas that the blues was defined and, as Kelley and Filene have demonstrated, that ideals over folk authenticity and modernist consumerism were contested. The increasingly globalized nature of popular culture in the postwar era also created numerous possibilities for links between past and present, and for people to "acquire memories of a past to which they have no geographical or biological connection."[47] This possibility for the cross-fertilization and diffusion of cultural forms means that it is possible to espouse an idea of cultural hybridity, explained by Paul Gilroy's concept of the "doubleness" of black cultural forms within and outside definitions of modernity in the "black Atlantic." Gilroy explains the duality of late nineteenth-century black musical forms as they reappear through interpretations in the twentieth: "The anti-modernity of these forms, like their anteriority, appears in the (dis)guise of a premodernity that is both actively reimagined in the present and transmitted intermittently in eloquent pulses from the past."[48] If we borrow this concept for the analysis of blues scholarship, the dialogue and interaction between past and present within a transatlantic context meant that the blues was at once divorced from its social and geographical roots by interpreters from afar, while being rooted back within an imagined African American world by the same writers.

In the postwar era the blues became a source of cultural capital for both white and African American observers. It is obvious that for many white European audiences, identifying with the music of a segregated minority was a means of anticonformism, of defying convention, of supporting the lower classes and thus rebelling against the establishment. This can be seen from Oliver's experience of being condemned for playing jazz music at college, to the "rebellious" behavior of the Rolling Stones during the sixties. Frith and Horne conceptualized this more eloquently by arguing that in Britain the combined effect of the end of colonialism, rapid industrialization, and the unstoppable rise of capitalist culture meant that native folk forms were always in decline, paving the way with identification with external sources.[49] However, even for some African American audiences of the postwar era and the second half of the twentieth century, the blues has been a source of racial pride, heritage, and artistic inspiration. While the "New Negro" movement of the Harlem Renaissance may have regarded the music as lowbrow, for many African American authors the blues has been a huge resource. Adam Gussow has demonstrated that some writers of the sixties Black Arts movement were vociferous in their disapproval of the blues as the primary form of black culture, and espousing a conception of the music as a symbol of the old accommodationist Jim Crow South (i.e., Frantz Fanon's description of the blues as a "black slave lament" and Ron Karenga's assertion, "the blues are invalid"). However, for many other African American writers, the blues was a "cherished ancestral root-stock, an inalienably black cultural inheritance that could be put to political as well as aesthetic good use."[50] For black theorists of the post–Black Arts era such as Houston Baker Jr., the blues became conceptualized as "matrix," the "enabling *script* in which African American cultural discourse is inscribed." The "godfather of rap," Gil Scott-Heron, also defined himself as a "bluesologist," referring to the importance of understanding the origins of African American song, of human expression in dire social and economic, and psychological circumstances.[51] Considering the blues as this source of cultural capital in an era that permitted the intermixture of imagined cultural categories, this book moves away from politically or racially motivated debates on whether white men can sing—or, in this case, really understand—the blues. It is less important to focus on whether cultural outsiders can comment on the blues, than to acknowledge the fact cultural outsiders *do* and *have done*.

Oliver's work on the blues will be examined from the early fifties to the end of the sixties—his writing on the subject since then has been used only with reference to his work during the revival. The are two main reasons for this. First, Oliver published the main bulk of his books by the end of the sixties, before the author decided to take a break from extensive blues research in the seventies; second, this period corresponds with Wald's assertion that revivalist conceptions of the blues had become fully established by 1970, roughly coinciding with Oliver's last major book of the period, *The Story of the Blues* (1969).[52] However, it is important to remember that conceptualizations of the blues and race would continue to be shaped after 1970, with future publications such the American magazine *Living Blues* (which began to be published the same year), as well as scores of other books on the subject.[53]

In addition to the body of his written work during the fifties and sixties, several personal interviews have been conducted with Oliver in order to supplement the historical background of this period and to consider specific issues. These were particularly useful in obtaining additional information regarding more obscure aspects of his scholarship, such as his work during the fifties when writing for the specialist jazz press, and in the details of his 1960 field trip to the United States. These interviews have been used in the full knowledge that Oliver's recollections of these events are subject to the biases and omissions of memory, and often refer to the British writer's present thoughts on his past. As the oral historian Alessandro Portelli argues, "Oral sources tell us not just what people did, but what they wanted to do, what they believed they were doing, and what they now think they did."[54] The interviews therefore exhibited some of the typical problems of using oral history, particularly given that Oliver had the difficult task of recalling specific details of events from more than fifty years ago. In addition, as I am sure many who know and have worked with him will agree, Oliver's great generosity is outweighed only by his modesty. He regards himself as a minor figure in the history of the blues, meaning that it was often difficult to discuss some of the specifics about his personal life and scholarship. I hope that this book will go some way in changing his mind.

The first two chapters focus on Oliver's blues writing prior to visiting the United States for the first time in 1960. Chapter 1 begins by giving a brief biographical overview of Oliver's beginnings as a blues scholar, and goes on to examine his writing in British jazz periodicals such as *Music Mirror*, *Jazz Journal*, and *Jazz Monthly* during the fifties. This period was characterized by a reliance on records, which Oliver had been collecting since World War II. Blues music in Britain was the domain of a small group of British jazz enthusiasts who embraced blues as the foundations of jazz. However, it is also the period that saw the early formation of revivalist conceptions of the blues as a folk music that was separate from jazz, with roots in the African American experience of the early twentieth century. Interestingly, Oliver began to explore the background of African American life that produced the blues through the lyrics of songs. As well as relying on the work of American jazz writers such as Mezz Mezzrow, Rudi Blesh, Frederic Ramsey, and Charles Edwards, he made use of contemporary black literature, such as that of Richard Wright and Ralph Ellison, to inform his understanding of black culture. This functioned to increasingly blur the boundaries between fact and fiction. In addition, Oliver decorated articles with his own illustrations based on the content of blues songs, adding a visual insight into his interpretations. Importantly, this decade saw the first visits to Britain by black American blues singers. Responses to their performances and interviews provided a means of confronting the real with the imagined. However, the impressions built around the visits of these singers were to be largely dependent upon the skill of musicians, such as Big Bill Broonzy, to negotiate the expectations of transatlantic audiences, and supply the demand for the imagined *real* bluesman.

Oliver's prolific work and record collecting in the fifties led to the publication of two books at the end of the decade, a short biography, *Bessie Smith* (1958), and the passionate exploration of themes in blues lyrics, *Blues Fell This Morning,* which is the subject of chapter 2. This book, like many of Oliver's publications, has not been considered in revisionist scholarship despite appearing shortly after Samuel Charters's *The Country Blues* (1959), considered part of the canon of revivalist scholarship. In contrast to Charters who focused on the lives of individual singers, Oliver's monograph examined the lyrics of over 350 songs and sought to relate them in thematic categories to the lower-class African American experience of the early twentieth century. While it received a mixed reception, many hailed it as the first scholarly assessment of the music, and acknowledged the fact that the book presented the reality of the African American experience and the sociological context of the blues in candid terms. It also received support in the form of a foreword from Richard Wright, who praised Oliver for his objective insights into African American culture. The analysis of lyrics and the association of their meaning with notions of truth and reality reveal the processes by which ideas about the music were constructed by an audience reliant on recordings. The blues Oliver described was very different from that which young skifflers and rock'n'rollers interpreted as blues, revealing that the music was also a contested space among British audiences. Importantly however, it was also divorced from the contemporary social and political struggles of African Americans in the late fifties, revealing the manner in which Oliver identified with a more distant and remote folk culture.

After the book was published, Oliver conducted a field trip to the United States that was partly funded by the American Department of State and the BBC. Along with his wife Valerie and founder of Arhoolie records Chris Strachwitz, he interviewed, recorded, and photographed over seventy singers across the country. The trip was an opportunity for Oliver to confront the world he had been describing with the reality, and he concluded that "the relation of blues to context that I had described [in *Blues Fell This Morning*] proved to be correct."[55] The book that was published as a result, *Conversation with the Blues* (1965, the subject of chapter 3), was the first in a long line of photo-documentary-style publications on the subject of the blues. Indeed, books filled with interviews and images of blues musicians continue to be published in the present day, most recently in William Ferris's *Give My Poor*

Heart Ease: Voices of the Mississippi Blues (2009). Oliver's *Conversation* is a fascinating attempt to give the singers back their voice in the telling of the music's history. Importantly, while the interviews took place in 1960, the memories of the selected and cropped oral responses in the book serve to create a nostalgic attachment to the past, demonstrating the way oral history could contribute to promoting a distinctive and constructed idea of the blues, but also demonstrating how blues musicians could be complicit in this process. This is complemented by Oliver's use of black-and-white photographs that in many instances evoke images of the Farm Security Administration (FSA) photographers of the 1930s New Deal era. The backward-looking focus of the book helps to demarcate the blues from the newfound popularity of the blues during the revival, which Oliver regarded as posing a serious threat to the survival of the genre. This is even more interesting considering that the book was published in 1965, following the entry of the blues into the main echelons of sixties popular music.

Oliver's final two books of the sixties became more directly focused on historical analysis. The late sixties were a period in which blues scholarship was becoming much more specialized following the increased attention generated by the revival and the expanding area of ethnomusicology. Oliver returned to the analysis of blues lyrics in *Screening the Blues: Aspects of the Blues Tradition* (1968). Here the writer expanded on a number of previously written articles to trace the development of a tradition and an evolutionary link with the past. Chapter 4 examines the manner in which the attempt to trace the blues tradition reified the blues as a definable category with an idea of the past that regulated the present. The emphasis on the blues' roots within the past acted as a prelude to *The Story of the Blues* (1969). Chapter 5 discusses the problematic formation of the "blues narrative," which tells the unique story of the music and the culture in which it emerged. It was a story that formed strong categorical boundaries by giving the music a history of its own, but also importantly, indirectly proclaimed the music's demise following changes in African American society and the white "discovery" of the music. Adopting White's conception of the historian-author, it is possible to appreciate this book as a narrative organized from historical elements, and one that constructs a *story*, but at the same time erases from history many elements that revisionist writers have recently attempted to revive. Therefore, the chapter examines how the book contributed to the iconography of the blues that had been established by the end of the decade.

Oliver's scholarship demonstrates that the "invention" of the blues was much more complex than simply a process of white middle-class enthusiasts describing a black music and culture that was very different from their own.

While revisionist writing has pointed to the nostalgia and romanticism with which American blues collectors, enthusiasts, and scholars enshrined the blues and the lives of blues singers, Oliver's focus on the relationship between the music and African American life through analysis of lyrics, oral history, photography and history-writing demonstrates that even the most rigorous research was susceptible to romanticism, something embedded in the study of popular music. Moreover, Oliver's writing also evidences the historical circumstances within which blues appreciation and scholarship developed, from the changing nature of popular music to social and political developments in the postwar era, and allows a more detailed understanding of how perceptions of race influenced the representation of the blues. While there were undeniable differences between the approaches and representations of American and British scholars, popular conceptions of the blues were shaped within a transatlantic context, and national and sometimes racial boundaries have more often been imposed on the categorization of blues research by the ideologies of individual writers.

1 • Beginnings

The Early Revival

> Suddenly the air seemed split by the most eerie sounds. The two men were singing, swooping, undulating, unintelligible words, and the back of my neck tingled. "They're singing a *blues*," Stan hissed at me. It was the strangest, most compelling singing I'd ever heard. . . . I wanted to know from Stan how he knew what they were singing and what it was?[1]

Born in Nottingham, England, in 1927, Oliver encountered African American music performed by African American GIs when he was a teenager in the summer of 1942 in Stoke-by-Clare, Suffolk. Oliver was working alongside his friend Stan in a harvest camp. However much this recollection has been touched by the hands of nostalgia, it captures the impact of the music on Oliver as a teenager. It also calls to mind W. C. Handy's memory of encountering the blues for the first time in 1903, and coming across "the weirdest music" he'd ever heard. But while Handy would go on to regard himself as the "father of the blues" following his "discovery," the British writer would neither seek the same recognition nor become labeled as such.[2] That Oliver's first experience of the music occurred during World War II is an example of the influence of black troops in the widespread diffusion of African American music during the war. The encounter with the troops sparked an interest in record collecting that would provide the backbone to a prolific career as a blues scholar and historian.

The Career of a British Blues Scholar

Oliver started attending Harrow Art School in 1942, where he eventually began to organize sessions where people with similar interests in African

American music could come together to share and play records. He recalls how this got him to trouble,

> My developing interest in Afro-American music nearly got me expelled. The head blew his mind when he heard me playing it and told me to "get that filthy muck out of the place or otherwise I was." He was shouting down the staircase at me in this big building. He felt that the music was obscene and demanded that I stop running my sessions of alternative music.

This replicated the experiences of British jazz and blues singer George Melly, whose school headmaster described the music on the radio as "filthy jazz."[3] Oliver left Harrow Art School to complete an Art Teacher's Diploma course at Goldsmith's College in London, and then took up the post of art teacher at his childhood school, Harrow County, in 1949, staying there until 1960. While there he undertook a part-time degree in the history of art at the University of London, which would act as a prelude to a future career in architecture.[4] Also while teaching at Harrow County School, Oliver set up the Harrow Jazz Purist Society with the help of his friend Bruce Stiles, based in the headquarters of the Fourth Harrow Rover Crew on Blaiwith Road. He also began to further his interests by reviewing for various jazz periodicals such as *Jazz Journal* and *Jazz Monthly*, which was also one of the main ways to supplement his part-time teaching salary. He was also able to apply the artistic ability he had been honing from a very early age to the design of record covers when the new ten-inch LP records arrived. He recalls this as a great source of extra income, paying around £15 per cover. Around this time Oliver was also a member a skiffle group called The Crawdads in which he played mandolin, although he did not have a high opinion of his playing and decided to quit. Interestingly, another reason for this was that he came to believe that the social and cultural differences separating him from the context of African American music were insurmountable: "I had a strong feeling that it wasn't for me to try and play guitarist (or mandolin player)—I had no association with the world of blues singers nationally, racially, environmentally, even by class." For Oliver, the only person who "had managed to bridge the impossible gulf between the cultures" was the English harmonicist Cyril Davies.[5] While this statement serves to highlight the early formation of ideas about who could and could not play the music, it also differentiates Oliver from young disillusioned Brits who felt a sense of "affiliation" with the world and culture of the blues. Andrew Kellett borrows this idea from the literary theorist Edward Said to describe the manner in which the blues provided a gritty alternative to the blandness of popular consumer culture and conformism in the fifties and early sixties.[6] While Oliver obviously experienced the manner in which young Brits in the art school environment associated themselves with a distant culture as a form of middle-class rebellion, he was representative of another audience for African American music, one that based itself on developing knowledge of African American culture and understanding the social significance of the music.

In 1960 and following his field trip to the United States, Oliver was appointed principal lecturer in art history at the Architectural Association School, beginning an academic career in vernacular architecture that eventually saw him become associate head of the Architecture School of Oxford Brookes University.[7] While the sixties marked the beginning of Oliver's professional career as an architect, the decade was also his most prolific as a blues writer. Following the field trip that was funded by the U.S. Department of State and the BBC, Oliver conducted a large exhibition presenting his findings at the U.S. Embassy in London entitled "The Story of the Blues" in 1964. This was then accompanied by the photographical oral history *Conversation of the Blues* (1965), which presented images from the field trip and excerpts from interviews. Oliver closed the decade by publishing a further three books on the subject, *Screening the Blues: Aspects of the Blues Tradition* (1968), *The Story of the Blues* (1969), and *Savannah Syncopators* (1970). The latter was the first in a line of Blues Paperbacks that Oliver edited, and saw some of the first publications of now established blues commentators such as Paul Garon, David Evans, John Fahey, Derrick Stewart-Baxter, Bengt Olsson, William Ferris Jr., Bob Groom, Bruce Bastin, and Tony Russell.[8] The author recalls taking a break from blues writing during the seventies, and while no books were published in this decade, Oliver continued to write articles for magazines such as *Jazz & Blues* and *Living Blues*. In the last three decades Oliver has continued to publish on the subject of blues and related African American music with new editions of all his major books of the sixties, and new books such as *Songsters and Saints: Vocal Traditions on Race Records* (1984), *Broadcasting the Blues: Blues in the Segregation Era* (2005), and most recently, *Barrelhouse Blues: Location Recording and the Early Traditions of the Blues* (2008). In addition, he was one of the original members of the editorial board for the journal *Popular Music*, contributing as an editor until 1990.[9] He also acted as coeditor for a number of publications including *Popular Music Studies: A Select International Bibliography* and *The Continuum Encyclopedia of Popular Music of the World*.[10]

It is remarkable that Oliver has had such a prominent career as a blues scholar considering that it has been secondary to his main profession as an architectural academic. However, his background in the art schools of the immediate postwar years allows us to place his interest within the broader context of the British reception of African American music. Simon Frith and Howard Horne point to the manner in which the art schools created a home for disenchanted British youth lost between the rigid choices of the elitist academic world and the more likely daily grind of manual labor. The schools acted as cultural nurseries for these "misfits" that would eventually go on to spearhead the British rhythm-and-blues boom of the sixties. Jazz in these art schools was

> something understood as a folk form, live music for dancing and community entertainment, became a recording cult, music for collectors, for an elite of jazz students, critics, musicologists and discographers. Solemnity not excitement defined true jazz fans, who self-consciously distanced themselves from the general public and were suspicious when anyone like Louis Armstrong became popular.[11]

Oliver belonged to a slightly older generation than the musicians of the eventual British rhythm-and-blues "boom" of the sixties, and the divergence in these generations would become evident in the reactions of blues scholars to the white imitations of the blues revival. The British writer was closer to the generation of jazz musicians such as Humphrey Lyttleton, who had attended the Camberwell School of Arts and Crafts following his discharge from the army after World War II.[12] Also, in contrast to many of the musicians who are the subject of Frith and Horne's study, Oliver was a teacher as opposed to a student. This educative function was to be reflected in his style of writing, which would seek to inform readers on the meaning of blues lyrics and the social and historical background of the music.

The principal point here is that the art school environment of the postwar years fostered the formation of distinctive ideas about art and mass culture, and that the folk music of African Americans came to be represented as "the soundtrack of disgust at the new 'affluent admass' society."[13] This sentiment would run throughout the writing of blues critics of the fifties and sixties. The representations created within this context made the blues into a "genre" as defined by Frith: "popular music genres are constructed—and must be understood—*within* a commercial/cultural process." While Frith was referring to the manufacture of genres into consumable commodities and *not* academic or musicological constructions, the representations of the blues in Oliver's scholarship were part of a larger cultural process that defined the blues as a distinctive genre. Consequently, Frith's argument that constructed genres "set up expectations, and disappointment is likely when they are not met *and* when they are met all too predictably," also applies to the academic and scholarly creations of the blues as a genre.[14] Importantly, the British art school context also points to the relationship between the contextual circumstances of the interpreters of the blues, and the blues itself. The manner in which the blues was represented in Oliver's scholarship was thus as much a product of the author's social, cultural, and historical context in the fifties and sixties as it was an analysis of African American blues from the interwar years.

But it is Oliver's writing on blues for British music magazines throughout the 1950s that is indicative of the early formation of views about the music in the immediate postwar period. His writing, alongside that of other commentators during this time, also demonstrates that an active audience for blues existed in Britain prior to the much more widely covered blues revival of the 1960s. Indeed, this early period was pivotal in the construction of concepts that would become prominent the following decade. On the one hand, the reception of the blues in this period was facilitated by the already established appreciation for jazz, particularly with the revivalist factions that saw the "moldy figs" privileging the African American music of New Orleans as opposed to the music of modernist beboppers. On the other, the postwar era saw the emergence of a folk revival, an interest in the culture of "ordinary people" that was coupled with a fear of "Americanization" following the growing role of American intervention in Europe in both political and cultural terms. Amid these revivals, it was possible for Oliver to promote the appreciation of blues as a distinctive musical form in its own right based on the fact that, on the one hand, it represented the foundations of jazz and, on the other, it was a representation of African American folk music.

The 1950s: Between the Jazz and Folk Revivals

Popular portrayals of blues history tend to concentrate on the late fifties and early sixties as the period in which the music of black Americans became fashionable with young white middle-class English youth. Given the commercial success and huge audiences, often of screaming teenage girls, that developed for the British invasion bands, this fact is unsurprising. In the 2011 BBC documentary *Blues Britannia*, a dust-covered, grey and austere 1950s Britain is depicted as "crying out" for something as an alternative to the "gutless" popular music of the time. Consequently, as rock'n'roll was on the wane in the late fifties (symbolized in the documentary by Elvis's enrollment into the U.S. military), these young British audiences "discovered the depth, power and authenticity they craved in a music they hadn't heard before, the very basis of rock'n'roll, black folk music from the American South—the blues." The show also hints at the emergence of a "secret society" of enthusiasts and record collectors, often referred to as "the purists."[15] Representative of this group were prominent jazz critics such as Max Jones, Ernest Borneman, Albert McCarthy, and Rex Harris, and from this collective would emerges a group of writers that would begin to examine blues exclusively.

However, the origin of dedicated attention on the blues has its origins in the more established and much older appreciation for jazz. Catherine Parsonage's survey of the diffusion of jazz in Britain describes the manner in which primitivism and exoticism meant that since the 1920s responses to the music had been characterized by "fascination" and "fear." This was especially manifest in the depiction of jazz as a black idiom in need of white refinement. It was not until the visits of Louis Armstrong and Duke Ellington in the 1930s that a reevaluation of these attitudes prompted "a deeper understanding of the artistic and cultural validity of jazz," which subsequently forged the notion that only black Americans would be able to deliver the genuine article.[16] This critical reassessment became manifest in American books such as Frederic Ramsey and Charles Edwards's *Jazzmen* (1939), Mezz Mezzrow's autobiography *Really the Blues* (1946), and Rudi Blesh's *Shining Trumpets* (1949). These books also began to place emphasis on the importance of the blues to jazz, which became synonymous with the African American experience that made jazz unique—as the musician Clarence Williams declared in *Jazzmen*: "Why I'd never have written blues if I had been white. You don't study to write blues, you 'feel' them. It's the mood you're in."[17] The blues represented the almost indescribable emotive quality that was intricately connected to the African American way of life. For this reason Blesh likened the rhythm of blues to "the human pulse." Much of this early writing on jazz was marked by the writers' clear sense of affiliation with the musicians"

> The chants and rhythmic calls always struck a gong in me. The tonal inflections and the story they told, always blending together like the colors in an artist's picture, the way the syllables were always placed right, the changes in the words to fit the music—this all hit me like a millennium would hit a philosopher. Those few simple riffs opened my eyes to the Negro's philosophy more than any fat sociology textbook ever could. They cheered me up right away and made me feel

> wonderful towards those guys. Many a time I was laid out there with the blues heavy on my chest, when somebody would begin to sing 'em and the weight would be lifted. Those were a people who really knew what to do about the blues.[18]

The blues was therefore the music of a race, bound to the lives of America's black population. As the cold war between modernist beboppers and traditional revivalists intensified in the immediate postwar period, the latter sought the idiom's roots in African American antecedents. In this context, the blues became not only a simple musical form based on the three-line stanza and twelve-bar progression, but also an emotive foundation that prioritized sincerity of expression over classical musical knowledge or technical dexterity.

In Britain, the revivalist faction was spearheaded by jazz bands such as George Webb's Dixielanders and musicians like Humphrey Lyttleton in the late forties.[19] However, the growing jazz press also provided a small but committed critical counterpart. The early British writing in *Melody Maker* and *Jazz Journal* duplicated the tradition of American revivalist critics. McCarthy, for instance, echoed the attitudes of *Jazzmen* by placing the authenticity of jazz in opposition to the large commercial swing bands of the time, and demanded the assistance of "serious music critics" to "save jazz from becoming a museum piece."[20] British jazz critics also upheld the notion of African American music embodying the antithesis of the Western classical tradition of highbrow culture, by reveling in "frankness" of black musical expression, of a music "shaped by emotion" rather than learned through dedicated study.[21] Importantly, British writers also began to emphasize that the blues was the "essence" of jazz, providing it with the emotive qualities born in the experiences of ordinary African Americans. Within this context, there was a growing appreciation that a firm understanding of blues, "the parent idiom of jazz," was fundamental to true jazz appreciation.[22] This was summarized by Iain Lang's *Jazz in Perspective: The Background of the Blues* in 1947: "the blues is not the whole of jazz, but the whole of blues is jazz."[23] Clear distinctions began to be drawn between authentic blues and commercial offshoots of the music. Jones argued that "the peak period of the blues (like jazz) on record was reached when the style had little attraction for any but coloured Americans."[24] Herein began to take shape images of a black world, rooted in a folk culture and portrayed in defiant opposition to white commercialism and popular taste. Offering an analysis for the European fascination for folk cultures such as blues, Francis Newton (aka historian Eric Hobsbawm) argued that it could be explained by nostalgia for a self-made, participatory culture, a need arising from "thin-blooded middle-class art . . . drained by systematic commercial debasement and over-exploitation."[25]

Newton's analysis draws in the romantic aesthetic of the postwar era folk revival, when A. L. Lloyd's *The Singing Englishman* (1944) became the symbol of a period that Georgina Boyes terms the "second folk revival." Following World War II and the United States's growing role on the global stage and particularly in the rebuilding of Europe, Boyes argues that a prevalent fear existed that England could become the forty-ninth state.[26] Michael Brocken develops this idea by stating that the sentiments of folk revivalists emanated from a convergence of a number of factors, among which were not only the spread of American institutions and culture, but also a nostalgia for the loss of Britain's former role as a global power. This arena fostered the development of a more politically leftist mood that favored a "rediscovery of working-class art."[27] This open attitude toward art from the lower echelons of society benefited the American folklorist Alan Lomax, who spent much of the fifties in Britain due to his exodus from the anticommunism of McCarthyism. During his British stay he produced radio programs for the BBC such as "Adventures in Folk Song" and "The Art of the Negro" from the body of his Library of Congress recordings. He also collaborated with prominent British "folkies" such as Ewan MacColl and A. L. Lloyd in promoting working-class music.[28] The American folklorist's programs on African American life and culture proved popular with audiences, demonstrating the manner in which black American culture was not viewed in the same light as its more mainstream and commercial white counterpart. In this context, given the emphasis on the music's African American roots, jazz was embraced as an uncommercial idiom, not tied to the growing global political power that was the United States. Thus, jazz also presented a cultural symbol for the subordinated, which made it compatible with the aesthetics of the postwar folk revival. The blues appeared as the idiom's "archaic" antecedent, providing a distant and obscure past from which jazz sprang into the modern era.[29]

Blues in the British Jazz Press

Amid this context of the jazz and folk revivals, a handful of blues commentators emerged in Britain in the postwar era. Oliver had been collecting records from his first encounters with African American music since the early forties, and the impression he had been building about the blues at this time challenged the prevalent notion that saw blues simply as a building block for jazz.[30] The music was still relatively obscure at this point, and familiar only to the few record collectors who had had the fortune of stumbling upon the rare records available in Britain since the twenties.[31] Derrick Stewart-Baxter's "Preaching the Blues" column in *Jazz Journal* became "a haven for British blues fans" from 1949 onward. This was accompanied by *Melody Maker*'s "Collector's Corner," which, following Sinclair Traill's takeover in 1949, began to devote more time to African American folk music.[32] A significant aspect of the jazz press during the postwar period is that correspondence from readers was vital to the direction that articles took. For instance, as early as 1946 Max Jones and Rex Harris were inviting readers to write in with any information on singer Peetie Wheatstraw, which contributed to a discussion and exchange of information regarding the singer over a number of issues of *Melody Maker*.[33] In a similar manner, Stewart-Baxter demonstrates the collaborative nature of the early days of blues appreciation:

> So many readers have asked for a bigger coverage of blues records in the column to supplement that already contained in the review section of this magazine that I have approached the various companies. Most of them have agreed to co-operate. . . . In future all important blues issues will be reviewed in "Preachin" the Blues."[34]

This active correspondence seems to have typified much of the postwar period. Oliver still sought assistance from readers in answering some fundamental research questions in 1960: "Who then: recorded the first vocal with traditional twelve-bar blues verses employing the characteristic repeated lines a) with vocal introduction, and b) with no introduction?"[35] Much of the readership, at least that which tended to correspond with the writers, seemed to have involved collectors of records rather than just the average listener. If they took the time and effort to write to the magazines, it can be inferred that they were fairly keen to obtain records and information on them. This means that the music magazines of this period were also forums for the exchange of information and knowledge on the subject of jazz, blues, and related music. It also suggests that locating records still relied on chance as much as it did on reissues from record companies. Therefore, rather than simply being antecedents of the present-day music press, these magazines seem to have been platforms for the avid listener and record collector, able to devote time and most probably money to music appreciation.

In the late forties and early fifties, Oliver began giving talks on the blues while teaching at Harrow County School, and he set up the Harrow Jazz Purist Society. In this period he began writing on the subject regularly for *Music Mirror*, *Jazz Journal*, and *Jazz Monthly*. The circulation figures available indicate that these magazines had a very small but stable readership. The average monthly sales for *Jazz Monthly*, for instance, rose from 4,601 in the second half of 1956 to 6,631 in the first half of 1958. This number gradually decreased to 4,997 in the second half of 1960. It is safe to assume that the figures for *Music Mirror* and *Jazz Journal* would have been similar, if not lower. These numbers seem to mirror the membership of the folk club known as the Ballads and Blues Association, which had grown to around 4,000 in 1959. This club aimed to present performances by American and British folk artists across the UK.[36] These were highly exclusive in comparison with publications such as the more popular weekly *Melody Maker*, which at its peak in early 1957 averaged 116,776, and the *New Musical Express* (*NME*), which in early 1958 had an average of 143,259.[37] Given the dominance of jazz in the smaller periodicals, blues was very much a limited taste in the late forties and fifties. It is perhaps likely that the relative obscurity of the music at this point, coupled with the dominance of the jazz and folk revivals during the postwar years, allowed Oliver a certain amount of journalistic freedom. The author recalls a friendly atmosphere between British collectors and commentators in this early period that made publishing articles on the blues relatively simple.[38] Blues records had been available to collectors able to devote their time to scouring junk shops, or who had the financial means of ordering expensive records from the United States at a time of national austerity. Despite the sluggish postwar recovery, where food rationing continued until 1954, the circumstances were not enough of a deterrent for Oliver, who recalls the logistical difficulties of collecting records during wartime:

> I was desperate to get hold of them, and in the war it was very difficult. I wanted very much to have a King Oliver record and I had to cross the whole of London to get to southeast London to a shop which I knew had got one. And yet, traveling at that time was extremely difficult, to go across London—it was very hard indeed.[39]

Therefore, having the resources to devote time to collecting and researching music was very much a niche and middle-class enterprise that fostered the creation of what has been sensationalized as a "secret society" in popular documentaries such as *Blues Britannia*. Schwartz has highlighted the manner in which groups of enthusiasts would meet, discuss music, and exchange knowledge on the music in specialist stores such Dobell's Record Shop in Charing Cross Road, London.[40] She also points to the evangelical quality of blues proselytizing in the late forties and early fifties, as suggested by the title of Stewart-Baxter's column in *Jazz Journal* and by Oliver's own admission:

> There was an evangelical element in my talking about the blues, I realize now, an urgent need to get the message across to as many people as I could in as many ways as I could. Like any enthusiast for a subject who feels passionately about it and about its neglect, I wanted the blues to be recognized and enjoyed.[41]

While Oliver's recollection exemplifies the evangelical quality of blues scholarship in this period, the writer's emergence within the context of the postwar art schools, and the jazz and folk revivals, meant that blues proselytizing was also "evangelical" in the preaching of stringent ideas about African American folk authenticity, and commercial music.

The African American writer Richard Wright would eventually praise Oliver's efforts to explain the meaning of the blues within the context of the black experience in the United States. Speaking about Oliver's *Blues Fell This Morning* (1960), Wright believed the social and cultural distance that separated the author from America allowed Oliver the freedom to work without the pressures of the American social and political climate, thus favoring a more objective and unbiased analysis.[42] This would seem to complement Oliver's philosophy: "I tend to keep myself out of the text, so that there's a focus on the subject of blues or blues singers, without any intrusion."[43] However, while Oliver may have been removed from the turbulent racial and political struggles of America in the fifties, this does not mean that his British context was unobtrusive or simply permitted an "objective" analysis. If, as Hamilton states, "every landscape is a work of the mind," then Oliver connected with the world of the blues by imagining its landscapes and its people through the sounds and lyrics of blues songs, in combination with the depictions of African American literary works of the mid-twentieth century.[44] The consequence of the physical, historical, and cultural distance separating Oliver from the music was that a large part of the experience was left to the imagination, and by imagining the blues there was also the possibility for exaggeration, marginalization, and as the language of revisionism now warrants, "invention."

Interestingly however, the pages of British jazz magazines in the fifties often included articles by American and European writers interested in jazz and blues records, ultimately suggesting that blues scholarship of the immediate postwar era was distinctly transatlantic in nature. *Jazz Journal* often included articles by the French jazz critic Hugues Panassie, but it was not uncommon, particularly in the late fifties, to see articles by American writers such as Samuel Charters, Mack McCormick, and coauthor of *Jazzmen* Frederic Ramsey Jr. Often these articles would provide firsthand accounts of interviews with blues musicians, or report on their experiences in jazz clubs and field trips. Interestingly, there are also articles written by the likes of African American writer Ralph Ellison, who contributed biographical articles in tribute to singers such as Charlie Christian and Jimmy Rushing.[45] Apart from Ellison's eloquent treatment of these singers and the blues in general, the inclusion of such an article demonstrates the links between American and European writing on African American music, and the range of perspectives that were included in the music press. Despite the transatlantic distances, Americans and European collectors corresponded frequently. Oliver recalls corresponding with Charters in the late fifties, prior to the American author's publication of *The Country Blues* in 1959. The fruits of this communication can be traced in the American journey of the French blues enthusiasts Jacques Demetre and Marcel Chauvard, whose tracing of blues singers in Chicago and Detroit in 1959 was facilitated by information provided by Oliver, before the British writer had ever visited the United States. Their experiences would be presented in a series of articles that appeared in *Jazz Journal* in 1960.[46] These transatlantic links begin to paint an image of blues scholarship less rigidly defined by national provenance. In Oliver's articles throughout the decade it is therefore possible to examine the manner in which aspects of the blues and African American culture were interpreted within a more open transnational dialogue, and in turn how these interpretations began to define the music as a genre in itself.

The "Negro World" of the Blues

In his very first article in 1952, dealing with the topic of religious music in African American churches, Oliver began to depict what he would often refer to as the "Negro world."[47] This is a world that is difficult for the outsider to access. The further removed the African American was from the influences of the white world, where the places were of a "darker hue," the more it was possible for him to be "unashamedly himself." The distance between black and white, and the separation of the races, were fundamental to an understanding of African American music. Ironically, Oliver was preaching a philosophy that would become the battle cry of Afro-centric African American cultural commentators in the late 1960s. He claimed the cultural and historical distance of the "Negro world" from the surrounding world was difficult to cross for the "outsider." An example is given in an article on Blind Lemon Jefferson, where there is a specific reference to the singer's anonymity in white America. This was in contrast to the "Negro world," where "the blues singer was valued and loved, for [Blind Lemon Jefferson] spoke to them who were members of his race."[48] Similarly, when discussing the significance of Peetie Wheatstraw's music, it was clear for Oliver that the music spoke strictly through racial lines: "Peetie's blues appealed to his coloured audience because they made no compromise. He sang in their language, he sang of his life which was their lives."[49] The question that arises here is how the writer could draw such conclusions about music in the "Negro world." For Oliver, although accessing this world was difficult, it was not impossible. As he argued himself, "there are, of course, exceptions as [Wheatstraw's] work tends to appeal only to the 'hardened' collector who has allowed himself to be absorbed by the idiom." There is no doubting that Oliver was completely "drenched in his subject." This can be corroborated by the evidence from his personal notebooks from this era, which reveal hours upon hours of laborious transcription from records, and the endless listing and referencing of record serial numbers.[50] While Oliver may have regarded the dedicated process of record collecting as an endeavor that served to narrow the ideological gap between the blues enthusiast and the music, the author's "absorption" into the "Negro world" was also accomplished through the use of literature.

As well as analyzing blues lyrics and scanning the available literature on African American life and culture in the U.S. Embassy in London, Oliver relied heavily on the literature of black writers such Claude McKay, Ralph Ellison, and, in particular, Richard Wright. In fact, Oliver had become relatively close to Wright while the author was living in Paris throughout the fifties. Together with his wife Valerie, Oliver would meet Wright on yearly visits to Paris, where he also met Langston Hughes and the American jazz musician Mezz Mezzrow.[51] While it is difficult to measure the full influence of the relationship with Wright on his perceptions of the blues, especially since the American author had regarded jazz and blues as being only "naive" and "mundane" forms of expression in his early career, Oliver described the Parisian "subculture of talking, writing and music" as highly influential, particularly to the writing of *Blues Fell This Morning*.[52] He also believed that these literary works could allow the blues collector "a clearer insight into the environment that produced [the blues singer's] music than he can find in any descriptive work of non-fiction."[53] Although the realism and immediacy that characterize the writing of these authors make this claim more than plausible, it was by no means unproblematic. For instance, despite the naturalist shades of Wright's autobiography *Black Boy*, as John Lowe argues, the narrative "is so consciously shaped and framed, editing out many aspects of Wright's actual life, and reshaping others, that it needs to be considered a fiction, despite the fact that most of the major incidents actually occurred."[54] Wright's autobiography was a literary work crafted by the hands of memory that negotiated the past in the author's present. The consequence of this representation of the past is that the boundaries between fact and fiction are blurred in the eyes of the reader. The use of the realism in African American literature has the effect of neutralizing the physical separation of the British writer from the context of the music. While Oliver's transatlantic context allowed him to bypass the racial politics of American society, the distance separating him from the United States favored the construction of an imagined African American world shaped by the writing of black authors and the lyrics of blues songs.

Ellison's *Invisible Man* in particular seems to have had a particular effect on Oliver's interpretation of African American life. Apart from the direct mention of the novel in his two articles on Peetie Wheatstraw, there are other more indirect but nonetheless significant references. For instance, in the novel the protagonist encounters a man on the streets of New York, who later turns out to be Wheatstraw:

> Close to the kerb ahead I saw a man pushing a cart piled high with rolls of blue paper and heard him singing in a clear ringing voice. It was a blues, and I walked behind him remembering the times I had heard such a singing at home. It seemed that there are memories slipped around my life at the campus and went far back to things I had long ago shut out of my mind. There was no escaping such reminders.[55]

The song invokes memories of the past, home, and "far back" in the protagonist. The blues plays the role of guiding the *Invisible Man* toward self-realization, one among many instances in which the protagonist is in "movement toward identity."[56] The music touches an innate, natural, but hidden part of his identity. This sense of African American atavism seems to be of fundamental importance in Oliver's depiction of music in African American life at this time. In his first article, for example, he mentioned that music "is . . . essentially a part of the coloured man's nature"; dancing was described as a "natural form of expression"; and in talking about the Delta singer Muddy Waters, he argued that "it was as natural to him as the desire to eat . . . [to] want to learn to play and sing the blues."[57] Herein is evident the similarity of Oliver's language to the descriptions of jazz revivalists of the thirties and forties, which rested on subtle racial stereotypes of innate sense of rhythm and musicality, a propensity for feeling music naturally rather than learning from study, and the ability of the blues singer to "sing[] of things as he sees them."[58] What emerges is a form of compensatory primitivism that valorizes not only the music of African Americans, but also the philosophical approach to life that is interpreted from the music.

Oliver portrayed the blues as being both the symbol and practice of a folk heritage that went deep into the heart of the African American experience, depicting blues as something as natural as breathing for African Americans. The examples demonstrate the manner in which Oliver's own imagination as a writer merged with the literary memory of the African American author in a layering process. The "Negro world" is therefore imagined in isolation; the African American experience is divorced from the social, political, and cultural context of the late nineteenth and early twentieth centuries. One of the major consequences of this divorce from context is that this world is idealized, and in Oliver's writing the evidence of this can be seen in his depiction of the African American "folk." He often made reference to the blues as "the common folk song of the African American Negro," and those who sang "the music of their people" were most often regarded as being more authentic and worthy of attention.[59] The explanation for this reasoning lies in the fact that, for Oliver, the blues was inextricably linked to the African Americans' subordinate position with the American social hierarchy:

> The Negro knows the blues. He can talk with the blues, walk with the blues. And for the coloured man confounded by his environment, puzzled and disappointed, the blues is not just an unwelcome associate: the blues give him consolation, enough to continue the fight.[60]

That the music functioned as a means of releasing tension and providing comfort amid the social problems affecting American life would be echoed in countless future examinations of the music in future years. For instance, for James H. Cone the blues enabled a "liberating catharsis" that helped both the singer and the audience to deal with the pressures of African American life through the process of performance.[61] For Oliver, however, the blues performance did not provide the means by which ordinary African Americans could fight back against prejudice and racial discrimination. In one sense, Oliver was also divorcing himself from the overt "negrophilie" of certain jazz revivalists, such as Mezzrow, that in jazz saw the ultimate cultural challenge to American social inequality.[62] However, his descriptions oscillate between the identification with African Americans as a class group enduring social and economic hardship on the one hand, and the racialized interpretation of a symbiotic relationship between African Americans and the blues on the other (evident in phrases such as "the Negro knows the blues"). Simultaneously, the author reduced the possibility for the defiance of Jim Crow laws in public spaces as in Robin Kelley's "theatres of resistance."[63] Music in Oliver's "Negro world," in contrast, was a coping strategy, a "safety-valve" for the release of tension and hardship. It was when Blind Lemon Jefferson sang about the problems of "his people" that he was a "true folk artist," displaying the folk heritage of African Americans.[64] It has often been a criticism of those studying the nature of folklore that the ambiguity of the term "folk" rests on the subjective definition of each individual observer, or as Richard Middleton argues, whatever the researcher says it means.[65] What is less ambiguous from Oliver's interpretation of the black folk world, however, is that true "Negro" folk music was in its purest form where white influence was lowest, and where music echoed the experiences of African Americans. Paradoxically, black folk culture was dependent upon the racial oppression of the white world, which maintained black isolation from the mainstream.

While attempting to navigate away from the overt idealizations of black life and culture, Oliver's descriptions of the fifties sometimes fell prey to fetishized descriptions of his subjects. A clear example is presented by Oliver's first book, the biographical *Bessie Smith* (1958):

> Bessie wore simple dresses that were boldly draped over her splendid figure, her hair was swept back and at her neck she wore a single strand of beads, sufficient to draw attention to the regular beauty of her oval features and her dark, moist eyes.[66]

The description is suggestive of an overt sexual voyeurism and exoticism for the female blues singer. Another example is provided by the imagined description of Peetie Wheatstraw:

> One can imagine him as he sings through thick lips scarcely open; his eyes, not quite straight, glinting from beneath lowered lids; the dimples on his dark cheeks belied by the backward tilt of his head and the hat pushed far off the domed forehead.[67]

The focus on the dark elements of the singers' physical appearance is suggestive of Oliver's exhibiting a moderate form of "negrophilia," but it also gives an indication of the author's level of personal fascination not only in the music, but in its people. This also becomes manifest in Oliver's analysis of lyrics, as for instance, in the explanation of the railroad theme in many blues songs: "And there was too, the fascination which a powerful, snoring engine always exerts on many men with its urgent rhythm, its fierce masculinity."[68]

Oliver's treatment of blues lyrics as the direct expression of the hardships of the African American experience, the primary method adopted in *Blues Fell This Morning* and widely used in subsequent research, helped to build the foundations of his "Negro world." He justifies this by stating that "the blues singer is seldom inhibited by any thoughts of the more delicate sensibilities of his listeners and his statements are frank and forthright."[69] The method's reduction of blues to a mere report or description of reality has been criticized for denying the lyrics their potential poetic value. Frith has also challenged the realist interpretation of song lyrics for the subjective and arbitrary distinction the cultural critic draws between the "real and unreal."[70] For Oliver, however, the blues singer's "subjective realism" paints an accurate picture of African American life. The "forthright" realism that Oliver imparts to the blues is reflected in many of the illustrations that he produced to accompany his articles. Figure 1 for instance, is an illustration of two African Americans working on the riverside. Their body language shows dejection, their facial expressions convey fatigue as well as melancholy, all in an environment that seems to resemble a bygone era. On the other hand, figure 2, which accompanied an article on the living conditions of African Americans, is a representation of urban family life in a tightly cramped living space. As Oliver wrote, " 'Hot-bed' apartments are rented by three families at once, each using the bed and room for eight hours of the day."[71] In the illustration a despondent elder member of the family sits on the bed with young children inside. The clean clothes hanging on the line over the bed seems futile considering the griminess of the walls. The image is reminiscent of a scene in Wright's *Black Boy*:

> Another change took place at home. We needed money badly and Granny and Aunt Addie decided that we could no longer share the entire house, and Uncle Tom and his family were invited to live upstairs at a nominal rental. The dining room and the living room were converted into bedrooms and for the first time we were squeezed for living space. We began to get on each other's nerves. . . . Rattling pots and pans in the kitchen would now awaken me in the mornings.[72]

The similarity to Wright's autobiography is coincidental. However, Oliver's illustrations show a distinct resemblance to social photo-documentary style of Wright's *12 Million Black Voices*, which used a number of images from the Farm Security Administration (FSA) photographers produced under the auspices of the New Deal's Works Progress Administration (WPA) during the late thirties and early forties.[73] The author was providing a visual reference to his articles at a time when images of blues musicians and the African American life were difficult to obtain. He states, "I just really wanted to communicate the content and where it took place and what it looked like, as far as I could tell, from the information I collected." These illustrations proved popular, as Oliver contributed some of his drawings to *Big Bill Blues*, the autobiography of the singer edited by Yannick Bruynoghe. He also illustrated an article by Rex Harris on jazz that appeared in *Radio Times*, perhaps highlighting the difficulty of obtaining actual photographs even for a popular national magazine.[74] Actual images of blues musicians would begin to appear more frequently in British music magazines in the late fifties when Frederic Ramsey Jr. would make photographs available from his field trips.

Oliver's illustrations represent snapshots of his vision of the world in which the blues had emerged and had meaning, and in this sense they bear a stylistic resemblance to the rural paintings of the nineteenth-century French artist Jean-François Millet, also drawing attention to Oliver's life as an art teacher. Millet's work came to focus on images of the French peasantry at a time of rapid urbanization that gave rise to a popular emphasis on the common man and the fate of the French countryside. Perhaps Oliver's image of a cotton picker looking resigned (perhaps due to the fact that a machine was beginning to take over his job) best represents the link to the rural art of post-1850 French painting or the nineteenth century Arts and Crafts movement (figure 9). However, some similarities in content can also be detected. Robert Herbert describes the "primeval innocence" in works such as *Man with a Hoe* and *Going to Work* that characterizes Millet's rural subjects. In the former in particular he argues,

> Instead of confirming the middle-class view that life on the farm is a happy round of healthy tasks, Millet brought the labouring peasant directly into the observer's presence, with a sense of the gruelling, wearing tasks he performs.[75]

A number of Oliver's illustrations portray subjects in similar circumstances. The despondency and fatalism in the expressions and body language displayed in figure 1 are also evident in the faces of the family of figure 3, and the ambiguous image of a black prisoner sitting in front of a white guitar player in figure 5. The difficulties of the manual labor that typified much of African American employment in the South is also manifested in illustrations of a horse and cart carrying tree logs through swampy terrain, and of bare-chested men working on the railroads (figures 6 and 7).

Portraits of singers also display similar dejected expressions (figure 8), highlighting the manner in which Oliver opted to portray the subjects of his illustrations as largely unable to effect change in their daily lives, but through the images able to inspire sympathy on behalf of the observer. The similarities with Millet's painting are most likely coincidental (although given Oliver's art history background, it cannot be discounted that he had come across the French artist's work and may have been influenced by rural paintings in some form), but nonetheless Oliver's illustrations share an affinity with the plight of the subjugated, and in the attempt to represent the reality of the experience faced by the subjects.

Oliver's images thus bring together his own artistic impression of African American life with the subjective realism of blues lyrics, interpreted in combination with the literary representations of black life in the South narrated in the books of Wright and Ellison. In this intermixture of sources and influences it is possible to consider Oliver's role as a *listening* subject. As Steven Feld argues, "the listener is implicated as a socially and historically situated being, not just as the bearer of organs that receive and respond to stimuli."[76] Thus the listener brings himself and his social and ideological circumstances into his experience of the music. Oliver's empathy for the plight of African Americans, the dignity he sees in the sincere expression of things as they appear, and the admiration for the folk come to pervade his descriptions of the "Negro world."

The personal involvement in the process of constructing the imagery of African American life is evident in Oliver's writing style, which takes the form of a series of short "narratives." An example can be seen in his exploration of the theme of departure in blues lyrics:

> Coming home when the sun goes down, hand thrust deep in empty pockets, gunny sacks tied about his feet, he pauses before his clapboard shack. The holes in the walls are patched with packing cases and rats live unmolested beneath the floor boards. His children greet him solemn-eyed. Their bellies are swollen with pellagra. Now busy with the hominy grits in the skillet his woman is waiting for him. Only partially does she appreciate why the pay packet is small and why so much of that is spent in the gin-mill at the back of town.[77]

The characters here are literal inventions, as they are not referring to any particular singer. Oliver's writing here is not sociohistorical or academic but more akin to a fictional literary style. The subtleties of the man's pause, the children's greeting, and the woman's attitude are imagined and seek to create the situation in which a typical bluesman would feel the need to depart. This example is complemented by two further illustrations that depict a man leaving his family (figures 3 and 4). It would be difficult to find a more stereotypical image of the wandering bluesman leaving his troubles behind and taking to the road. This style is highly representative of Oliver's articles in the fifties, and considering the writing is journalistic, the creative literary writing style could be understood as attempts to engage readers. Nonetheless, the illustrations are literary images, works of the imagination that aim to present the reality of African American life, but instead, like much realism in art, are closer to *re*-presentations of that reality.

The portrayal of the realism in blues lyrics and their relevance to African American life seems to be an attempt to validate the music as being worthy of more attention. Indeed, Oliver even bemoaned the way African American intellectuals snubbed the music for being "backward," claiming "they have yet to recognize the beauty of their own tradition."[78] Oliver may have been referring to younger African Americans who begun to turn their attention to newer genres, such as soul, or perhaps even those black intellectuals of the Harlem Renaissance who renounced blues and jazz as "popular" entertainment that did not conform to their standards of high civilized art.[79] Oliver had become familiar with an array of African American writing from this period by spending time at the U.S. Embassy's library in London. A notable example would be Alain Locke's "New Negro" movement, to which "Afro-American music had always been a source of embarrassment . . . [and their] feelings about urban spirituals—the blues—and about jazz sometimes verged on the unprintable."[80] Oliver's sentiments seem to mirror those of Zora Neale Hurston and the poet Langston Hughes, who were exceptions to the predominant view of the low-art credentials of African American music. Hughes in particular "was noted as one of the first poets to celebrate the beauty of the blues as an American art form," and was often criticized for it.[81] It is a characteristic of those who study folk cultures to feel the need to rescue that culture from extinction, and feeling that the blues was being disregarded and forgotten, Oliver defiantly declared that "it has not gone yet" and "there is still time. . . . Blind Willie McTell still walks the streets of Atlanta with his guitar and his tin cup." This was a cry not only for preservation, but for research that consisted of direct contact with the people involved, because, at the time it was still "living folk-lore."[82]

The *Real* and the *Imagined*

The reliance on recordings had undeniably fostered a desire for British blues enthusiasts and collectors to see the real thing, and the fifties saw many singers making the trip to Europe and the UK, despite a British Musicians Union ban on foreign musicians since 1935.[83] When African American singers such as Big Bill Broonzy, Lonnie Johnson, Josh White, Sonny Terry, Brownie McGhee, Muddy Waters, Otis Spann, Little Brother Montgomery, and Brother John Sellers did come to Britain, the anticipation in the press was palpable. This was apparent with Josh White's imminent arrival to Britain, as *Melody Maker* included an advert for "Josh White at Foyle's" in Charing Cross Road in London to sign records prior to his 1951 tour. Similarly, *Jazz Journal*'s Albert McCarthy expressed excitement at the prospect of Lonnie Johnson's first show, and Derrick Stewart-Baxter described the arrival Big Bill Broonzy in 1951 as "a date with the blues."[84] The performances of these musicians, most often as "variety" acts during performances by British jazz bands, was the time when British blues critics could compare the "real" thing to the records they had been listening to for years. As was to be expected, the construction of a reified idea of the blues as a static genre derived from record collecting meant that the live performances were judged in accordance with a number of preconceptions, and some musicians fared much better than others. Oliver's experience was typical of this, and as Jeff Titon argues, the "fascination with the recorded artefact produced a distancing that the 'real thing' (hearing the music live) couldn't quite dislodge."[85] Therefore, the responses to the appearances of blues musicians provide an insight into the prevalent attitudes of British critics formed in the early years of blues music appreciation.

The most notable "failures" in the eyes of the British blues enthusiasts were undeniably Lonnie Johnson and Josh White. Sinclair Traill viewed Johnson's performance with some skepticism for the inclusion of "too many of his own ballad compositions." Meanwhile, as Elijah Wald highlights, despite becoming very popular in Britain during the fifties with numerous radio and television appearances, White could not win over the core of jazz and blues critics. Max Jones's review in *Melody Maker* entitled "Josh White pleases the mums and dads," exemplifies the idea that the singer was pandering to popular taste by including songs such as "Lord Randall," "Waltzing Matilda" and "Foggy Foggy Dew." Audiences were also less than pleased at the arrangements of the performances with a backing band, and such was the pressure applied by readers of *Melody Maker* that White's next performance on March 17 in 1951 was arranged as a solo concert in order to satisfy the need for the more authentic folk-blues sound based on White's recordings from the thirties.[86] Later in the decade Muddy Waters also experienced the demanding nature of British blues audiences that had developed stringent expectations about how the blues should sound. This is recalled by the Rolling Stones' Keith Richards"

> So you had that traditionalist blues thing going. I once saw this fought out in the Manchester Free Trade Hall between an audience who watched Muddy Waters play acoustic guitar for an hour, applauding magnificently, only to boo him off when he came on with his Chicago band.[87]

Interestingly, the event would be echoed eight years later at the same venue by the now infamous cries of "Judas!" at Bob Dylan's concert with a full backing band.[88] In his 1958 performances across the country, Waters evoked similar responses from audiences that did not respond kindly to his electrified sound. Tony Standish attempted to compensate for this reaction by printing an interview with the singer, who explained that it was difficult for him to sing the same blues as he did years ago, given that his life had virtually gone from rags to riches.[89] It therefore seems evident that the British blues cognoscenti had developed clear ideas as to what constituted authentic and inauthentic blues during the fifties, and were not shy in pronouncing their views.

Having devotedly collected records and reviewed them since the forties, Oliver was no exception. He described Lonnie Johnson singing "Stardust" as "a pathetic picture." Although he was sympathetic to the singer's circumstances of having to operate within the music industry, Oliver also argued that Josh White had "suffered from a . . . popularising process" and had "drawn increasingly from a commercial repertoire . . . at the expense of a certain degree of authenticity and quality." He would maintain this memory of the singers for many years:

> Josh White had worked with Leadbelly, so he came to Europe and toured in Britain. The boy who had led a score of blind blues singers through the South and recorded as Pinewood Tom was a virtuoso guitarist and sang with a glottal catch. He sang *The House of the Rising Sun*, or *One Meat Ball*. Almost as disappointing was Lonnie Johnson, who had once accompanied Texas Alexander, as he smiled his way wistfully through *I Lost my Heart in San Francisco*. And then Big Bill Broonzy arrived.[90]

As the closing sentence of the quotation indicates, no singer seems to have had the impact that Big Bill Broonzy had in helping to form these stringent conceptions of blues. The singer dominates blues writing in the British jazz press during the fifties and beyond. Les Pythian argued that "[Big Bill Broonzy] is the first authentic representative of the 'genre' ever to hit this neglected land of ours. . . . His is the art of the true folk artist." This appreciation for Broonzy was effectively replicating the depiction of the singer by the French jazz critic Hugues Panassie:

> He is a plain blues singer, always sticking to the pure idiom of the early blues; by this, I mean the blues as they were sung and played before jazz music really started, and as they are still sung and played today way down in the State of Mississippi and other states in the South of the USA.[91]

It is apparent that Broonzy was much better at negotiating the demands of British audiences than some of his contemporaries, and the marker he set became the basis against which all subsequent live blues performances would be judged. It is very difficult to find a review of a blues performance or record without reference to Broonzy, and more often than not a major victim of this was Josh White: "It's fortunate that in blues singing the voice is least important . . . for a good voice and polish, we'll listen to Josh! Here [Broonzy] is the real thing, the style and feeling which are all-important." Oliver agreed, arguing that "[Broonzy's] hollering made Josh White seem slick and effete."[92] In addition to his performances, Broonzy also seems to have been a highly personable and charming character:

> He was quite different from the other singers because he talked to the audience almost as if they were his friend and it was the way in which everybody felt he was talking to them, so to speak. He just had an extraordinary stage manner and very relaxed and yet played so well. So I think his personality was one that was, you know, kind of engaged the audience.[93]

Oliver recalls that the singer "held audiences in the palm of his hand for hours," and his magnetic character is corroborated by the fact he became very close friends with a number of British blues enthusiasts, particularly Alexis Korner, with whom Broonzy actually lived for a short while. Korner described the singer as "a very human person," but also indicated a sense of awe at his otherworldliness: "But Bill Broonzy is from another world than ours and it is with his own people that he will always be happiest." Oliver also holds fond memories of his encounters with the musician, recalling the time when Broonzy visited for Valerie Oliver's birthday and insisting on cooking for the occasion.[94]

As Wald suggests, Broonzy's style in this period did have a more folk-based sound, and the singer had reverted to an older repertoire in order to satisfy the needs of his English audiences. Bob Riesman's recent biography highlights the singer's versatility and adaptability from the manner in which he managed to fill Robert Johnson's shoes for the Delta blues slot at John Hammond's 1938 "From Spirituals to Swing" concert at Carnegie Hall. This was after a period in which Broonzy had been developing a progressive urban blues sound by playing with groups in Chicago. Broonzy's experiences of the American race records industry throughout the 1930s, with the decline in record sales and, consequently, the radical drop in the number of blues recordings during the Great Depression, are indicative of the world within which blues actually existed. Images of Broonzy and scores of other blues artists sharply dressed in pin-striped suits during the late 1920s and 1930s, as well as the abundant advertising of the era, are representative of the recording industry that the blues was inherently part of in the interwar period. Indeed, Wald has used this as further evidence that the blues was the *pop* music of its time, and that blues musicians sought to make a living from their music, and were not as averse to commercial success as their postwar fans believed. What is more interesting here, however, is that the context of the race records industry, and the manner in which the recordings they valued so highly were produced, seem to have been either disregarded or forgotten in the minds of revivalist blues aficionados. This is particularly striking, given their reliance on recordings, and Broonzy seems to have played an instrumental role in helping to divorce the blues from the music industry. Despite having an almost unrivaled career as a blues artist, recording 744 titles for black audiences and exhibiting a range of musical styles and personas, Broonzy was able to portray himself skillfully to the British media as the archetypal bluesman with roots firmly within rural black life of the South.[95] In this sense, Broonzy becomes an extremely interesting character due to the fact that he played an active part in creating a sense of the blues based on a more "country" style that also depended on a lifestyle associated with black life in the rural South, highlighting how blues musicians could promote images of the music. He argued: "you got to be born a Negro in Mississippi and you got to grow up poor and on the land."[96] Manfred Mann guitarist Tom McGuiness even recalls the singer dressing in the typical southern sharecroppers' dungarees in order to portray the correct image to his British audiences.[97] Consequently, most blues musicians who made the trip to Britain in the fifties were compared to Broonzy for their authenticity, and all too often they struggled to achieve the same level of recognition.

However, Broonzy had also managed to cultivate his image as an authority on blues history, and given his African American origins and proficiency with the music, there were few to question him. In this context, in much the same way as Korner, Oliver came to accept the singer as "representing the living past." In his persona as a bluesman and a blues historian, Broonzy supplied a wealth of biographical, historical, and discographical information to collectors. For instance, Oliver recalls the time when Broonzy mentioned Muddy Waters as an up-and-coming blues singer at a time when very few had heard of him. Oliver therefore advocated the use of the singer's testimony for blues research by promoting the value of the autobiography, *Big Bill Blues,* compiled by Yannick Bruynoghe in 1955.[98] The stories that Broonzy told would become gospel to many British blues commentators, helping to form the rigid ideas of what the blues was, where it came from, and whom it belonged to.

Interviews and encounters with blues musicians were to become an important part of Oliver's career as a blues scholar, and in the fifties he began the process of interviewing visiting blues singers in Britain:

> Well, I mean, obviously I was very interested in interviewing them and they, I think, were genuinely surprised how much I'd known about them—I was trying to collect any bit of information I could from everywhere. And I generally had them come over to stay with me at least overnight.[99]

These encounters allowed Oliver not only the chance to obtain as much information as possible, but also to get to know the blues musicians on a more personal level, as was the case with Brother John Sellers.[100] Although recordings formed the basis for most of Oliver's research in this period, he acknowledged at the time that the transcription of records could never fully account for all the subtle qualities the recordings contained. He also often stressed the fact that African American folk music was rooted in the oral tradition of the folk culture, in which improvisation was the "golden rule." [101] Therefore, analysis of records could only reveal so much, and oral history could have a large part to play, especially considering the relative obscurity of the music at this time, and only a handful of its exponents were known to be still alive. Indeed, it was Broonzy who perpetrated this myth: "But the real old time singers who worked in the fields, there's almost none of them left now."[102] Consequently, the large amount of biographical information in articles that focused on singers, especially on those from the more distant past, such as Blind Lemon Jefferson and "Ma" Rainey, were dependent on the recollections and reconstructions from interviews with visiting musicians. Oliver often acknowledges that the interviewees could not always guarantee certainty in their recollections, and were often liable to exaggerate or exclude certain facts, and these are common consequences of using oral history.

Perhaps more than any other time, British blues scholarship in this period prior to the boom of the sixties was dealing with a significant lack of physical evidence that forced a reliance on record collecting, the use of secondary literature, and interviews with a handful of musicians. However, the obscure past of the music fostered a mysteriousness that was undoubtedly compelling for collectors. In fact, Oliver was intrigued by the immeasurable possibilities that the enigmatic lives of singers presented and the unknown element in the music's history, "for therein lies much of its fascination":

> But as the blues collector stares at the record label or listens whilst the needle summons again three lost minutes of a man's life some thirty years ago, he cannot help but speculate at times on the possible chain of circumstances that finally brought him from the city sidewalk and before the crude recording apparatus. . . . Where did he come from; who were his parents; when did he leave home? One wanders and falters, as the limitations of one's own personal experience make it almost impossible to imagine.[103]

This passage not only provides an example of the stimulus given by the "unknown" to the blues collector, but also highlights Oliver's acknowledgment of the imaginative qualities of listening as an activity. In a study on the role of radio in African American society, Tona Hangen argues that the role of listening through radio allowed African American listeners to "renegotiate racial boundaries." The medium allowed entry into a sensory experience that could ignore racial barriers, something not as easily tangible in the reality of the South, for example.[104] It can be argued that listening to records was a similar experience in the sense that it could allow Oliver to transcend the transatlantic gulf separating him from the South. Listening was also a key factor in the recording of oral history. Interviews with singers would often lead to the recollections of obscure singers from a lost era who were never recorded, leading Oliver to dwell on the identity of those on record label discographies labelled as "unknown."[105] The lack of physical material to discover the unknown elements may have facilitated the quantity of guesswork. However, the fascination of enthusiasts with the more obscure elements of blues history could help to explain the enormous interest during the blues revival in singers who had recorded little and were not widely known in their time, such as Robert Johnson, but who died in mysterious circumstances.[106] During the fifties, then, the blues was a puzzle in which a large proportion of the pieces were missing, pieces that scholars such as Oliver attempted to recover by analyzing records and interviewing visiting musicians.

Importantly, as Broonzy helped to shape the interpretation of black folk music in the eyes of British blues enthusiasts, popular music was opening its doors to the emerging sounds of rock'n'roll and rhythm and blues, which provided the soundtrack to the rise of an increasingly youth-orientated era. In 1954 the vocal group The Chords was the first African American group to cross over into the white best-seller charts with their hit "Sh-boom."[107] At the same time, Bill Haley and the Comets had some success with "Shake, Rattle and Roll" in December 1954, but with their next hit of October 1955, "Rock Around the Clock," which featured in the 1956 movie *Blackboard Jungle*, the group really caused a stir. The film was banned in many British cinemas, but the success of Haley's songs paved the way for Elvis Presley to take center stage the following year. At the same time, Mike Dewe notes how *Melody Maker*, formerly the magazine that carried the subtitle "for the best in jazz," began giving more column space to popular music following the increased competition offered by the *New Musical Express*'s pop charts.[108] For many of the writers in the jazz and blues press, these developments were either viewed with contempt or disregarded altogether:

> Just as Elvis Presley and his ilk have borrowed from the Negro—with disastrous results—the Negro youth in his turn has been influenced by the various facets of cheap commercialism with which we cannot help but come into contact.

The effect was to further demarcate the boundaries between pop music for entertainment and for the mindless youth, from the authentic folk music of a people unconcerned for commercial success, and who sang for "the sheer joy of making music."[109] This helps us to explain the apparent lack of consideration for how the blues of the 1920s and 1930s operated within a large recording industry. It lends weight to the argument that British blues scholars of the 1950s *chose* to emphasize the music's folk character, at the expense of understanding how the blues functioned within the modern phenomenon of the entertainment industry. Paradoxically, however, as the products of the race records industry would allow future generations from both sides of the Atlantic the opportunity to discover the blues, the music of the newer generations—Elvis, Buddy Holly, Chuck Berry, and Fats Domino—would be an entry point into the world of American music for many younger British listeners and musicians. As Tom McGuiness explains,

> I came to blues from a completely different perspective; I came to it from rock'n'roll. I wasn't into folk music particularly of any sort. I

> grew up with a bit of Irish folk music going on all round me, inevitably, but rock and roll just opened my eyes, opened my ears. Suddenly it was all there, and Big Bill Broonzy I didn't discover until much later. . . . I loved Chuck Berry, a fantastic song writer, fantastic guitar player, and that led me into the whole Chicago thing. I liked Muddy, I liked Wolf, I liked John Lee Hooker—I know he's not Chicago but same thing. I loved Buddy Guy, Magic Sam, Otis Rush. I love tough, hard rhythm and blues, so Big Bill and that whole area really didn't get to me, but now I see.[110]

Nevertheless, the emerging genres of the fifties that seemed to borrow from the blues were seen as the corruption of tradition and the loss of sincerity of expression. The marginalization of youth culture from the music press of this period further reinforces that the readership was more focused on the serious practice of collecting than on consumption.

An interesting challenge to the purism in blues scholarship came in the form of skiffle, which had been brewing in the UK since the late forties up to the "craze" period in 1956. A considerable proportion of skiffle was based on the songs of Woody Guthrie and predominantly Leadbelly. McGuiness remarks that "a whole generation" picked up guitars because of Lonnie Donegan following the success of "Rock Island Line" in January 1956.[111] This seemingly homemade music based on American folk songs and ballads indicates the popularity of American music in Britain in this period. However, while young "skifflers" looked to genuine folk sources in the eyes of jazz and blues critics, their efforts could not reach the level of their American progenitors. Oliver had already aimed some criticisms at British jazz musicians by arguing that the "whole British jazz movement is built wholly on imitation." Skiffle musicians suffered similar disapproval. Oliver held various criticisms for British musicians attempting versions of African American songs. British musician Ken Colyer was described as "singing without feeling," and Lonnie Donegan's failure to impress was given to the fact he was not "born of a folk heritage."[112] A description of Donegan's success years later exemplifies the writer's attitude toward skiffle:

> But no one expected the runaway success of Lonnie Donegan's Rock Island Line. The voice was Cockney/Deep South, the song was Leadbelly's, the singer's name was half Lonnie Johnson's. But the banjo player from Chris Barber's Jazz Band made a "skiffle" record which stood at number five in the charts in the United States within weeks, and eventually received the accolade of mimicry of Stan Freberg.[113]

It is evident that Oliver, as well as other "blues evangelists" and proselytizers of this period, had developed a clear notion of "how it was imagined the music of rural African Americans ought to sound," and clearly whites, especially British, were not able to replicate it.[114] In a later article Oliver would attempt to explain the popularity of American music at the time of skiffle by attributing it to the fact that whites had long since lost their own culture, and thus needed to "borrow" from another.[115] Thus, much the same as the pop music of Elvis, the skiffle boom in Britain was mostly regarded as a symptom of the Western cultural crisis by blues purists. By borrowing, British musicians could not be as sincere as someone like the pianist Champion Jack Dupree, depicted here in album review by Max Jones:

> Jack Dupree is a realist. Nothing in this album is remotely sentimental; indeed, as one American has written, nothing is romantic or even nostalgic. . . . I like it and believe it to be an example of "Come in and hear the truth."[116]

The contempt for popular music and approximation of black music by white musicians helps to contextualize the emphasis and fascination with African American folk culture that characterizes much of Oliver's writing. In many instances Oliver's descriptions take on a distinctly ethnocentric hue, as they echo the sentiments expressed earlier on in the twentieth century by W. E. B. DuBois, who argued that "the true Negro folk-song still live[d] . . . in the hearts of the Negro."[117] The underlying implication is that music as a form of expression had become unnatural for white Western culture, with musical production being too intricately tied to commerce and capitalism. Therefore, African American folk culture in its purest form was considered "unpalatable" for the white observer.[118] The blues of Blind Lemon Jefferson, although appearing primitive, crude, and unrefined to the white world, was "starkly dramatic, stripped of all superfluities," and "uncompromising" to the African American.[119] Similarly, Peetie Wheatstraw "sings for the coloured people with no thought for discographers or a white world."[120] The true folk blues singer, then, for Oliver, consciously rejected the materialism of the white world, and this is something that stands in contrast to the efforts of Big Bill Broonzy to prolong his recording career across the Atlantic. Oliver's interpretation of the "Negro world" and its folk culture was thus defined by its opposition to white Western culture. British skifflers like Donegan and Colyer could attempt African American songs, but in Oliver's eyes they would never be able to match the real thing. It would seem that later in the decade Oliver's writing was more orientated toward identifying cultural and class distinctions, moving away from the racialized tones of *negrophilie* which characterized some of his earliest descriptions of the African American world.

Despite the physical, cultural and historical distance marking Oliver's scholarship during the fifties, the interpretive methods for the analysis of blues, from the sociological interpretation of African American literature, the subjective realism of blues lyrics, the reception of the first blues visitors to Britain, to the activity of listening, allowed him and other blues enthusiasts to transcend "the cultural separation" separating them from the land of the blues.[121] It was then possible to imagine a "Negro world" within which the blues was one of the ways singers and audiences were able to cope with the strains imposed by the harsh realities of life in the American South. Music functioned as both a practice that allowed the African American to go on, and as a symbol of the undying folk heritage of the African American community defiant in the face of white capitalist oppression. Importantly, blues is seen as representative of an African American culture and approach to life that values human relationships and sincerity above any notions of commercial success or materialism. By contrast the music was reliant upon the white world pushing the "Negro world" further into obscurity, strengthening the group solidarity of a black music and culture. Ironically, while the blues existed within a place that seemed dislocated from the modern world, the objects used by blues collectors and writers were produced within the very modern context of a large recording industry, in which African Americans bought millions of records each year, where record labels operated very much as they do today and sought to produce the next hit, and where blues musicians often held very contemporary aspirations of "making it."[122]

However, the pervading folkloric perception that colors Oliver's writing in this period, presents the reader with images of a world where the boundaries between historical fact and fiction are often unclear. This lack of clarity is created by the romantic desire for a music beset by the enigmatic lives of singers, combined with a sense of loss of folk heritage in the modern postwar world. It is also characterized by an idealized view of black musicians and singers, who are often represented in a passionate language that sometimes borders on exoticism, and at other times identifies with African Americans more as a class than as a racial group. Importantly however, the influence of romanticism in Oliver's blues writing is not to be understood as a trait that devalues the worth of his research, but instead should be interpreted as one of the underlying features of the reception of African American music in this period. The level of personal involvement in Oliver's writing in the fifties reflects the personalized experience of the listening process and demonstrates the difficulty the blues writer faces in disengaging with his tastes. Oliver's writing in this period is crucial to understanding conceptions of the blues and African American culture years before the revival of the sixties, when the names of Robert Johnson and Charley Patton as beacons of authentic blues would become the norm, and the British invasion bands would begin paying homage to their idolized blues masters.

Figure 1. "Sources of Afro-American Folk Song 1—Down the Line," *Music Mirror*, vol. 1, no. 1, May 1954

Figure 2. "Chocolate to the Bone," *Music Mirror*, vol. 1, no. 7, November 1954

Figure 3 and 4. "Another Man Done Gone," *Music Mirror*, vol. 1, no. 4, August 1954

Figure 5. "Hometown Skiffle," *Music Mirror*, vol. 3, no. 11, February 1956

Figure 6. "Sources of Afro-American Folk Song 1—Down the Line," *Music Mirror*, vol. 1, no. 1, May 1954

Figure 7. "Down the Line," *Music Mirror*, vol. 1, no. 2, June 1954

Figure 8. "Devil's Son-in-Law," *Music Mirror*, vol. 3, no. 2, March 1956

Figure 9. "Boll Weevil Blues," *Music Mirror*, vol. 1, no. 3, July 1954

2 • *Blues Fell This Morning*

The Blues and Black Life

Oliver's *Blues Fell This Morning: The Meaning of the Blues* would have been the first dedicated book on the blues had it not been for a six-month printer's strike. The delay meant it appeared shortly after American folklorist Samuel Charters's *The Country Blues* (1959). For most researchers and writers of the 1960s and beyond, these two very different publications unofficially marked the beginning of blues being studied as a separate genre from jazz. Former editor of *Blues World* Bob Groom argues that these two publications "were the milestones" of blues research at the time.[1] Importantly, they also exemplify the simultaneous emergence of dedicated attention to blues scholarship on both sides of the Atlantic. It is also apparent that Oliver's book appealed to more than "serious" enthusiasts and budding ethnomusicologists. Guitarist of The Groundhogs Tony McPhee decided to hold a copy in his hand while dressed as a priest for the cover of the album *Blues Obituary* (1969), which invites the conjectural suggestion that for some white blues musicians the book was of "biblical" importance.[2] Since then, it has acquired an almost legendary status among blues writers. As Paul Garon recalls, "*Blues Fell This Morning* was the single most important work for my blues education." At the time of its release the book was an insight into a culture and world of experience that offered an alternative to what Alan Balfour, a contributor for the magazine *Blues & Rhythm*, called "the sanitized version of American history I was taught at school."[3] Interestingly, *Blues Fell This Morning* appeared in the same year as Harper Lee's Pulitzer Prize–winning novel *To Kill a Mockingbird* (1960), which shone a bright light on the racial discrimination and institutional injustice experienced by black Americans during the 1930s. Oliver's book was remarkable as it also sought to bring to light the life of African Americans in this period, although its central theme was very different. It also represented one of the first instances of British writing on the life of African Americans. As the photographer and jazz historian Val Wilmer recalls, at the time there was little writing on the subject in Britain that had examined the cultural and political implications of African American music.[4]

In many respects the book focused more on the context that produced the blues than the music itself. Oliver's passionately written and highly accessible narrative presented the lyrics of 350 blues songs, mostly taken from his personal collection of records from the 1920s to the early 1950s, and described the meaning those lyrics held within the context of the African American world. Explored are the most prevalent themes in blues songs such as work, relationships, sex, gambling, health and disease, poverty, superstition, natural disasters, and migration and rootlessness, but Oliver approaches each theme from the sociological condition that lyrics suggest, rather than analyzing the lyrics directly. The book brought together the bulk of Oliver's work throughout the fifties, which was aided by fellow record collectors and blues enthusiasts who helped to transcribe lyrics, find records, and provide contextual information.[5] However, in the pursuit of the meaning of blues lyrics and establishing blues as a musical genre worthy of study in its own right, *Blues Fell This Morning* highlights the reification of the blues and African American world that produced it, a process of "construction" that was gathering steam following a decade of blues scholarship, the tours of numerous blues musicians in Britain, and an increasingly diversified musical landscape.

Blues Fell This Morning makes it clear that rather than just representing a form of entertainment, the blues was intrinsically tied to social and economic circumstances of ordinary African Americans: it had a *meaning* for a specific people, and was thus worthy of scholarly attention. However, as this chapter will demonstrate, by relying on the lyrics of blues recordings, the book further reified the blues as a definable and identifiable category that set it apart from other music, be it jazz or the music of the new teenage generations beginning to take control of the charts in the late fifties. Oliver's methodology also saw the evolution of the image of the bluesman as a spokesperson for African Americans, the strengthening of the idea that blues mirrored their experiences, and fostered the notion of a more sincere and honest relationship between African Americans and the natural world. These motifs were upheld by an ever-present but subtle undertone of disillusion with the modern world symbolized by the commercial music industry. The focus on the conditions of African Americans in the first half of the twentieth century also begins to trace a narrative of the African American experience. In *Blues Fell This Morning* this is constructed in the combination of a sociological, and at times anthropological, survey of southern and urban black life in the United States, and the lyrics of blues songs. The result is a reality blurred with fiction that becomes manifest in poetic descriptions of nameless and imagined characters that are brought to life.

The "Outsider" Debate: Afrocentrism versus Paul Oliver

Importantly, *Blues Fell this Morning* is narrated by a British blues record collector and enthusiast yet to visit the United States. As his decision to stop playing music had demonstrated, Oliver was well aware of the possible misinterpretations this distance may have caused:

> Though possibly no further removed from my subject in distance than the historian is removed from his in time, I am acutely aware of my remoteness from the environment that nurtured the blues. The help given me by visiting blues singers has therefore been invaluable and I would like to express to them my heartfelt thanks for their patient interest and kindly forbearance of my endless questions. In many hours of conversation Big Bill Broonzy drew from his inexhaustible fund of memories of half a century; Jimmy Rushing recalled at length the hey-day of the twenties; Brownie McGhee and Sonny Terry reminisced on blues and blues singers of the thirties and forties, demonstrating many points, and Brother John Sellers gave me the benefit of his wide knowledge of the blues in the post-war years.[6]

Despite his "remoteness," Oliver was confident that his experiences with musicians visiting the UK, combined with a detailed survey of blues lyrics and the use of extant literature on African American society, would go some way to bridging the knowledge gap. The author also believed that dedicated record collecting was a means of infiltrating the world of the blues. While the accounts from blues singers like Broonzy and Sellers were invaluable, the intermixture of sociological description and memories from oral histories also created the possibility for realities to become blurred with nostalgia, or romanticism, something that became much more evident in *Conversation with the Blues* (1965) following Oliver's field trip in the summer of 1960. However, the issue of the blues critic's race *and* national origin was raised by the passionate appraisal for Oliver's work in the book's foreword, written by the African American author Richard Wright:

> As a Southern-born American Negro, I can testify that Paul Oliver is drenched in his subject; his frame of reference is as accurate and con-

> crete as though he himself had been born in the environment of the blues. Can an alien, who has never visited the *milieu* from which a family of songs has sprung, write about them? In the instance of such a highly charged realm as the blues, I answer a categoric and emphatic Yes. Indeed, I see certain psychological advantages in an outsider examining these songs and their meaning: his passionate interest in these songs is proof that the songs spoke to him across racial and cultural distances; he is geographically far enough from the broiling scene of America's racial strife to seize upon that which he, conditioned by British culture, feels to be abiding in them; and, in turn, whatever he finds enduring in those songs he can, and with easy conscience, relate to that in his culture which he feels to be humanly valid. In short, to the meaning of the blues, Paul Oliver brings, in the fullest human sense, what courts of law term "corroborative evidence."[7]

This calls to mind the Carnegie Corporation Board's selection of the Swedish sociologist Gunnar Myrdal for the sociological survey of the African American condition that resulted in the classic study *An American Dilemma*. Myrdal recalled that

> the whole [race] question had been for nearly a hundred years so charged with emotion that it appeared wise to seek as the responsible head of the undertaking someone who could approach his task with a fresh mind, uninfluenced by traditional attitudes or by earlier conclusions, and it was therefore decided to "import" a general director.[8]

Similarly, according to Wright, Oliver's "remoteness" was a distinct advantage, allowing the British author to examine the blues in a more objective light, free of any politically charged bias that may have clouded an American scholar. This was the self-confessed case of Charters, who recalls being motivated by the need to highlight the creative qualities of African Americans in order to challenge the racial and social injustice of America.[9] By contrast, Oliver could focus more on the aspects of the songs that made them unique, "humanly valid," and therefore universally appealing. Wright's conception of the blues is framed in the context of beauty emerging from tragedy, of the tenacity of the human spirit against insurmountable odds. He emphasized the fact that the African American history of slavery and racial oppression meant that the blues "ought not to have come into being."[10] In this sense, Wright espouses Oliver's thesis that the music was born of "a certain cultural separation," that

> the blues has grown with the development of Negro society on American soil; that it has evolved from the peculiar dilemma in which a particular group, isolated by its skin pigmentation or that of its ancestors, finds itself when required to conform to a society which yet refuses its full integration within it.[11]

The British scholar therefore believed that the black experience of Jim Crow segregation and racial discrimination were intrinsically bound to the story of the blues. For Wright, however, Oliver's sociocultural distance from this experience—the "milieu" of the blues—could be bridged by the fact that the content of the music was of universal character. While the music was the product of the African American experience, it gave voice to experiences that communicated across racial boundaries.

There are, however, many cultural critics that disagree with Richard Wright, arguing that Oliver's distance from African American culture has led to many misrepresentations and errors of judgement. More vociferous than any other has been Jon Michael Spencer, who has argued that "Oliver has done more than any other writer to impede the understanding of the blues and the race of people who were its creators." Indeed, he passionately challenged Wright's judgment that an "alien" could adequately write about the blues. To that question "the answer . . . is a categorical and emphatic No."[12] For Spencer, as well as many other ethnocentric commentators, external commentary has led to misrepresentations of the music due to the fact that in order to understand the blues, it is necessary to be native to the idiom—African American and from the South. However, this stance serves to perpetuate rather than challenge stereotypical clichés such as "White people can't sing the blues." While it is inevitable that the physical and cultural remoteness of white blues writers during the revival caused misrepresentations and romanticized ideas of the blues and black culture, to follow the ethnocentric argument presented by Spencer would nullify the validity of most kinds of social, anthropological, or historical research. The strict divisions drawn between white and black cultural categories as hermetic and separate from one another also tends to minimize the fluidity of cultural forms, as suggested by Hagstrom Miller's study. As Brian Ward suggests, the "Afrocentrism" that emphasizes the hermeneutic nature of black culture and seeks to overturn centuries of racial subordination can often work in favor of legitimizing the racial discourses of segregation.[13] Indeed, the ethnocentric debate also serves to minimize the impact of African American culture on white audiences, and the subsequent interaction of the two in the formation of ideas on the blues. The very existence of blues and jazz appreciation and scholarship in Europe from the twenties onward demonstrates that African American music had managed to establish a connection with peoples far beyond black America, giving evidence to the interpretation of Richard Wright. While the music of black artists and musicians became a multi-million-dollar industry at home, the music traveled well beyond the borders of the United States, and was therefore open to interpretation and representation from outside its "natural" home. Spencer's stance also places the responsibility of misrepresentation on white blues scholars, without acknowledging the role that blues singers themselves often took in creating the genre. As I have already suggested, blues singers such as Big Bill Broonzy were fundamental in transatlantic conceptions of the blues, and as Bob Riesman's biography demonstrates, the singer was a master of reinvention and of giving his audiences what they thought they wanted. It would be a bold assertion to suggest that only Broonzy did this. Oliver's scholarship on the blues—largely influenced by meetings and interviews with numerous singers—can help to bring to light the complicit role of singers in constructions of ideas about the blues during the revival.[14]

Paradoxically, a significant proportion of "white" writing shares many characteristics with the ethnocentrism of African American writers. Ironically, much in the same way that writers such as Spencer, Cone, and Murray have attempted to defend the blues from white appropriation and dilution, many white blues scholars have emphasized the fact that the blues belongs firmly within African American folk culture in order to defend the music from white cultural colonialism. Charters, for instance, argued that to understand the blues was to empathize with the "fabric of Negro life itself."[15] So much was the blues vital to the existence of African Americans, that the music was seen as being synonymous and representative of the African American experience. Richard Middleton also emphasized the importance of the African American experience to understanding the blues by arguing the music represented "the Negro's strategy for living" in an oppressive world.[16] William Barlow adopted a similar interpretation by placing the emphasis on a history from below, and arguing that a distinctive and separate African American culture, such as the blues represented, was vital to the survival of African Americans during and after slavery. Black folk songs were seen as being made up of past experiences and acted as "cautionary folktales" to solidify group cohesion. The lives of blues singers themselves were interpreted as representative of the separation from the mainstream: "Blues personas achieved mythical stature in the black community, constituting a black pantheon separate from—and in many ways antithetical to—the white heroes and heroines of middle-class America."[17] Even Oliver was effectively preempting the thesis of LeRoi Jones (Amiri Baraka) when he argued that "the blues has grown with the development of Negro society on American soil." In *Blues People* (1963), one of the most well-known books on the black American music, Jones equated the birth of the blues (albeit with a looser definition that blurred blues with jazz) with the emergence of a distinctive African American identity in the post-Emancipation era. He argued that the blues "represented a clearly definable step by the Negro back into the mainstream of American society," and that "the term 'blues' relates directly to the Negro, and his personal involvement in America."[18] As a consequence, most often white blues writers of the revival, as opposed to young white musicians, believed that white imitators and interpreters would never be fully capable of either replicating the music's function for African American communities or getting at the heart of the message the blues was believed to carry for its black audiences. The Afrocentric criticism of blues historiography therefore tends to divert attention from the more important questions on the nature of blues scholarship. What is of more interest is the fact that the music did become the object of study on both sides of the Atlantic, and Oliver's observations became highly influential in future representations of the music.

Mixed Reception

The early days of postwar blues writing were characterized by transatlantic correspondence and cooperation, which represented the fact that the blues was no longer limited to African American audiences. While disagreements in approach between American, European, and ethnocentric African American writers did emerge and persist into the second half of the twentieth century, the reactions to *Blues Fell This Morning* demonstrate that debates were as much internal (i.e., in the UK) as they were between nationalities and ethnicities. As Adam Gussow has shown, writers of the Black Arts movement of the late sixties and early seventies were divided on the role of the blues within a modern African American social and cultural consciousness.[19] In another example, African American author Ralph Ellison had argued that LeRoi Jones's narrative was too strongly dictated by the militant attitudes developing among certain black factions during the sixties, and for this reason he suggested that *Blues People* was more indicative of Jones's attitudes toward white America and the civil rights issue than it was of the blues. Interestingly, Ellison disagreed with Richard Wright regarding Oliver's approach to the blues. He defined *Blues Fell This Morning* as "a sadly misguided effort," arguing that the music had been better served by Stanley Edgar Hyman's essay "The Folk Tradition."[20] Hyman was reluctant to examine black culture as inherently oppositional to white and instead promoted the analysis of folk traditions as part of a more inclusive model of modern western literature. He had argued that when African American culture seemed closest to its African folk roots and ancestry, it was also transcendent of national or racial traits, and thus more "human."[21]

In Britain, the mixed reception that met the release of *Blues Fell This Morning* highlights the fact that the use of term "blues scholarship" could be misleading for the reason that it suggests some consensus in approaches, or established guidelines for research. Many of Oliver's "colleagues" were full of praise for the book. Fellow *Jazz Journal* critic Derrick Stewart-Baxter claimed it was a "remarkable documentary" and that the author was "a serious writer . . . for the serious student." *Jazz Monthly's* G. E. Lambert agreed, claiming that Oliver's monograph was "the best writing which has yet appeared on this subject."[22] More numerable were the criticisms, demonstrating that the interpretation of the music was highly subjective. Oliver recalls that Alexis Korner was one of the first to comment on BBC radio by stating, "This was not the book we were expecting." While it is unclear what Korner *had been* expecting, it seems likely that he shared the views of Bob Dawbarn, whose review in *Melody Maker* was entitled "This Could Have Been the Book on the Blues." Dawbarn was skeptical of the book's strict focus on the literality of lyrics and the social deprivation of African Americans, and argued that "all too often [Oliver's] text is a mere paraphrase of the verses he has quoted." Poet and jazz critic Philip Larkin concurred and stated that Oliver often fell into no more than "a mournful paraphrase of his material." Charles Fox echoed these sentiments by stating that the lyrics "are mainly used to illustrate the author's conclusions," and had expected more emphasis on the music and the singers than Oliver's sociological survey of African American life had allowed. Fox was also critical of the choice of songs selected for the book's accompanying record, arguing it was of "academic rather than aesthetic interest."[23] This prompted an article in response from Oliver, who justified his method of interpreting lyrics in relation to the lower-class black experience, and the selection of songs for the record: "I hoped to illustrate as many different *forms* of folk blues expression as possible."[24]

These reactions demonstrate that by 1960 the blues was being interpreted in differing ways by various British blues collectors and enthusiasts, and there were very different views about the type of research that was required. Oliver's record was obviously not enough to appease readers who had expected more information on blues singers and on the musical element. However, as Oliver's response to criticisms indicates, the author was convinced that an understanding of the social conditions in which African Americans lived was vital if any insights were to be gained on the meaning of the blues:

> For the majority of collectors, it may be fairly suggested, the appeal of listening to blues records lies mainly in the appeal of their musical qualities and often quite apart from the meaning of the verses themselves. But the music is the vehicle of expression; the true blues singer does not sing needlessly and his song is the medium by which he expresses what he intends to say. To appreciate the music without appreciating the content is to do an injustice to the blues singers and to fail to comprehend the full value of their work. In view of his peculiar social status and the complexities of the racial relations in the United States the world of the blues singer is circumscribed. His blues have meaning for him and he has ideas to express; it is impossible either to enjoy or to understand the blues to the full through the musical qualities alone.[25]

Here Oliver was essentially differentiating the music from other more popular genres. Blues singers did not sing "needlessly," and therefore there was more to the music than the rhythm that caused a foot to tap or a head to nod in time. There was meaning in the blues that needed to be communicated, and thus, discovered.

Blues Fell This Morning

Much of the early jazz literature in Britain that devoted space to the study of blues had laid the foundations for Oliver's main line of inquiry in the book. The thematic study of lyrics was the most common method employed by jazz writers seeking to unlock the music's African American roots. This was due to the fact that most jazz and blues critics were not musicologists, and also—given the British scholar's forced reliance on records—partly because lyrics were one of the few sources of "raw" materials available for interpretation.

The practice of associating the lyrics of songs with the lived experience of the singer's themselves was in many ways an inevitable outcome of the association of blues with its African American origins, and a result of the superficial link formed between the music's aural, or "blue," characteristics, and the African American position in American society. Many blues scholars have developed highly convincing arguments from this form of enquiry. Garon, for instance, approaching his analysis from a surrealist perspective, argued that the blues contains "an explosive essence of irreconcilable revolt against the shameful limits of an unlivable destiny," and that the music's appeal was due to "the universal nature of the forbidden wishes it expresses." In another important study, Angela Davis used the lyrics of three blues women, Gertrude "Ma" Rainey, Bessie Smith, and Billie Holiday, to reveal the existence of "a historical feminist consciousness that reflected the lives of working-class black communities." Guido Van Rijn also continues to examine blues expression in relation to historical realities, such as the American presidents.[26] Most analyses of blues lyrics are pervaded by what Frith refers to as "reflection theory," that is, the faith in the lyrics of folk songs to convey the real world. However, as Frith's critique of this theory argues, what has become ever more apparent in the realist interpretation of words in songs is that the method has suffered overwhelmingly from the arbitrary subjectivity of the interpreter. The extent to which certain songs convey reality more than others is largely determined by the person examining their meaning.[27]

This problematic aspect of the interpreter's subjectivity must also be considered alongside the nature of the music on record. The enormous body of blues songs available for analysis, the three decades or more the recordings span, the effects of the boom of the 1920s, the Depression of the 1930s, the range of styles this encompasses, the varying audiences to which blues have been directed, and the idiosyncratic approaches of individual singers to composition are just some of the factors that contribute to the idiom's accessibility from a range of standpoints. In essence, blues lyrics deal with such an overabundance of subjects and employ such wide-ranging techniques that the blues writer's selection of songs, combined with their organization into a narrative, becomes emblematic of a constructed representation of the subject. Also, it needs to be remembered that until recently, most blues historians including Oliver have assumed that the record industry of the interwar years was able to record thousands of singers and sell millions of records *while* managing to preserve a folk music on record. Oliver acknowledged the scale of the music industry in this period, noting that it is highly likely that five to six million records were bought annually by African Americans in the mid-twenties.[28] Nonetheless, the manner in which blues musicians performed, recorded, and wrote lyrics *within* and *for* the music industry has not received the full attention that the blues' folk origins have. As uncomfortable as it has been for many blues aficionados, Elijah Wald's thesis in *Escaping the Delta* has forced us to acknowledge that many blues singers did see music as a means of making a living, as a way out of sharecropping and manual labor, and had very familiar aspirations of material success and "making it." This was something that most blues writers of the revival were either unwilling to admit or unable to see, highlighting the inherent subjectivity of analyzing blues lyrics.

The room for invention in the interpretation of blues lyrics is not dissimilar from the deconstructionist theories of historical practice. Questioning the classical notions of historical knowledge based on empiricism, Friedrich Nietzsche asserted that "history is the work of the dramatist: to think one thing with another, and weave the elements into a single whole, with the presumption that the unity of plan must be put into objects if not already there."[29] Much in the same way that poststructuralism refuted the subject's complete grasp of *the* historical truth, there is no absolute historical truth or meaning to blues that is not created at some level by the interpreter. This is not a denial of the existence of a truth to the blues or its meaning, but an acknowledgment of the blues scholar's inability to obtain its reality fully. From the selection of songs that exist, as much as historical artifacts or documents, in "a pre-jigsawed state," the blues writer weaves the various and sometimes disparate elements that constitute the lyric content of songs and brings them into a unified narrative. The author then actively controls and directs the blues singer's gaze to reveal a specific vision of the world, which ultimately is more indicative of the author's vision of the object he is seeking to describe. It must be said that in later editions of *Blues Fell This Morning* Oliver dropped the definite article from the subtitle, now "Meaning in the Blues," perhaps in order to avoid drawing absolutist conclusions on the significance of blues songs.

Nonetheless, Oliver's analysis in the first edition of *Blues Fell This Morning* is an example of this subjectivity. Writing in the late fifties, Oliver was using material that was predominantly from the interwar period and mostly from his personal collection to offer a cross section of the genre, and to show that "the thematic content of the blues related to many aspects of black experience."[30] Oliver was careful to avoid overgeneralizing and was fully aware of the selectiveness of his sample. While pointing out that omissions of certain singers were "in no way an indication of personal prejudice," the book still clearly identifies a particular kind of blues, predominantly what Charters referred to as "country" blues and what Titon later termed "down-home" blues.[31] Oliver was thus effectively demarcating the boundaries of the genre by making clear what was *not* blues. The discography in the book reveals that most of the songs are from the late twenties to the thirties, and the few numbers that date after that period are from singers whom Oliver regarded as representative of the same tradition of country-style blues, such as John Lee Hooker, Muddy Waters, Big Bill Broonzy, St. Louis Jimmy, and J. B. Lenoir. This selection points toward the development of a blues narrative that would take shape in Oliver's *The Story of the Blues* (1969). This effectively traced the origins and diffusion of a blues tradition that ran alongside the African American experience of the Great Migration from the 1920s through to the late 1940s.[32] This narrative has the tendency to marginalize the changes in the nature of the recording industry from the classic blues craze of the 1920s to the Great Depression, or, more importantly, the changes in the behavior of audiences—what records African Americans bought and why. This is an important aspect that is worth noting. While the focus here is on the transatlantic reception of the blues, there is much more to be learned about black audiences and their appetite for records during the interwar years. Again, it is Wald who attempts to highlight the workings of the race records industry in this period, demonstrating how record companies sought to produce the next big hit through "hip" and "urbane" acts. He gives the examples of Leroy Carr, and the duo of Tampa Red and Georgia Tom, who had respective hits with "How Long—How Long Blues" and "It's Tight Like That" in 1928. Indeed, it was this slicker "barroom" model of artist that record labels sought in order to sell records throughout the next decade.[33] The commercial side of the blues records industry, the desire of labels and musicians to be successful or even please audiences, is something that sits uncomfortably with Oliver's categorization of folk blues in *Blues Fell This Morning*.

Oliver's categorization marginalises the newer, electrified, and blues-derived styles that had emerged at Oliver's time of writing. So the blues-infused genres of rock'n'roll and rhythm and blues of musicians such as B. B. King, Chuck Berry, Little Richard, Fats Domino, Ray Charles, or even Nat "King" Cole, which were increasingly popular with black audiences in the immediate postwar years, have marginal space in the book. Interestingly however, the music of many of these performers was much closer to that which appealed to young British musicians. Mick Jagger and Keith Richards both recall developing an interest in music in their late teens by listening to the hybrid styles of Elvis, Buddy Holly, Jerry Lee Lewis, and Chuck Berry.[34] Oliver recalled that he had omitted this music because it had "reduced its content," in the sense that it no longer had a meaning to communicate to its audiences and had simply become a form of thoughtless entertainment.[35] Thus, *Blues Fell This Morning* begins to highlight the widening rift between the blues as interpreted by Oliver (and other blues scholars) and the world of popular music. This rift had a certain generational aspect. The end of the fifties and beginning of the sixties witnessed younger audiences engaging with music derived from the blues, and young musicians emulating the sounds of American rhythm and blues. As Alexis Korner had acknowledged, "America has 'invented' The Teenager. . . . The younger fans want new voices. They are on the whole, an audience that likes to know but does not want to learn."[36] The more purist elements of blues writings were highly territorial, as Keith Richards recalls fairly cynically:

> The real blues purists were stuffy and conservative, full of disapproval, nerds with glasses deciding what's really blues and what ain't. I mean, these cats *know*? They're sitting in the middle of Bexleyheath in London on a cold and rainy day, "Diggin' My Potatoes." . . . Half of the songs they're listening to, they have no idea of what they're about, and if they did they'd shit themselves.[37]

Oliver would comment years after that "it was no coincidence that the black audiences quit the blues like it had never been, when the Beatles and the Stones topped the charts."[38] Having lost its relation to the black community and become a form of entertainment for white audiences, the blues was seen as having lost its original raison d'être. These cultural conflicts help to understand the manner in which *Blues Fell This Morning* roots the music firmly within the context of the black experience, an attempt to establish the meaning of the music by relating it to African American reality.

The Blues as "Mirror"

> Only the American Negro, whether purple-black or so light-skinned as to be indistinguishable from his sun-tanned White neighbour, can sing the blues.[39]

Oliver's book is centered on the premise that the blues are largely a reflection of the social and cultural context of the African American world. This belief emanates from a long-standing view of the deterministic relationship envisioned between folk music and its environment dominant in the work folklorists and revivalist jazz critics throughout the early twentieth century, to which Oliver adhered strongly: "the folk singer is influenced by his environment, and his work is largely a reflection of it."[40] In the case of the blues and the African American experience, there existed a greater potential for this relationship to be emphasized given the backdrop of Jim Crow segregation and the social deprivation characterizing black life in the United States. As the quote above indicates, Oliver maintains the imagined racial integrity of the music, but not without some element of irony, as his own work upholds the view that it is possible for white observers to analyze the music, even though they may not be able to sing it. This motif is reinforced by Wright's foreword that frames the story of the blues as one of beauty arising from misery. Thus, the music in *Blues Fell This Morning* is seen as giving voice to the African American experience:

> In the blues were reflected the effects of the economic stress on the depleted plantations and the unexpected prosperity of the urban centres where conditions of living still could not improve. In the blues were to be found the major catastrophes both personal and national, the triumphs and the miseries that were shared by all, yet private to one. In the blues were reflected family disputes, the upheavals caused by poverty and migration, the violence and bitterness, the tears and the happiness of all. In the blues an unsettled, unwanted people during these periods of social unrest found the security, the unity and the strength that it so desperately desired.

Oliver's belief was that it was precisely the African American experience that forced meaning upon the music, signifying that "the true blues singer does not sing needlessly," and making the lyrics of blues songs "socially significant."[41] He wanted to demonstrate that African American life—the experiences of social, economic, and psychological hardship that characterized the existence of black Americans—gave birth to the blues.

He achieves this by detailing the physical and psychological conditions of a particular situation, such as the search for work in the aftermath of Reconstruction, and then follows the description with the lyrics of a song that give the situation a voice:

> The last quarter of the nineteenth century saw an ever-increasing movement of Negro workers from state to state. By 1910 nearly one and three-quarter million Negroes had left their home states for others and of these some had moved West and half a million had gone North. As the pressure of hostile opinion and legislation became even greater, Negro workers sought new employment and travelled long distances in order to find it. In the ensuing years they were to be followed by thousands more.
>
> REFRAIN
>
> 2. Poor boy, poor boy, poor boy, long ways from home.
> I was down in Louisiana doin' as I please,

Now I'm in Texas I got to work or leave.
Poor Boy, *etc.*[42]

Another example is presented in the context of the 1930s and the New Deal, when schemes such as the Public Works Administration (PWA) and the Works Progress Administration (WPA) provided some employment for African Americans during the Depression:

> Though the men were not driven as many of them had been on the Southern plantations and the work was not by these standards hard, yet the road grading, the drilling and manual labour involved in many of the construction schemes was heavy enough, and the work paid only moderately well. Faced with the high rents that are charged in Negro sectors, and the debts incurred by having goods on credit in lean times, a labourer still had good reason for anxiety.

34. Working on the project with holes in all my clothes, (twice)
Trying to make me a dime, to keep the rent man from putting me out doors.

I am working on the project, trying to make both ends meet, (twice)
But the pay-day is so long, oh well, well, until the grocery man won't let me eat.[43]

It is evident here that Oliver did not base his focus on the lyrics themselves, but rather used the content of the songs as expressions of real situations. In this sense, Oliver's use of lyrics takes the shape of a "semantic soundtrack," much in the same way as the score of a film or documentary. This is made even clearer in Oliver's exploration of common health problems experienced by African Americans, such as the malady of pellagra, which is followed by lyrics that do not explicitly mention the disease, but are suggestive of ill health: "I'm in a bad condition, and I'm still going down slow."[44] There are numerous examples of blues singers who experienced some of the realities described by Oliver, such as James "Boodle-It" Wiggins, who was brutally lynched after he failed to step off the pavement as a white woman walked past him. There are also numerous blues songs written in response to specific events experienced by singers as well as millions of African Americans, such as the numerous songs on the 1927 Mississippi floods, or "Working on the Projects," as in the latter instance.[45] However, as the pellagra example indicates, many songs show only tenuous links with the physical reality that Oliver describes. What this highlights is that while the relationship between blues lyrics and reality is in some cases self-evident, in many others it is somewhat forced by the author, thereby helping to construct the idea that the blues function as a mirror of contemporary black life.

The perceived link between the music and reality comes from the manner in which the *language* of the blues was interpreted. For years, blues lyrics had been viewed as equal to speech, that is, sincere and direct. Max Jones argued that "the real blues sings out directly, unconcernedly, of life as it really is." Iain Lang and Rex Harris had also stressed the directness of blues lyrics and the comment they provided on the world as it appeared to the singer. This was perhaps best summarized by Francis Newton (Hobsbawm) who stated: "Nobody beats about the bush in the blues."[46] *Blues Fell This Morning* was no different, with Oliver declaring the blues to be "forthright and uncompromising" in all subjects: "the blues singer sings in the language that he speaks," and thus "[blues] expression was a natural and uninhibited one."[47] This pervasive view of blues expression was built upon the interpretation of the difference of African American language from that of Western popular music. Oliver often makes the effort to explain the difference, warning readers that to those who are unaccustomed with this form of expression, the lyrics could appear crude, coarse, and sometimes offensive: "the forthright, uninhibited language of the blues must be accepted, and what is more, accepted without reserve or apology, for it is a natural transposition of the everyday language of both users and hearers."[48] This sets up a dramatic binary opposition between the blues and popular music: "in popular song and in particular the concoctions of 52nd Street euphemistic phrases are sung and winsome, sentimental, erotically evasive symbols are universally employed."[49] The blues is therefore natural, unadorned by masquerade and sometimes brutally honest, unlike its direct opposite, which is "concocted" and, thus, false and dishonest.

Bluesman as Spokesman and the Blues as Catalyst

Oliver's representation of the blues as a reflection of the African American world, sung in a language that resembled everyday speech, places the blues singer at the heart of the story. The blues singer effectively takes on the role of the spokesperson for the race, giving voice to shared experiences,

> He is a realist, intimately concerned with his subjects but having no illusions about them. . . .

> In the sharply defined images of life that the blues reflects are mirrored the minutiae of experience of the ordinary Negro man. The words that the blues singer utters, the thoughts, passions, and reactions to which he has given voice are those that are shared by countless thousands of his fellows.[50]

The realism that Oliver reads in lyrics stems from his the view that the blues singer "sings from experience rather than sentiment."[51] With this affirmation the image of the bluesman begins to take shape, as a figure who has experienced being black in a white country, and has the capacity to articulate those experiences through song. The literal interpretation of blues lyrics with the "I" either embodying the autobiographical voice of the singer or representing the shared experience of the folk, works to form the image of the blues singer as the voice of all ordinary African Americans. The music was not simply a matter of pleasure, or entertainment, but spoke *to* and *of* a people, and it is in this sense that Oliver interprets blues as folk music, with the songs expressing the experiences and thoughts of the individual blues singer as well as the black community. A historical situation is presented such as the migration northward caused by World War I:

> The cessation of the influx of European immigrants coincided with Henry Ford's pronouncement, in 1914, that none of his workers would earn less than five dollars per day, and it was in that year that he commenced to employ Blacks on his assembly lines. As his huge plants in Detroit continued to expand and more coloured workers were taken on, the news reached the remotest corners of the South and attracted men who had been living in penury.
>
> 22. I'm going to Detroit, get myself a good job, (twice)
> Tried to stay around here with the starvation mob.
>
> I'm goin' to get me a job, up there in Mr. Ford's place (twice)
> Stop these eatless days from starin' me in the face. [52]

The lyrics of the song are presented to express the experience of the situation, with the blues singer singing of his personal involvement experience, which becomes also that of all African Americans who migrated. This example is complemented by another, which describes the fact that not all those who migrated found the improved conditions they had hoped:

Negroes who had gone North to find better employment became disillusioned; the South that they had left in bitterness now seemed less cruel. Cotton prices had risen to nine cents in 1940, to fourteen cents in 1941 and were to rise to twenty cents in the following year. Many were attracted southward. Sang Roosevelt Sykes:

38. (Spoken) Well I'm going back down South, where men are men, and

    women are glad of it
    Oooh—I've got those Southern blues, (twice)
    Cotton prices going higher, an' I ain't got no time to lose.[53]

In these examples it can be seen that Oliver saw these songs as expressions of the reality of African American life. The blues singer was heard as a voice of "real" experiences, giving the music value as a form of oral history, with the blues singer as the storyteller.

From the manner in which Oliver summarizes the sentiments of "Negroes who had gone North," it could be argued that the author was narrating a rather simplistic form of history, which suited the fairly vague and sometimes general lyrics of songs. Indeed, to say that the millions of African Americans who migrated were generally "disillusioned" with conditions in the North and regarded the South in a new light would be to simplify a number of historical experiences, expectations, and responses to the Great Migration. Between 1.5 and 2 million black Americans moved out of the rural South in the half century between World War I and the mid-1960s. The reasons for moving were multifaceted, from the labor demands caused by the effects of two world wars, flight from violence and discrimination, the collapse of cotton prices, to the simple desire for a better life.[54] In the case of Roosevelt Sykes, for example, the singer was singing as much of women who were glad of men being men, as he was of cotton prices. This perhaps demonstrates the selective and subjective character of interpreting lyrics as the mirror of the real world. But in *Blues Fell This Morning*, the relationship between the blues and the African American world takes many forms. For instance, Oliver describes the relief from hard labor that people sought in barrelhouses and gin mills, places that were often pervaded by violence, and uses the blues singer's experience of a similar event as an example: "I took a gal to the beer tavern, things was lookin' hot / But my ole lady took her pocket knife and cut out my baby's heart."[55] In another instance, Oliver describes some of the conditions forcing African Americans to wander and drift on the road during the Depression:

> The droves of coloured men, women and children who were to be seen scuffling along the dirt roads were unwelcome to both White and coloured communities. As the years wore on and money became scarce, when the poverty of those who wandered in the streets was almost equalled by that of the residents of homes for which they could not afford the rent, the begging cup of the hobo "bumming his chuck" and seeking a "handout" became more resented.
>
> 56. I have walked a lonesome road ill my feet is too sore to walk (twice)
> I beg scraps from the people, oh well, till my tongue is too stiff to talk.[56]

The use of lyrics in this paraphrased style force the link between the social reality of the African American experience and the blues. The blues singer is regarded as having lived the life of which he or she sings, which in turn, gives the singer an incontrovertible authenticity not only as a musician, but as a storyteller, a historian, and the voice of a people.

Interestingly, the "direct" and "uncompromising" language read in the lyrics is interpreted not only as a form of communication, but as a philosophical stance, the blues singer's approach to life. This is presented in the case of the Depression where African Americans, particularly those living in the rural South, had been hit hardest by stock market crash of 1929. In fact, these represented half of the nation's black population, and most suffered the effects of the drop in cotton prices from 18 to 6 cents per pound between 1929 and 1933. As a result, by then most African Americans struggled to find any kind of employment.[57] Oliver chronicles the difficulties of finding work using Walter Davis's 1945 recording of "My Friends Don't know Me":

> Negroes found that at first they were still George Schyler's "mudsill of America" and in the struggle for employment they had lost ground even in the hated "jobs." Accustomed to the fight for survival, they accepted the situation philosophically.
>
> 30. I woke up this morning laughing, laid down last night a-crying, (twice) Lost all my money, broke and didn't have a dime

When I had money, I had friends for miles around,
Hmmmmm-mmm I had friends for miles around,
Ain't got no money, my friends don't seem to know me now.[58]

The sincerity of the lyrics is read as an expression of the African Americans' acceptance and endurance of whatever life brings forth, in this case the unemployment and poverty caused by the effects of the Depression. This model is repeated throughout the book. Oliver describes the deprivation of black housing and the risks of disease and destruction that plagues the living conditions of African Americans, and in turn outlines that the endurance of these conditions justifies the "Negro's despairing fatalism." Additionally, blind blues singers, crippled by their disability, "seldom seek sympathy" and instead produce songs that state facts and sing of things as they are without complaint. This is exaggerated in the stark image Oliver portrays of a man dying with his wife at his bedside: "Fatalistically, the sick man faces death and, trying to spare the suffering of those that he leaves behind, asks only that he be remembered with love and not with tears when he is laid in the cold ground."[59] Thus the blues singer also assumes a heroic sense of stoicism, accepting the world as it is and enduring any hardship, including impeding death, without self-pity or protest.

The heightened and idealized representation of blues singers as spokespersons that is constructed in Oliver's interpretation of lyrics helps to explain the important role they and the music play in black society: "The blues acted as a catalyst for the blinding anger and frustration that sought to demolish the moral codes and spirit of a man, and the act of artistic creation brought satisfaction and comfort both to him and his companions."[60] From this comment it is clear that Oliver reiterates the value of blues as a "folk" in terms of its function of allowing a release of anxiety for the black performers and audience as a whole. Oliver argued that blues was popular among African Americans precisely because the music "had meaning not only for the singer but for every Negro who listened."[61] Despite the fact that Oliver had been careful to point out early on that "the blues does not reflect the whole of Negro life in the United States," this is often contradicted by the representation of blues singers as central figures in African American communities: "The death of a blues singer is a tragedy within the Negro race and its repercussions are little felt by other Americans."[62] Not only is the image of the blues singer presented almost as a messiah, but the distance of black culture from the dominant white mainstream of American society is firmly established. Therefore, the blues—functioning as a coping strategy for those "close to moral and mental disintegration"—is also distanced from the perceived function of popular music, whose sole purpose is imagined as resting in fickle and insignificant entertainment.[63] The framing of the blues as folk music in *Blues Fell This Morning* is therefore achieved as much in terms of its opposition to contemporary culture, as it is the music displaying certain musical or aesthetic traits that distinguish it as folk. Despite the inherent contradictions in defining the blues as folk, one of the principal ways in which Oliver attempts to do this is by describing the African American world as one different from the reader's, and therefore in need of deep description and explanation.

The Real and the Imagined

Blues Fell This Morning is in many ways an interpretation of African American life from the end of the nineteenth to the middle of the twentieth century, as much as it is an exploration of the blues idiom. This was in line with the author's objective of gaining an insight into the social, cultural, and economic background that produced the music. Oliver made use of a range of sources in order to describe in detail various facets of African American life, from the research of anthropologists such as B. A. Botkin and Melville Herskovitz, the sociologist Gunnar Myrdal, African American writing such as that by W. E. B. DuBois, Richard Wright, and Adam Clayton Powell Jr., to the statistics on the African American population provided by the United States Information Service (USIS). As a result, each chapter gives a detailed account of the social and economic and conditions of African Americans. Oliver details the physical harshness of the various types of manual labor faced in both rural and urban settings; he describes the disenfranchizing systems of sharecropping and debt peonage locking black laborers; the experience and impact of large-scale events such as the Depression and the two world wars; the social, economic, and racial push-and-pull factors conditioning migratory movements; the experience of violence, whether through the forces of race prejudice or those caused by desperation and anxiety; he examines the nature and composition of the African American family; the role of religion and superstition in black culture; he provides an account on the African American appropriation of popular stereotypes, such as the caste system, upheld by the black community as much as it is perpetrated by racism; and he provides a grim account of the social deprivation that causes the increased level of health problems among the black population. It is unsurprising that in his review the jazz critic Philip Larkin described the book as "a drab and depressing recital."[64]

However, it was Oliver's intention to demonstrate that the negative aspects associated with African American life, such as increased rates of crime and violence, promiscuity and disease, lack of hygiene, laziness and rootlessness, were products of the social and economic circumstances that deprived them of adequate housing, employment opportunities, education, and sanitation. He effectively wanted to argue that

> Psychologically, biologically, and anthropologically the belief that the Negro is inferior to the White man and incapable of the higher emotions is fallacious and insupportable. The capacity for love, for devotion, for courage, for selflessness is no less than that of any other group, even if conversely he is as prone to similar weaknesses of rapacity, avarice, or hatred as are others.[65]

The author attempts to nullify misrepresentations of African Americans by giving sociological and psychological explanations. A clear example is made in the case of the propensity for superstition among African Americans:

> Victimized by circumstances over which he has no control, facing adverse conditions with no conception of the events that have brought them about, witnessing friends and relatives falling sick and dying with no cause that he can comprehend, the primitive and uneducated man falls readily into superstition. Observing a sequence of events or noting the coincidence of happenings strange or unexpected in themselves, he will satisfy his desire for understanding and seek to quieten his disturbed mind by drawing illogical but acceptable relationships between them. Frequently it is the lack of even a rudimentary education rather than inferior intelligence or intellectual capacity that causes a man to invent or accept such superstitions as a substitute for knowledge.[66]

Similarly, the inclination that many African Americans seemed to have for gambling can be explained by the underlying lack of social mobility and unstable economic status. With regards to the higher rate of health problems among the black population, Oliver argued that "the Negro is often more openly exposed to illnesses of many forms because he is insufficiently equipped to oppose them."[67] In this sense, Oliver adopts a descriptive style that oscillates between the sociological and anthropological as it aims to dispel racial stereotypes by arguing that the social and environmental conditions marginalizing African Americans are at fault. It might be supposed that Oliver sought dispel some popular myths at a time when racial stereotyping in Britain had been conditioned by a number of factors. World War II was not a distant memory, and the presence of African American GIs in the UK and the "brown baby" legacy had caused substantial friction in different parts of the country.[68] While Alan Lomax had gone a long way to producing educational programs on African American culture for the radio, the representation of black culture on television was somewhat different. *The Black and White Minstrel Show*, a program with whites dressed up in blackface performing song-and-dance routines, began to air on prime-time television in 1958, and would continue to do so for two decades. The same year also saw the spilling of racial tensions on to the streets of Nottingham in August, and in London with the Notting Hill race riots of September.[69] Therefore, in *Blues Fell This Morning*'s educational tone became most evident the "scholasticism" of British blues research, heavily focused on fact and empirical evidence.[70] Oliver's descriptions attempted to humanize the African American population by suggesting that their condition is forced upon them, rather than being a manifestation of a different and inferior race. This is also suggestive of Oliver's focus on the African American population as a coherent and distinctive class group, shifting away from some of the more overt *negrophilie* of his articles in the fifties.

While Oliver aims for this inclusive approach in one sense, he also assumes a descriptive style that encourages the interpretation of the African American as "other." This appears in the detailed explanations that deal in particular with African American systems of behavior. In the following extract, Oliver attempts to explain the motivation behind certain feelings that are described as if alien to the reader:

> As the extremes of mental capacity, of madness and genius sometimes seem to converge, so too the extremes of emotion seem closely allied. Outbursts of anger may come when the heart is bursting with affection; pain and pleasure are inextricably interwoven; the deepest feelings of love may readily turn to the cruellest hate. Humiliation, frustration, bitterness and selfishness are bound up in the complex emotions that are experienced by the lover whose partner has been unfaithful.
>
> 118. If I was cold and hungry, I wouldn't even ask you for bread
> (twice)
>
> I don't want you no more, if I'm on my dying bed.
> At one time I loved you, but sure do hate you now, (twice)

Baby, you are the kind don't need no good man nohow.

Ev'ry man in town knows about your ornery ways (twice)
Cain't nobody change you now, 'cause you've been a devil all of
your days.[71]

Once again the lyrics function to convey the presence of these "extreme" emotions among African Americans. Not only does the author attempt to explain these emotions, but also inherently promotes the idea that the intensity of these feelings is less prevalent in the world of the reader, as in the case of love:

> The blues singer brought a basic simplicity of mind to the subject: he seldom attempted to unravel the problem but states his condition of heart in uncomplicated terms that in their sincerity lost little.
>
> 99. Don't leave me, baby, 'cause I'm so down and blue (twice)
> Deep down in my heart, baby, my love is only for you.
>
> You are the only woman ever got into my heart, (twice)
> Lawsy, how would I live, baby, if we were to part?
>
> I'm down and blue an' I'm as blue as I can be, (twice)
> Because your love, baby, means all this world to me.[72]

What begins to emerge in Oliver's description of the African American world is an almost supernatural relationship of the black community with the instinctive aspects of human emotion. Indeed, the author was unconvinced by the Victorian modes of thought evidenced in early writing on the blues (such as Lang) that had adopted stereotyped views of the "depressed classes [as] incapable of spiritual love."[73] As a consequence, Oliver takes this to extreme lengths by depicting the lower-class African American as possessing natural human qualities that have been erased by modern life in the West. This is replicated in the relationship that Oliver envisions between the African American and the natural world:

> Since the Negro appeared in any appreciable numbers on the West Coast, there have been no earth tremors of any consequence and away from the Pacific volcanic perimeter ring such subterranean movements are not a serious problem in the United States. But though

> earthquakes do not bother him, the Negro still feels very much at the mercy of the earth; for so many of his fellows their entire lives have depended upon its fertility. The lives of a large proportion of Negroes are closely associated with the fundamental elements of the Ancients: with Earth, Air, Water and Fire.[74]

This presumed understanding between African Americans and the land aligns Oliver with the romanticism pervasive in the folk revival, which longed for a long-lost connection to the natural world. It allows the possibility for some assumptions regarding the desires of ordinary African Americans, as in the case of black prisoners: "they prefer to be in the state farms than in the jails where the congestion, the inactivity, the boredom destroys the soul. They can smell the earth, see the sky, sing, and work with their companions."[75] Thus, Oliver's description and explanation of African American life has an inherently paradoxical quality. Historical and sociological facts that pertain to the realities of African American life are intertwined with the psychological assumptions made from the interpretation of lyrics, demonstrating the convergence of fact and fiction.

Reality and imagination become indistinguishable particularly in Oliver's semifictionalized descriptions of scenarios that attempt to explain the African American state of mind. Continuing this manner of narration from his articles throughout the fifties, in *Blues Fell This Morning* it occurs most vividly in the exploration of relationships between men and women, and infidelity in particular:

> For the man who has struggled hard to try and secure for his wife a better home and standard of living, and in doing so has been forced to spend all his waking hours at work, "doubling" his jobs to secure extra pay, her unfaithfulness is especially bitter. Fundamentally, his neglect of his wife and his inability to give her the tenderness and love that she as a woman demands with her whole being, has been because her interests were uppermost in his mind. Knowing that he loves her, she never shares his love and in her own-first in easy distractions, finally by giving herself to another man whose attentions are flattering and liberal because his responsibilities to her are negligible.
>
> 113. I work all day long for you, until the sun go down,
> I work all day long for you, baby, from sun-up until the sun go down,

An' you take all my money and drink it up and come home and
want to fuss and clown.

I worked for you so many times, when I was really too sick to
go,
I worked for you, baby, when your man was slipping in my
back-door,
I can see for myself so tell your back-door man I won't be your
fool no more.[76]

Oliver builds this mini-fiction from the lyrics of songs on similar themes, often using material from different singers recorded at different times in a format that adopts the songs as a dialogue between the man and the woman concerned, as can be seen in the next stage of the story:

> When next he sees her she is leaning back in a sleek Cadillac Eight, the arm of another man about her shoulders. Whilst she is enjoying the pleasure of luxuries that he has never been able to offer and her laughter still echoes in his mind, he tries to convince himself that she will soon return.

115. I saw you ridin' roun', you ridin' a bran' new automobile,
(twice)
Yes, you was sittin' there with your hustler-driver at the wheel.[77]

It also incorporates the personalized writing style that includes the repeated use of "he" and "she," reminiscent of, among many others, Melville Herskovitz's descriptions of the African American in *The American Negro*. For instance, Herskovitz's chapter titles included "The Amalgam He Represents" and "His Significance for the Study of Race."[78] The effect of this style is to build a narrative-like quality to Oliver's description of the African American world, which effectively blurs the boundaries between the real and the imagined. More than mere description, the people become characters that the reader can identify and sympathize with, as in the case of a nameless black convict who recorded a few songs in ambiguous circumstances in 1936:

> His voice was rough, uncultured and intensely moving, as he sang his only testament. There is no blues more poignant, none that reproaches

> more directly the indifference of those who hear and do not attempt to comprehend, or see and do not recognize, than this simple and beautiful creation of a Negro convict. But it was the blues of a man with spirit but without hope, who has been so long severed from the outside world that Oklahoma was to him still the "Territory" of the Indian nations; and who has been paying a debt to a society that had given him nothing. "You heah me talkin' to ya, buddy, what made ya stop by heah?" he demands of the listener as a certain man might well have done of those who passed by on the other side of the Jericho road.[79]

Here is an instance where the author is openly romanticizing "the simple and beautiful creation" of the African American prisoner; indeed, no blues was more "poignant." While revealing Oliver's identification of authentic blues as the music of those at the bottom of the social hierarchy, and who had had nothing from society, this passage also perfectly summarizes the author's preoccupation with the most obscure material from the interwar era. It further evidences the manner in which the music is both imagined and contextualized in Britain. The singer is made to appear as beckoning from a long-lost time, to sing not for commercial reward or the possibility of freedom (although either could have been true), but purely because the blues is the form of expression that is most natural to him, and in this case probably his only form of response. The obscurity of this singer's recordings is mirrored by the songs present on the record that accompanied Oliver's book. Although some of the names on the record, such as Bukka White, Skip James, and Blind Boy Fuller would be familiar to many blues enthusiasts today, the recordings of other singers such as Barefoot Bill, Tallahassee Tight, and Kansas Joe would have been extremely rare to everyone other than dedicated collectors at the time of publication.[80] The obscurity of these recordings, together with the example of the nameless black convict, demonstrate how the selection of blues for the book placed the genre far back enough historically to be detached from the corruption of contemporary culture, but was also real enough in its existence through recordings to be reconstructed as an idyllic folk genre in the present.

What also emerges from these fictionalized descriptions is the prevalent depiction of African Americans as downtrodden victims of an oppressive and disenfranchizing world. The language varies little from "disappointed" and "disillusioned," with the typical blues singer seen as "victimised by circumstances over which he had no control." Oliver thus reserves little space for reaction or activism in African American agency. He argued that direct protest of social iniquities was not prevalent in blues lyrics, and that indirect protest could be more easily read in the sense of protest against the situations and feelings to which segregation gave rise.[81] Although Oliver's analysis allows for the building of community cohesion, there is little beyond "having the blues" that African Americans are able to do to ameliorate their condition. This means that the images of Oliver's characters stand in stark contrast to the life of illiterate sharecropper Nate Shaw, who was able to experience some success as a farmer despite numerous setbacks, or even Robin Kelley's examination of everyday responses of ordinary African Americans in the Jim Crow South.[82] It also in appears in opposition to the "modernist black aesthetic" consciousness that Roger House, for instance, reads in the music of Big Bill Broonzy.[83]

The reduction of African American agency in *Blues Fell This Morning* may have been behind Ralph Ellison's criticism of the book as a "sadly misdirected effort." The criticism may have been aimed at the resigned acceptance of fate that Oliver's interpretation imposes upon his subjects. Others writers keen to stress the strength of African American folk culture and the resistance it posed to oppression have embraced Ellison's vision of the blues as a transcending force by facing hardship head-on. Daphne Duval Harrison built on this by identifying the blues as "a driving force" that allowed the resolution of the "inner conflict" of identity.[84] Although many blues writers have since shared Oliver's regard for the blues' cathartic quality, some regard the context of performance and dance as more expressive of communal resistance against the oppression of the white world.[85] But whereas a proportion of writers have approached the subject of blues research from an evidently ethnocentric perspective, that is, seeking to emphasize African American agency and creativity—along with the contribution of black cultural forms to American society—the writing of British blues enthusiasts in the fifties and sixties is characterized by a certain detachment from the political discourses surrounding the study of black culture during the 1950s and 1960s. Years after the book was published, Oliver recalled that the period in which the book was written was a time of great social, political, and cultural upheaval, but that he had only mentioned issues pertaining to civil rights in the revised edition published in 1990.[86] The analysis and description of the African American experience in the first edition is almost ahistorical in this regard. The events of the growing civil rights movement, the emergence of black grassroots activism in the bus boycotts, and civil disobedience receive scant acknowledgment, and thus appear as largely unconnected to blues culture. As W. G. Roy has recently demonstrated, the blues was of little relevance to the civil rights movement; it was instead the freedom songs of the

1930s and the Old Left along with church music that played a much more central role in activism.[87] Oliver is more concerned with the sociological, economic, and psychological conditions that arise from the pre-civil rights era, such as the experiences of disenfranchizing labor systems life of the South, the migrations as a result of agricultural decline and the two world wars, and the effects of the Depression. This disassociation with the political struggles of African Americans in *Blues Fell This Morning* is indicative of the scholarly interest in the blues at this time. The blues as it was imagined in the earlier part of twentieth century was closer to its folk origins, and more distant from the commerce that began with the race records industry, thus representing the longing for a culture that was more human, closer to nature, and untainted by modern ideals. The "discovery" of the music from the past and the reconstruction of an African American world of meaning and experience was therefore part of a response to the crisis of modernity.

The Absent Presence of Sound

Some of the criticisms directed at *Blues Fell This Morning* seem to have been aimed at the book's almost total lack of musical analysis, and for the most part the study of lyric content in the book is divorced from any element of sound. Musicologists have often been critical of studies that separate semantic content from musical techniques. For instance, Middleton has argued that lyric analyses often assume an oversimplified relationship between the words in lyrics and the reality to which they refer. This assumption neglects the fact that lyrics can sometimes perform subordinated roles to sound where, for instance, borrowing from Simon Frith, familiar, everyday words are "defamiliarized" to "invest the banal with affective and kinetic grace."[88] Oliver, as was common in his considered approach, had pointed out that "above all other forms of music, folk song is to be heard rather than read."[89] Nonetheless, his approach in *Blues Fell This Morning* places the focus entirely on *what* is heard in terms of lyrics, rather than *how* it is heard. Middleton reminds the reader that it is contradictory to omit a sonic consideration of the manner in which lyrics in songs are communicated, and that their significance can often be subservient to the music that envelopes them. It is undoubtedly true that blues lyrics were often a reflection of the world in which they emerged, and that singers would sometimes comment on the world as they saw it, as many of Oliver's transcriptions demonstrate. However, the simplification to which Middleton draws attention exemplifies the nature of blues criticism that in Oliver's case—as in many others—

was subservient to subjectivity. The blues' sonic characteristics are stripped from the lyric core without an acknowledgment of the complex and varied relationship lyrics have with music, or how the totality of both elements combine in the receptive experience.

The presentation of lyrics as the mirror of the African American experience masks the fact that words of songs were not as easily accessible to the average listener. On a superficial level, the laborious and costly tasks of record collecting and transcription that the book entailed are somewhat hidden from view, and the book thus indirectly champions the content and meaning of blues lyrics as the primary form of expression. The selection of blues songs for the record that accompanied the book seems to have also been dictated by the accessibility of the lyrics. The fourteen songs chosen are accompanied by detailed notes on the sleeve, which give each song a real-life context, strengthening the music's relationship to African American experience. For instance, Bukka White's "Strange Place Blues" (1940) is described as an example of how the content of the song is "close to the bitter facts of life and death." The eloquent notes on the sleeve reiterate the interpretation of blues in the book:

> Inextricably bound in the drama of their own environment the composers of the blues sang of their immediate world: of their work, their personal relationships and private predicaments and in doing so gave expressions to their loves, hopes, repressions, superstitions and fears.[90]

The lyrics on the record are fairly accessible to the untrained ear, allowing the listener to engage with Oliver's subject matter relatively easily, a characteristic that is not always shared by records from the 1920s. However, the accessibility of the song lyrics marginalizes the primary form of reception characterizing the experience of the music.

As with all music, the initial response is characterized by the listener's reception of the music *first*, with the lyrics in many cases digested at a secondary stage. This almost certainly would have been the case with the records Oliver used for his book, as words were often undecipherable. More importantly, however, Oliver's analysis of the records is indicative of a form of listening that was only for the select and dedicated few, representative of the small and largely middle-class community of blues aficionados that Keith Richards recalls so critically. As opposed to the "hardened" collectors, for a normal, white, and uninitiated audience the music would be "frightening" and provide "grim listening."[91] This perspective seems to erect a barrier that prevents those who fail to take the music seriously from really understanding the music. This explains the book's attempt to render African American expression, which "to the European ear . . . is as difficult to understand as the 'Geordie' of the Tynesider is to the Londoner," accessible.[92] In this sense, the book attempts to translate the music for a wider audience, while at the same time demarcating the boundaries of authentic blues and serious blues appreciation from any notion of commercialism. Therefore, outside the world of the blues singer and its typical audience, the music only had meaning for those willing and able to delve deep enough.

The primary method to achieve this level of knowledge for people interested in the blues was to collect records. As described in the first chapter, Oliver had spent many years collecting records by mail order from the United States, and visiting secondhand shops across a blitz-torn London. As Middleton has argued, the work of folklorists has often been characterized by a sense of mission, to rescue folk music from vanishing forever, and by collecting blues records from the interwar period and pressuring record labels to reissue the recordings of forgotten singers, blues enthusiasts on both sides of the Atlantic were not only salvaging the music, but, as Oliver's work demonstrates, constructing meanings from their findings.[93] Collecting is to all intents and purposes a participatory process in which the collector assumes a sense of ownership over both the object and the subject. It is also a means by which categorizations are made and lines are drawn between what is deemed of value and importance, and what is not:

> Blues record collectors occupy a cultural insider/outsider status, their collections simultaneously representing a public display of power and knowledge and a private refuge from the corrupting influences of contemporary popular culture. . . .
>
> . . . the participants often combine gendered insularity with wilful obscurantism and a scathing repudiation of contemporary mainstream popular culture as an authenticating strategy that reifies collecting as inherently oppositional.[94]

The "insider status" that collecting allows was particularly significant in British blues writing as knowledge of the African American South would have been more obscure. More importantly, however, collecting itself became a substitute for the lack of participation in the culture that was being observed. Newton argued that white interest in jazz was originally attributable to the music's affinity with a historically self-made, participatory form of culture, and the jazz fan's desire to recapture those elements.[95] Thus, collecting could provide that element that was missing from modern life, as stated by Marshall McLuhan: "the Western world is visually lopsided and sorely in need of audible-tactile stimulation."[96] By contrast, then, music in the contemporary world was regarded as one in which participants were merely observants, passive recipients and consumers of cultural forms produced for consumption, as conceptualized by the French literary theorist Roland Barthes:

> Passive, receptive music, sound music, is become the music (that of concert, festival, record, radio); playing is no longer manual, muscular, kneading physical, but merely liquid, effusive, "lubrificating". . . .
>
> In short, there was first the actor of music, then the interpreter (the grand Romantic voice), then finally the technician, who relieves the listener of all activity, even by procuration, and abolishes in the sphere of music the very notion of *doing*.[97]

This vision of contemporary musical culture echoes the thoughts of German philosopher Theodor Adorno, who argued that the mass distribution of music "seems to complement the reduction of people to silence, the dying out of speech as expression, the inability to communicate at all."[98] Blues record collectors aimed to invert the state of music consumption, which Adorno claimed had gone from a "bottom-up" (participatory) to a "top-down" (handed down) form. This process, as also suggested by Hamilton, was inherently paradoxical.[99] Blues scholars relied on commercial recordings to reconstruct an idiom that was regarded as untainted by commercialism or the industry of the music market. Nonetheless, collecting records from another era would thus allow serious blues enthusiasts, or "hardened collectors," a way of increasing their distance from the corruption of the modern world, but at the same time narrow their distance to their object of desire. Blues collecting meant not only participation by preserving the idiom and communicating that they were reacting to contemporary norms, but also, importantly, was the means by which fragments of blues from the past could be organized into an image of the blues in the present.

The systems of thought associated with collecting were complemented by the interpretation of lyrics, which allowed the framing of the blues as a folk music. From the outset of the book, Oliver emphatically declared that "if blues had never been recorded in any form, it would have thrived as a folk music."[100] It is on the basis that blues was the music of its people that writers began to carve out arbitrary categorizations that separated it not only from newer forms of jazz, but more importantly from the commercial and market-driven world of popular music. The music could be therefore be saved from becoming extinct, preserved as an idiom that was regarded as having cultural and historical value rather than being a commercial commodity for consumption. In defining the music as folk, however, the music has to be imagined as it was in the past, when the blues was solely the music of African Americans. Collecting records that were predominantly from the interwar period facilitated this imaginary process. This is perfectly summarized in Dougan's conception of the constructive nature of creating the folk category: "Despite folk's emergence from within contemporary practices, the contemporary 'real' did not suit. So the real, the continuity, was substituted, arranged and engineered until an ideal disengaged past was itself 'real.'"[101] In other words, by authenticating and reifying an idea of the blues from the past, blues writers could justify the preservation of the blues as a folk music that had meaning in relation to the experience of African Americans, and thus be separated from the music of the masses in the present day.

In a wider sense, the separation of folk blues from popular entertainment, and the distancing of African American culture from mainstream Western culture, suggest that the work of blues scholars around the end of the fifties and into the sixties was fiercely driven by a sense of disillusionment with modernity. This means that it may be possible to think of blues scholarship in this period in a similar manner to Gertrude Stein's "lost generation."[102] The sense of aversion for the commodification of cultural forms manifested in Oliver's analysis of the blues and its opposition to modern mass forms of culture is not too distant in its ideology from the work of writers such as T. S. Eliot and Ezra Pound, poets canonized as part of American modernism. According to Seth Moglen, these writers were disheartened by "the logic of the market [that had] come to permeate virtually all aspects of life," and by the sense that such forces were irresistible.[103] Blues critics shared this experience of disenchantment with manifestations of modernity such as the entertainment industry and the world of popular music. Having no link to a *real* or extreme experience like that of African Americans, the content of popular music was reduced to embellishment and sentimental notions of love and romance that appealed to youngsters and were thus aimed at profitability. Oliver places a gulf between the sentimentalism of popular music and the expression of the blues, which is "natural and uninhibited." African American culture possessed the "erotic and affective connection" of real human relationships, of which modernist poets had mourned the loss.[104] Importantly, however, much in the same way that the lost generation "felt that a healthy relationship with the past is essential for the highest quality of life . . . in the present," it also reveals the method in which blues appreciation was a manifestation of the disillusionment with modernity through its attempt to reclaim an idealized past.[105]

Blues Scholarship as Archaeology

According to Stephen C. Tracy, "that shred of hope in the face of tremendous weight of accumulated moral, ethical, social, and political outrages and indignities" which characterizes the spirit and essence of the blues, is similar to the desire of modernist poets to piece back together a world from the wounds of consumer capitalism. He also describes Ezra Pound as "essentially an archaeologist bent on reconstructing our perception of past history so as to radically alter our present."[106] It is possible to argue that Oliver's work on the blues could be interpreted in this way. *Blues Fell This Morning* is as indicative of what has been *done* to the blues, as it is of African American life in the first half of the twentieth century. By collecting and interpreting records from a bygone era Oliver was conducting a form of "musical archaeology." Records were unearthed in junk shops and second-hand stores, traded in specialist magazines, and used as foundations for a reconstruction of the past from which they emanated. The records were used as historical documents, with lyrics used as a "mirror" to form an image of a world that echoed its past reality. The power of blues singers to sing of the world as it appeared allows Oliver to frame the African American world in *Blues Fell This Morning* as a folk community, one that appears to have maintained humane characteristics that the modern world of mass culture has lost. The idealization of this imagined world is communicated through a series of narrative descriptions in which the author creates empathy for nameless characters who are representative of the folk ideal. But in studying the discovered object, the blues, the object was also reconstituted. Thus, while the records he collected and the lyrics they contained evoked the black world of the early twentieth century, this world could never be grasped fully. As Wald argues, the work of enthusiasts created "a rich mythology that often bears little resemblance to the reality of the musicians they admired."[107] Oliver's writing in the book did not work toward creating the same mythology that the "blues mafia"—the New York–based group of collectors that would promote the canonization of Delta musicians—would promote in the early sixties.[108] However, the combination of a sociological survey of the African American experience and the lyrics of blues songs helped to create another version of the "Negro world" that was dependent on the author's attitudes to modernity and commercialism.

In a similar way that English folk song collector Cecil Sharp discovered a British past in America that he thought had been lost, Oliver was representative of a nucleus of British scholarship that had found an idiom across the Atlantic that retained qualities that the modern world was rapidly losing.[109] Unlike Sharp, Oliver had yet to visit the United States, but would be able to confront the world he had described in the book with the physical reality in his field trip in the summer of 1960. *Blues Fell This Morning* is representative of Oliver's generation of blues scholars, separated from the object of their studies not only historically, but also socially and culturally. However, this physical separation was not simply the cause of misinterpretations, as more ethnocentric commentators have argued. After all, to most blues enthusiasts, collectors, and critics of the sixties, the world of the blues was as alien for Europeans as it was for most white Americans. *Blues Fell This Morning* represents the manner in which Oliver negotiated and reconstructed his subject. Importantly, this negotiation is characterized by Oliver's existence in the present, what White terms the author's "here and now," meaning the image of the music presented in the book was as much a product of the contemporary forces driving the author as it was the sum of the blues records used.[110] Oliver's dialogue between his contemporary present and the blues "as it was" helps to create the image of a world from the past, an echo of the past reality. Thus, the image in *Blues Fell This Morning* is of a world in which the blues is the expression of an African American folk community that is closer to nature, more in tune with real human emotions, antimodern, uncorrupted by forces of consumer capitalism, and embodying a philosophical approach to life that accepts the world as it is. Unfortunately, this means that African Americans in Oliver's narrative are largely unable to effect changes in the world that oppresses and segregates them. This is not to suggest that Oliver's representation of the world within which the blues existed is incorrect, or that the boundaries between fact and fiction are completely blurred. *Blues Fell This Morning* remains a remarkable work that brought to light not only some of the grim truths of African American life in the United States, but also brought attention to hundreds of blues songs and singers that would have been lost to the silence of history.

3 • "You asked me about it, so I'm tellin' you"

Representation through Oral History and Photography

Blues Fell This Morning had helped to establish Oliver's reputation as one of the leading writers on the blues,[1] and by the time *Conversation with the Blues* was published in 1965, the author was being described in the British magazine *Jazz Beat* as "one of the foremost authorities on the blues scene."[2] The book presented excerpts from interviews with over sixty-five singers, accompanied by eighty-four photographs from his field trip to the United States in the summer of 1960. Unlike any other writing on the blues up to that point, the book appeared to give the creators of the blues the chance to tell their side of the story. Critics hailed the fact that in *Conversation* Oliver took a step back and let "the true experts" have their say.[3] British photographer and jazz critic Val Wilmer praised this methodology, arguing that Oliver was "highly successful in his conversations with the people who make and live the blues, surprisingly so in an area where the enthusiastic aficionado is so often a victim of the 'put-on.'" Wilmer also argued that Oliver's book was for blues what Nat Shapiro and Nat Hentoff's *Hear Me Talkin' To Ya* (1955) had been for jazz. Interestingly, these jazz writers had suggested that blues was deserving of more attention in its own right, paving the way for Oliver's scholarship that was to follow.[4] *Conversation* therefore seemed to offer a more authentic history, one narrated by the protagonists in their own environment, rather than by alien observers from afar. The appreciation for the book's engagement with direct sources was still championed more than thirty years later when the second edition of *Conversation* was published in 1996. Mervyn Cooke argued that the book represented "a classic in the reportage of oral history."[5] As mentioned in the introduction, Oliver's book has been a model to scores of similar photo-based publications that have appeared in the half century since, such as Paul Trynka's *Portraits of the Blues* (1997), Samuel and Ann Charters's *Blues Faces: Portraits of the Blues* (2000), Raeburn Flerlage's *Chicago Blues: AS seen from the Inside* (2000), and even William Ferris's recent *Give My Poor Heart Ease: voices of the Mississippi Blues* (2009). The photographs of the singers, where they lived and worked, have seemed to strike a chord for readers, perhaps in the way that the images heighten the authentic quality of the story by offering a window into the geographical realities of the blues.

In essence, Oliver's *Conversation* presented the home of the blues as a world ridden with poverty, hardship, and socioeconomic deprivation. For this reason, many readers were forced to face their imagined, romanticized and perhaps idealized perceptions of the blues and the African American world. In her recent survey of the reception of blues in Britain, Schwartz argues that the desire of sixties blues aficionados "to be in the bluesman's shoes" was virtually eradicated by *Conversation*.[6] However, the trip itself was an opportunity for the author to verify his descriptions of African American life in *Blues Fell This Morning*. In this sense it provides a unique opportunity to examine the role of fieldwork, particularly in terms of interviews and photography, in the reconstruction of ideas about the blues. While the function of oral history in blues scholarship has received some scholarly analysis, such as in the work of Barry Lee Pearson, the power of images and blues photography to shape stereotyped representations of musicians and African American culture has been neglected.[7]

This chapter will examine Oliver's highly selective and edited presentation of oral accounts from the singers interviewed on the trip, and discuss the manner in which the memories and reminiscences in the responses contributed to the creation of a specific idea of the blues, an idea rooted firmly in the past. It will also concentrate on the pivotal role of the book's photographs, which function to heighten the sense of nostalgia for the past and disconnection with the present. Many of the images deceptively recall the documentary-style of the 1930s and the New Deal–era photographers, particularly in their presentation of the harsh realities of African Americans as a context for the development of the blues. However, as in all documentary photography, what can appear as a direct representation of an objective reality can often be the result of manipulation and transformation. This chapter will therefore examine the outcomes of the problematic confrontation between the real and the imagined through the use of oral history and photography.

First, however, given that Oliver's trip and the publication of *Conversation* are separated by a five-year period, it is necessary to place Oliver's field trip within the contemporary context of blues scholarship in 1960, and consider how it related to other fieldwork. Also, as the book was published in 1965, it is important to acknowledge how the rapidly changing social, cultural, and political context of the first half of the sixties, which involved the intensification of both the civil rights movement and the blues revival, influenced the editing of the book and its reception.

Origins of the 1960 Field Trip

Oliver was by no means the first to visit the American South or the northern cities to record and interview blues singers. Alan Lomax had been conducting trips since the thirties, and in 1959 had completed a five-month folk song collecting tour of the South accompanied by the English folk singer Shirley Collins. Samuel Charters had also visited the South throughout the fifties, and coauthor of *Jazzmen* Frederic Ramsey Jr. had made several trips across the South in the same decade, which were later represented in the photo-documentary essay *Been Here and Gone* (1960).[8] Although Ramsey's book is similar to *Conversation* in its use of photography, Ramsey narrates a description of African American life in the South rather than relying on oral accounts from interviewees. Europeans had also been visiting the United States in pursuit of singers and recording information. A year before Oliver's trip, French jazz critic Jacques Demetre and discographer Marcel Chauvard visited New York, Detroit, and Chicago and wrote of their experiences with singers and in blues clubs for *Jazz Journal.* Oliver also recalls that Yannick Bruynoghe and George Adins from Belgium had undertaken self-financed trips to the United States in the hope of gaining biographical and discographical information on singers. Some of the findings from these expeditions had begun to generate substantial interest among British blues writers. Stewart-Baxter called for the gathering of funds to support another field trip in the hope of locating forgotten singers and authentic blues: "the work will be hard and the monetary reward small, but I am certain the adventure would pay dividends in pure folk singing. . . . Is anyone interested?"[9] Oliver gladly answered the call.

His expedition was made possible with the financial support of a Foreign Specialist Grant provided by the bureau of Educational and Cultural Affairs of the U.S. Department of State. Having worked in the American embassy in London for extended periods and making use of the United States Information Service (USIS), Oliver was made aware of the funding and recalls receiving around $1,000.[10] Schwartz argues that at this time American foreign embassies had a desire to promote "cultural goodwill" due to the contemporary social and political strains caused by the growing pressures of the increasingly visible civil rights movement and the Cold War. It is also possible to consider the Foreign Specialist Grant an extension of the State Department's sponsoring of jazz as a cultural export during the Cold War era. As Penny Marie Von Eschen's study shows, jazz had become a useful tool in the promotion of American modernism where traditional propaganda had proven ineffective, although the sponsorship of tours by African American musicians such as Dizzy Gillespie and Louis Armstrong at a time of deeply entrenched racial inequality was not without major contradictions. Nonetheless, government officials were attracted by the power of jazz as a culture-transcending high-art form, but also sought to distance the music from its African American roots, something that the musicians themselves often contested.[11] By contrast, however, blues was certainly not considered a vehicle for displaying modernistic ideals of high art, and had not gained the respectability of jazz in popular culture. Oliver's objective was also to examine the strictly African American roots of the music, so while there exists a link with the State Department sponsorship of the jazz tours, the sponsorship of Oliver's field trip cannot be considered a similar exercise of Cold War–era propaganda.

The BBC was also keen to obtain material that could be used for the production of radio programs on the music. Lomax had already helped to produce a series of broadcasts on American folk music during his time in Britain, and Oliver had managed to establish a working relationship with the BBC as he had presented a few radio shows in the late fifties. They provided a midget tape recorder, and would eventually use some of the material in a series entitled *Conversation with the Blues* on the Third program.[12] In addition, the BBC provided funds equivalent to $25 for each interviewee. Oliver, however, refrained from mentioning any payment before the interview in the fear that the proposed transaction would color the outcome. After recording the interviews he provided interviewees with a form with which they could apply for the funds directly to the BBC.[13] Following Stewart-Baxter's encouragement, fellow blues enthusiasts and writers also set up the "Blues Recording Fund" with the aim of recompensing singers who had been "ruthlessly exploited in the past."[14]

This attitude toward blues singers of an older generation serves to illustrate the mood among the purist strain of British blues scholars in the late fifties and early sixties. The feeling that the actual creators of the blues—the black singers of the South, or those who had migrated north—had been marginalized at the expense of young white pretenders who had appropriated the music, be it through skiffle, rhythm and blues, or rock'n'roll, was dominant among British writers. Popular music periodicals such as *Melody Maker* were extremely disparaging toward these newer genres in the late fifties.[15] In a sentiment prevalent among critics (as in the example of Alexis Korner in chapter

2), Stewart-Baxter sensed the threat to the blues caused by a new generation of young, white rock'n'rollers:

> There is more to it than a few talentless youngsters earning sums entirely out of proportion to their ability. As I have tried to point out, it is because these highly publicised young men are allowed to yell themselves hoarse that the real singers suffer hardship, and many of the great bluesman of yesterday have virtually disappeared. Some have drifted into employment, while others . . . ?[16]

There was also a growing sense that the blues was in rapid decline, and that what remained had to be recorded and preserved. This fatalistic view of the blues' decline increased following Oliver's trip to America, and a few months prior to the publication of *Conversation*, he argued that "some forms of the blues have moved away from the Negro world to that of the white folk world."[17] He felt that the popularity of music regarded as blues among young white musicians was "derivative," was merely a "blood transfusion," and thus would only serve to postpone its demise. In a more personal attack on white imitators, the headlines they grabbed and their music—he argued—made for "gruesome reading, not to say, listening."[18] It was not only white appropriation that was feared, but as *Blues Fell This Morning* had indicated, modernity itself, represented by the developments in technology and mass popular culture that had taken their toll on the music:

> For the folk collector the changes in the nature of the blues, the increasing use of amplification and stereotypes of sound mark the deterioration of the music whilst the lessening of social themes to the common denominator of sexual prowess and unrequited love mark a diminution of the blues as a vehicle for social comment.[19]

The feeling was that time was running out to find out about the history and nature of the music "from the lips of those who made it," and importantly in those places where the music retained the power of "social comment."[20] In addition, after more than a decade of collecting and interpreting blues records Oliver was motivated by a desire to explore the physical world of the blues for himself. He acknowledged that in the attempt to separate blues from jazz "[he] may have distorted the picture," and therefore wanted the opportunity to confront the world he had imagined and described in *Blues Fell This Morning* with the reality of African American life. The author was also keen to visit and survey places of the American South that had received less attention, such as Texas, encouraged by the growing concentration on Mississippi as the epicenter of the blues.[21]

Part of the need to communicate with blues singers had developed from the practice of interviewing blues singers in the UK in the previous decade. Oliver was among a small group of blues writers who was able to meet and interview singers on their visits to Britain, taking the opportunity to enquire about recordings, lyrics, and blues history. For many of these, Broonzy came to represent the antithesis of what was regarded as popular or commercial. The romantic image that Broonzy had nurtured for his own survival as a musician became the image that governed a considerable part of Oliver's searches. The author actively sought out the "natural context" where the blues singer was "at one with his environment."[22] From this view point, it was firmly believed that true story of the blues was in the rural and African American South, far removed from the world of popular music where young white audiences began to embrace rhythm and blues, skiffle, and rock'n'roll in the postwar era. This became evident in Oliver's desire to lesser known figures: "I was anxious to meet singers who were unknown to me or to the recording studio, but who were significant in their own milieux." This "milieux" meant the most obscure and lower-class aspects of African American society: "In total the story of the blues is one of minor singers rather than major ones, of men with small acquaintances, limited aspirations and humble talents."[23] Among these African Americans in the remotest and obscure parts of America the meaning of the blues would be discovered.

The trip therefore served to place the music within a specific time-place context, and at the same time create a clear division between that context and contemporary popular culture of 1960. Much in the same vein that historian Paul Thompson regards the practice of oral history as one that "enriches and enlarges" history by "break[ing] barriers between chroniclers and their audience," Oliver believed that by speaking to older singers he would uncover a more realistic history of the blues.[24] By interviewing, he also believed he would be able to engage with the oral tradition that characterized lower-class African American culture: "Blues is a folk-music—a music of the people, and much of its history is folk-lore, the mixture of truth and belief that must pass for history in an oral, unlettered tradition."[25] In this sense, *Conversation*'s content and methodology were in line with the academic currents of the decade that saw a shift from traditional studies of the center to the margins of power, as exemplified by the Italo-French school of microhistory, and influential sociohistorical works such as E .P. Thompson's *The Making of the English Working Class* (1963). Importantly, the sixties saw the relatively small but highly significant emergence of oral history as an academic discipline with the establishment of the Oral History Association in 1966, and the increase in funding available for oral history projects.[26] One of the most celebrated oral history works of the era, Studs Terkel's *Hard Times* (1970), which contained reminiscences and memories from people who experienced the Great Depression or its legacies, seemed to follow the resurgent interest in the social documentary works of the thirties. Alan Tratchenberg suggests that leftist youth movements of the sixties went in search of "a radical heritage," and many found this in the experiences of ordinary Americans presented in the visual works of New Deal–era photographers from the thirties. Originally produced under the auspices of the Farm Security Administration (FSA), works such as James Agee and Walker Evans's *Let Us Now Praise Famous Men* (1941), and Evans's *American Photographs* (1938) were rereleased in 1960 and 1962 respectively.[27]

In its use of oral accounts from largely unknown and ordinary African American musicians, and visual representations of their often squalid circumstances, *Conversation with the Blues* was remarkable for the manner in which it represented the convergence of the histories from below and the revival of Depression-era photography. As reviews of the book demonstrate, blues scholars regarded the book as a "document," a resource that allowed access to the social and cultural circumstances that gave rise to the music. John Szwed regarded the book as "a complete immersion into the context of the blues" that provided the contextual reference from which to understand the "meaning" of the music.[28] As Schwartz has also highlighted, the book became a key text of blues scholarship as it challenged some of the naive stereotypes held by enthusiasts. However, while the book has often been praised for its revelation of the physical realities of African American life, the use of oral history and photography and their relationship to these realities require closer examination. Both mediums are often presumed to represent a more direct and unmediated line of communication to historical realities, but, interviews and photographs often represent a tampered and subjective version of the real. In this sense, the memories of blues singers and images of their surroundings in *Conversation* play a prominent role in the reconstruction of ideas about the blues and lower-class African American culture.

However, this reconstruction was produced on either side of some major social and cultural changes. When Oliver began his trip in 1960, the blues revival was yet to peak. Singers such as Mississippi John Hurt, Sleepy John Estes, Peg Leg Howell, and Ishmon Bracey had not yet been "rediscovered."[29] The group of blues collectors known as the "blues mafia" had not yet established the Origins Jazz Library that would catapult Robert Johnson and

Charley Patton into blues legend.[30] In Britain, it would be another couple of years before the Rolling Stones would lead the British rhythm-and-blues boom, and before German promoters Horst Lippmann and Fritz Rau would launch the American Folk Blues Festivals across Europe.[31] At the time of the trip, the blues of the interwar period that Oliver had examined in *Blues Fell This Morning* was still the domain of a relatively small niche of collectors. These regarded this historic music as a bastion of authenticity based on its apparent anticommercialism and existence in a world that they believed the industry had never been able to colonize (not without irony, it was the commercial race records industry that produced the recordings British enthusiasts would collect).

However, by the time *Conversation* was published in 1965, the musical landscape had been almost turned on its head. The British invasion bands had raced up the charts with their adaptations of American rhythm and blues. Blues musicians had visited the UK frequently and toured with British backing bands. Blues songs had even featured on popular television shows such as *Hullaballo* and *Jazz 625,* and the Rolling Stones had had a number one hit with a cover of Howlin' Wolf's "Little Red Rooster" in 1964.[32]As Schwartz has observed, the rapid surge in the popularity of blues in the early sixties meant that this was on the wane by 1965. The American Folk Blues Festivals failed to attract the large audiences of the preceding years, and singers such as John Lee Hooker had begun to lose their novelty factor. At the time, Oliver was disappointed at the low turnout for the Blues Festival shows in Croydon in 1965. Notwithstanding, the number of dedicated blues enthusiasts and record collectors had risen, and within a year of its first edition, Oliver's *Conversation's* was reprinted for release. This followed the emergence of dedicated publications such as Simon Napier and Mike Leadbitter's *Blues Unlimited* in 1963, and Bob Groom's *Blues World* in 1965. Large record outlets also began to stock recordings that had previously only been available in specialist shops such as Doug Dobell's shop on Charing Cross Road in London. Schwartz notes how Dobell even opened a specialty store called the Folk and Blues Record Shop containing both domestic and foreign material on the subject.[33] Taken alongside the positive praise for the book, the reissue of *Conversation* indicates that Oliver had hit a nerve for this expanding blues intelligentsia. The immersion into the physical, social, and geographical reality of the music through the oral accounts of the people interviewed, combined with their images, permitted readers to engage with a representation of the context of the blues that could not have been more distant from the commercial successes of the blues revival.

Interviews in Blues and Jazz Scholarship

"What you want—history?" he muttered. "Well, I know it."[34]

The process of interviewing singers and musicians among jazz and blues critics was not uncommon by the time Oliver went to the United States in 1960. In Britain writers rarely missed the chance to interview visiting singers throughout the fifties. It presented an opportunity to not only meet highly esteemed musicians, but the possibility to learn about the origins of the blues, the lives of blues singers, recording information, and the meaning of lyrics. Interestingly, following his transatlantic success as an exponent of the "real" blues that European audiences desired, Broonzy had been interviewed at length by Yannick Bruynoghe in order to compile his autobiography *Big Bill Blues* (1955). In the United States interviewing had become extremely important in jazz scholarship during the thirties. Alan Lomax had learned the potential for discovering an alternative history of jazz by interviewing New Orleans pianist Jelly Roll Morton in Washington between May and June 1938. As his impassioned description of the pianist suggests, it allowed the story to be told by one of the makers of history:

> With not a moment's pause—as if all his life had been waiting for this and treasuring up the sentences—Jelly Roll began to think out loud in a Biblical, slow-drag beat....
>
> These sessions were important to him. He was renewing his self-confidence as he relived his rich and creative past for a sympathetic audience that didn't interrupt; he was putting his world in order; but, much more to the point... New Orleans and her boy, Jelly, were getting their hearing at the bar of history itself.[35]

The potential of firsthand accounts was the motivation that led jazz aficionados Charles Edward Smith and Frederic Ramsey Jr. to use interviews with New Orleans musicians to create *Jazzmen* (1939). As Hamilton notes, this endeavor was marked by the philosophy of the Federal Writers Project of the New Deal era, and so the authors sought to compile a "folk history" made up of the stories and reminiscences of the musicians who had created the music.[36] This was followed by Shapiro and Hentoff's *Hear Me Talkin' To Ya: The Story of Jazz as Told by the Men Who Made it* (1955). The authors believed that the stories of jazz musicians would cut through unrealistic depictions of the music in popular culture:

> This portrait, happily, is not anything like the caricatures of jazzmen too often found in the movies, daily press and even in many otherwise accurate magazines and books. As you will hear in the voices to come, the musicians of jazz are citizens of a strong and original creativity, with deeply felt traditions of expression and a richly experienced way of life.[37]

Studs Terkel also used firsthand accounts of jazz musicians in order to compile his *Giants of Jazz* (1957).

Given the greater popularity of jazz among white scholars, interviews with blues singers were less frequent prior to the fifties. Again, it was Alan Lomax who pioneered the method. As John Szwed has observed, Lomax became more interested in blues in the postwar period as he began to see it as another form of folk music.[38] Following his experiences with Morton, Lomax used interviews to learn about the lives of singers and the origins of the blues, as for instance in his now legendary discussions with Memphis Slim, Sonny Boy Williamson, and Big Bill Broonzy in New York in 1947.[39] In his almost endless search for America's folk past, Lomax believed oral history was the medium that would allow the submerged folk voices of America to be heard. Thus, interviews with the participants of history allowed the documentation and recording of events from previously unheard voices, a philosophy of the oral history method shared by Thompson:

> Oral history is a history built around people. It thrusts life into history itself and it widens its scope. It allows heroes not just from the leaders, but from the unknown majority of the people . . . [It] offers a challenge to the accepted myths of history, to the authoritarian judgement inherent in its tradition.[40]

In this sense, oral history provided the means of democratizing history, of telling the story from the bottom up, and allowing a more direct connection to historical sources through oral communication. Lomax's scholarship and methodology would have a significant impact upon British jazz and blues music scholarship during the fifties, given his work with the BBC on American folk music. This was summarized by British folk singer and playwright Ewan MacColl in his reference to *Mister Jelly Roll* as "the first great work of Socialist Realism" in 1950.[41]

It seems evident that Oliver's research on the field trip of 1960 was highly influenced by the work of the Lomaxes. A clear example is Oliver's visit to the Mississippi State Penitentiary in Parchman, where he may have been hoping to replicate John Lomax's discovery of now legendary figures such as Huddie Ledbetter, or "Leadbelly." With regards to interviewing, Oliver was driven by a similar desire to allow those at the foot of the historical ladder to have their say. He argued that "the blues reveals much of the patterns of behaviour and thought of an underprivileged minority group in a modern state," and that the real story of the music was that of the "minor singers" who were for the most part "still unknown."[42] It was through oral history that this story could be obtained:

> If blues musicians explain their music best in their performance, their recollections do much to add to our knowledge of the blues. The reminiscences of the individual and his relationship to his community are still the raw material of social research and remain so when this embraces folk-music, explaining the importance of the music in that society, its function, its raison d'être.[43]

It is important to stress that this ideology was motivated by the pervasive folkloristic approach to popular music studies, prevalent among jazz and blues scholarship at the time. Oliver clearly regarded the popularization and mass production of the blues in hybrid forms such as rhythm and blues, skiffle, and rock'n'roll as deteriorating its function as a "vehicle for social commentary."[44] It was therefore necessary, he believed, to engage with those who had seen little or no commercial success, and who had been untouched by the fickle demands or rewards of the entertainment industry. To seek out their stories and histories would give a clearer picture of the blues' origins and significance among the African American folk. This interpretation itself points to an element of construction, or what revisionist writers now call "invention," as Oliver favored the unknown and commercially unsuccessful to build an interpretation of a music that had become, as Simon Frith claims, available to transatlantic audiences precisely because it had penetrated the mainstream.[45]

Recalling his trip at the turn of the twenty-first century, Oliver noted that in his interviews he was "determined to let the singers give their accounts and make their observations with the minimum of direct questioning." As his treatment of the BBC funds available for interviewees indicates, Oliver attempted to minimize the risk of influencing the responses and "wanted to keep in the background as much as possible."[46] However much he may have desired anonymity, the very collaborative nature of oral history makes the historian an active participant in the production of the oral accounts. According to Ronald Grele, oral history is a "conversational narrative," where the interviewer's research goals drive the process. Alessandro Portelli expands on this by arguing that oral history is "the result of a relationship, of a shared project in which both the interviewer and the interviewee are involved together."[47] In the process of interviewing Oliver helped to produce the oral accounts given by singers. Essentially, however, it is important to consider that Oliver's oral history was conditioned by a multitude of factors in two stages: first in the interview process, and second in the editing and presentation of the oral accounts in the book.

In terms of the actual interviews, a myriad of elements that are impossible to detect could have influenced the outcome. For instance, each interviewee would have differed in his attitudes to being interviewed and recorded, depending on his experience of interviews, or his expectations of potential outcomes. As was customary for the British author, Oliver carefully acknowledged these possibilities by arguing that the "limited horizons of many of the singers produced their own perspective distortions. Time and pride may [have] cause[d] them to embroider some narratives and leave others as sketches."[48] These varying attitudes would have affected their willingness to disclose sensitive information. It is impossible to quantify the accuracy of recollections and the imaginative additions or revisions of those memories, shaped by personal experiences and attitudes to the past. The time and place of interview may have also dictated the outcome of an interview, or the presence of others during the recording process may have conditioned the responses.

Some factors, however, can be examined and appreciated. For instance, Oliver argues that his European origins, combined with the presence of his wife, proved to be an advantage rather than a hindrance, lending weight to Richard Wright's view that a cultural outsider would be best equipped to study the music, due to his or her distance from the racial strife that troubled American society. Oliver stated that his European provenance managed to form the basis for a bond with African Americans who had been stationed abroad in wartime.[49] While this is more than feasible, it is also true that many may have regarded a European as more open toward African Americans, especially following the rumors of cultural acceptance across the Atlantic and the exodus to Europe following McCarthyism. Shirley Collins also experienced positive reactions to her nationality in her field trips with Alan Lomax.[50] On the other hand, coming from the UK seemed to give Oliver a naïveté that meant he was less daunted than other white Americans in visiting black areas, such as in the case of Harlem in New York:

> Having got to New York, Val, my wife, decided we'd go up to Harlem, and we were quite taken by the number of people who warned us and

> said it was very dangerous and so forth. Neither of us felt that was really true, yet we didn't quite know why. We thought, well, we'll risk it and get across and see what it's like. So we did, and in fact it was really quite okay. People were a bit surprised to see a young couple, white, especially when they spoke to us and discovering we weren't even American.

The presence of Oliver's wife was most probably a huge help building relationships. Oliver has commented that she would sometimes spend time with singers' wives while he interviewed or recorded singers or visited barrelhouses, as in his experience with Wade Walton.[51] Conversely, it could also be argued that some of Oliver's assistants on the field trip exerted some form of influence on the interviews. Aside from his wife Valerie, Oliver was aided by many "enthusiasts," such as Bob Koester, the founder of Delmark Records, and John Steiner in Chicago; Charley O'Brien in St. Louis; blues historian Mack McCormick in Texas; Dick Allen and Bill Russell in New Orleans; and the founder of Arhoolie Records, Chris Strachwitz, whom he met in Memphis.[52] The latter went on to record and launch the careers of many singers whom Oliver interviewed in the South, such as Mance Lipscomb and Lightnin' Hopkins, and it is therefore not unlikely some may have been affected by the lure of a recording contract.[53]

In his analysis of interviews with blues singers, Barry Lee Pearson argued that the content of the oral accounts could oscillate between the "businessman's side of the story," that is, the self-promotion as an authentic exponent of the genre, and the "artistic narrative," in other words, the respondent's "performance" of his life and memories through speech.[54] Pearson brings to light the various forces that could have shaped the responses of his interviewees and acknowledges the fact that, in the same way the interviewer brings his own set of assumptions to the process, the blues singer evaluates his reasons for speaking and his expectations. Pearson argues, therefore, that the interview response can result in a songlike "performance," where "the bluesman creates an artistic version of his past."[55] It could be argued that Broonzy was one of the major "performers" in this regard: "Broonzy had been canny enough to corner the nascent British blues market while he could, allowing willing recipients of his wisdom to believe in the romance that here was, indeed, the last of the Mississippi blues singers."[56] Thus, through the blues interviews it is important to remember that, while the representation of the interview was in the hands of the interviewer, blues singers were active participants in the production of oral histories: they alone decided on the nature of the accounts they gave. Conversely, this does not mean that they communicated transparent truths or fabricated a life story for themselves in order to gain something from the interview. Broonzy provides an example where the amount of fabrication and complicity in "invention" could be measured at least to some extent. However, for many of Oliver's less well known interviewees, it is fair to assume that the oral accounts may have varied greatly on the mixture of fact and fiction. It is therefore more useful to adopt Titon's notion of the interview as the production of a "life story" that is a more of "a self-contained fiction" produced in the interaction of the interview, and determined by social psychological and cultural contexts, than a simple biographical report.[57]

The editing process also conditioned Oliver's representation of the blues in *Conversation*. In the first instance, Oliver's desire to reduce his influence on the oral accounts by presenting them without comment is contrasted by the presentation of the interviews in carefully selected excerpts. The lack of authorial comment lends a stream-of-consciousness quality to the book, but despite the fact there are no chapter headings, a faint thematic organization resembling the layout of *Blues Fell This Morning* is detectable. The oral accounts are grouped in a rough order beginning with ideas on the nature and meaning of the blues, descriptions of the "old days" (childhood, family, learning music), work experiences, leisure time activities (Saturday nights and role of music), violence and tragedy experienced in their lifetimes, the experiences and memories of female singers, and the singers' experiences of recording. This organization reveals Oliver's editorial hand at work, contrasting the attempt to let the singers have their say. In addition, the absence of contextual commentary means there is no clear indication as to the questions asked, or whether the excerpt represents the full extent of the singer's response. Given that many singers appear throughout the book more than once, it seems that each excerpt was carefully selected and extracted from the entirety of the interview. This means that each excerpt selected for the final copy of *Conversation* was deemed to be of greater value and as having a greater effect. In this sense, the author aims to direct the reader toward a reconstructed and manipulated interpretation of the blues. What is selected for publication and what is excluded say as much about the author's attitudes toward his subject as they say about the subject.

Finally, the inevitable reproduction of the interview in the written word marks one of the problems of representing oral history. As highlighted by Portelli, the transcription of oral accounts represents more of a translation in which many of the oral elements are morphed into "segmentary traits."[58] Important aspects of the oral responses, such as emphasis, tone, pauses, become essentially lost in translation. The excerpts therefore contain a certain fragmentary quality, never able to faithfully reproduce the original oral accounts, and thus morph into spectral echoes of African American voices from 1960. Importantly, while elements of physical speech are lost in translation, the transcriptions add other elements to the oral responses. Oliver's reproduction of the dialect and parlance of his interviewees by adopting unconventional spelling and the dropping of "g" at the end of words, as will be highlighted below, is demonstrative of his attempt to faithfully convey "authentic" African American voices. As Jeffrey Hadler's essay on the representation of black voices highlights, this process of reproduction based on unorthodox language, which he terms the "Remus orthography," sees the combination of fact and fiction. Historically, similar transcriptions of African American speech have been overshadowed by an inherently racist ideology.[59] While it is safe to say that Oliver's representation of the black voice was in no way related to notions of racial prejudice, the oral transcriptions of *Conversation* are nonetheless characterized by the paradoxical blend of reality and imagination. In other words, they at once approximate the reality of the oral responses by focusing on how they are spoken, but at the same time "construct" identities based on the reader's perception of stereotypes. Therefore, the voices of the respondents are as much real as they are dependent on reader's reconstruction of an *imagined* real. Overall, the ambiguous nature of Oliver's fragmentary excerpts favors the distortion of the physical reality of the field trip into an imagined and constructed interpretation of the blues and African American life.

Oral History in "Conversation"

It is in the opening paragraph that it is possible to truly understand the romanticism underlying Oliver's appreciation of the blues:

> It was a burning July morning and the relentless sun drained the colour from the sidewalk signs, the shop fronts and drawn shades on 4th Street. Inside the Big Six barber shop it was close and the electric fan, the size of a cartwheel, could not dispel the perspiration that glistened on fore-arms and ran down foreheads and chests. Immaculate in putty trousers and tan shirt the barber, Wade Walton, seemed least affected by the oppressive heat. He fingered a slow blues on the guitar for it was Sunday and Clarksdale was quiet.

Described in the style of narrative fiction so typical of Oliver's writing throughout the fifties, the image of Walton playing a blues sets the scene. Here, the blues appear as part of daily life for an ordinary African American with some spare time on what seems to be a lazy Sunday morning. The blues is presented as a means of expression and pastime that is turned to whenever time permits. The story progresses as two more African Americans come into the shop and one of them also begins to play a blues. Without saying whether he asked any questions, Oliver begins to report back the conversation between the two singers, Walton and Robert Curtis Smith.[60] From this passage, it seems that Oliver has managed to stumble upon both a performance and a discussion, precisely what he had been searching for, the blues appearing spontaneously in its natural environment. For the most part, this situation reflects Oliver's approach to finding singers by word of mouth, and following leads generated by other blues enthusiasts and collectors. He had also used place-names in blues songs to find singers:

> Yes, well if by any chance there was a blues record that they made which had the name of a place in it, I would often go to the place to see if it was associated with it, and so forth, because there was only a hunch that there might be but in fact that worked out quite well, and I found quite a lot of people that way actually.[61]

However, the representation of the discussion between Walton and Smith sets the tone of *Conversation* by making the music appear as both natural and spontaneous expression, and furthers the attempt to root the blues firmly within the lived experience of ordinary African Americans.

In line with this attempt, the selected excerpts focus on elements that are seen to characterize the blues and differentiate it from other more popular forms of music. One of these is honesty and the expression of truth. Although the responses of the singers gave varying interpretations of the feelings that gave rise to the blues, most regarded the music as a means of communicating those feelings directly. For instance, Robert Curtis Smith led with the ideas of honesty and sincerity, that the blues is unadorned with dramatic effect or sentimentality, but instead is a vehicle for truthfulness. Smith stated that he sang his blues "straight from the heart," and that therefore those listening would understand that "[it]'s me as I is." Similarly, Boogie Woogie Red claimed that "the blues is something that you have to play coming from your heart," and John Lee Hooker declared, "When I sing the blues . . . I really means it."[62] Again, it is conjectural to attempt a measurement of the actual sincerity of these responses. The singers could just as easily have been telling Oliver what they thought he wanted to hear, as they could have been giving their honest opinions. What is significant however, is that Oliver chose to emphasize the theme by selecting excerpts in which truthfulness and sincerity were mentioned.

The emphasis on the honesty and directness of the blues stems from the association of blues scholarship with ideas prevalent in folk music studies. Alan Lomax's work, for instance, had regarded the music produced by ordinary people as a reflection of folk cultures, therefore expressing the reality of those cultures. As demonstrated throughout the fifties and in *Blues Fell This Morning*, Oliver regarded the lyrics of the blues as an expression of African American life, a window through which that culture could be observed. A clear marker of this ideology was the belief that folk music was more of a natural ability than a learned craft, and many singers' responses included in the book exemplify this belief. Former singer of the Mississippi Sheiks Sam Chatman argued that most people of his generation had learned "just by ear," and Willie Thomas made the case that the African American didn't learn the blues; instead "God give it to him." In a caption to a photograph of a recording studio, Oliver also argued the case: "Blues singers have no use for sheet music and music stands."[63] It is also important to note that at the time of his trip, most of the people interviewed were unknown or had recorded very little as musicians. Mance Lipscomb, for instance, had never recorded prior to his encounter with Chris Strachwitz on Oliver's trip.[64]

The interpretation of blues as a form of folk music explains the means by which the realities of African American life come to play such a prominent role in the book. Some of the most common responses in *Conversation* focus precisely on lived experience, particularly on the harsh realities of poverty, the toil of manual labor, and experiences of violence. There are numerous examples of singers emphasizing the state of poverty that characterized most of their lives. For instance, Blind Arvella Gray told of his never having worn shoes as a child; Willie Thomas recalled the Depression era, "when there were eight of us eatin' out of one pan at the white folk's house"; and James Butch Cage described the poverty of living with his widowed mother and twelve siblings, which meant he was required to work instead of going to school as a child.[65] Significant emphasis is given to accounts that focus on the singers' experiences of manual labor. For example, Robert Curtis Smith described working from "sun-up until sundown," J. B Lenoir told of doing "just about everything a person could name for to make that money for a livin'," and Jewell Long told of his working wherever there was work to do.[66] However, the majority of accounts that discuss work experiences concentrate on the nature of the sharecropping system, which in 1930 provided work for just under 400,000 blacks. This system of farming, which most often left black laborers at disadvantage to landowners, had been particularly hard hit during the Great Depression and the numbers of black sharecroppers fell by almost a quarter over the course the 1930s. Mechanization and the labor demands of World War II had also affected rural work, and thousands were forced to seek employment in the urban centers of the South, North, and West. While in the postwar years black Americans would become predominantly an urban population, there will still many residents in the rural South who survived by sharecropping.[67] The singer Lil' Son Jackson recalls his own experiences:

> We sharecropped out on a farm and more or less that's the onliest way we had of makin' a livin'. I mean my father follered that kind of labor; I mean that's the onliest labor he ever knew. And which and why that was the hard side of life, because in sharecroppin' you work all the year and when the year ends and everything supposed to be divided up, why then you supposed to get half and he's supposed to get the other half. And you don't have but one thing to do and that's go along with him take whatever the figures showin' whatever you have. You can't argue. You can't prove nothin' so you just go along with him. So you make it whatever way you can—make it go further.[68]

Interestingly, this oral excerpt is slightly different from the sound recording present on the accompanying record to *Conversation*, but also clearly demonstrates Oliver's attempt to faithfully represent Jackson's speech through unconventional language. Oliver had also chosen to crop the small parts of the responses in order to make them more readable in the transcriptions.[69] While even here it is evident that Oliver's editorial hand had modified the oral accounts, the numerous responses testifying to the experiences of sharecropping demonstrate that many African Americans of the South who played the blues experienced disenfranchisement, hard labor, and exploitation. However, in *Conversation* the concentration of these accounts lends weight to the idea that in order to play the music, it is essential to have lived a certain life, particularly one related to that of ordinary African Americans, which is also represented by Jackson's peculiar speech. In the book's closing excerpt, Edwin Buster Pickens states that "[the] nach'al blues come directly from a person's heart: what he's experienced in life, what he's been through."[70] But while Pickens may have been referring to personal experiences in a more general sense, the thematic organization and cropping of the responses focuses the reader's attention on the specific experiences of harsh manual labor and disenfranchisement.

The oral responses in *Conversation* therefore appear to match an image of the blues singer that took shape in the fifties with the testimony of Big Bill Broonzy—that the blues was music not only of sharecroppers, but of African Americans in the Jim Crow South. Effectively, they helped to demarcate the boundaries between blues as interpreted here in the folkloristic sense, and the other genres deemed more popular, whether pop, rhythm and blues, or rock'n'roll. Oliver's representation of the blues in *Conversation*, which prioritizes the memories of aging and lesser-known musicians, has the effect creating a temporal, as well as musical, cultural-aesthetic boundary. The blues has not only been separated from jazz as a distinct musical category worthy of attention, and divorced from newer versions and evolutions of the genre, but effectively placed firmly within the realm of the past. The temporal separation of the blues from more contemporary genres is to a large extent steered by the backward-looking focus of the oral responses of the singers. A large proportion of the excerpts in the book are reminiscences of the past, whether they are about learning to play an instrument, childhood, work, sharecropping, recording, or songs. For instance, Muddy Waters recalled a fairly enigmatic and "restless" Robert Johnson in one excerpt, and in another talked of his early experiences around Clarksdale prior to trying his luck in Chicago; Will Shade described Beale Street in Memphis back in "them days"; Bo Carter, Speckled Red, and Gus Cannon all reminisced of their experiences in the traveling medicine shows of the twenties; Sam Price, Jesse Crump, and Norman Mason recalled the heyday of the female classic blues singers; and the list goes on. It is extremely rare to find a response that describes what any of the musicians were doing at the time of interview, what their opinions were about newer music, or how they were living in 1960.

In his review essay of Terkel's *Hard Times*, Michael Frisch argues that "memory . . . moves to centre stage as the object, not merely the method of oral history."[71] In considering *Conversation* a similar enterprise, it is important to acknowledge the problematic notion of accepting memory as historical fact. Oliver was careful to acknowledge in his introduction that there "were stories not without contradictions, not perhaps without errors of fact," whether caused by age, limited horizons, or pride.[72] However aware he was of the possibility for sketchy histories or fictive tales of past times, Oliver could not prevent the interpretation of the excerpts as a form of history. Indeed, as Portelli rightly makes the case, with memory as (unofficial) object, whether the oral account is based on historical fact or is mere fiction becomes irrelevant. It is what the informants choose to tell and what they believe that becomes history.[73] The oral recollections may not therefore refer to the historical reality that Oliver may have sought, but are equally indicative of what the respondents thought of that history, which also draws attention once again to the participation of the respondents in the reconstruction of the blues in *Conversation*.

Portelli's reference to the "now"—the present—becomes crucially important in the analysis of the oral responses. As Frisch argues, "Contemporary pressures and sensitivities encourage people to screen their memories in a selective, protective, and above all didactic fashion."[74] In other words, the respondents' reminiscences of their experiences in the past have been shaped, filtered, and manipulated by their life since then, and therefore come to indicate as much about the present as about the past. This means that the collection of memories and recollections in *Conversation* is paradoxical, since the selection of excerpts prioritizes the past by marginalizing the present. But while invisible, it is in the social, cultural, and political context of 1960 that the memories in *Conversation* were immortalized on record. It is also not impossible to imagine that, given the evident circumstances of many of the interviewees at the time, some may have been motivated by the possibility of reaping some financial reward of recording music again, and therefore built their responses in order to gain credibility. While this is difficult to quantify, what is certain is that in seeking to separate blues from contemporary popular cultures and promoting the appreciation of blues as a form of folk music, Oliver's book is an attempt to effectively travel back in time through the memories of the respondents, to an era when the music was known only to the African American folk, when it carried more weight as a "vehicle for social comment," and was therefore at its most "authentic."

Consequently, through *Conversation* it is possible to regard Oliver as another of Filene's "memory workers," a group that includes Alan Lomax, Willie Dixon, and Samuel Charters. However, while Filene's group helped to establish the idea of the blues, particularly that of the interwar period as "roots" music, that is, as part of America's musical heritage, Oliver was less interested in nurturing the historical foundations of American folk music. Nor was he focused on promoting the role of British interest in the preservation of the blues. The oral recollections of the past promote the idea that blues was a creation of the early twentieth century, and that it was intricately tied to the daily experiences of ordinary African Americans. At the same time, the memories of the past indirectly suggest that the music is in decline and on the verge of vanishing in the present day. Therefore, Oliver's emphasis on the past in *Conversation* puts distance between the "then" and "now." This temporal dislocation could be interpreted as a deliberate attempt to create categorical distinctions between the intricately tied music and lived experienced of African Americans of the interwar years, and the contemporary world of popular music in the mid-sixties. Simultaneously, the reliance on memories and reminiscences of the past is suggestive of the nostalgia for an idealized past that hangs over the scholarly analysis of the blues.

Another feature of the emphasis on the blues from the past is that it is indicative of the belief that the blues was in decline, and dying out with the aging singers who remained. The blues in *Conversation* is in a world that is rapidly vanishing. This means that Oliver's scholarship also disconnected the music from contemporary African American life and culture. Unlike Lomax's, Oliver's writing lacked the leftist political ideology that emanated from the thirties Popular Front, and was much more timid on the racial struggles of African Americans. Lomax, for instance, was much more outspoken on issues of social injustice and had been openly critical of Ben Botkin's *A Treasury of Southern Folklore* (1949) for its failure to acknowledge the culture of lynching that pervaded the South.[75] Oliver, on the other hand, had interpreted the blues as lacking a political voice primarily from the absence of direct protest against Jim Crow or discrimination in blues lyrics, arguing that political issues were only ever present as an "aside."[76] Consequently, Oliver's point of departure in *Conversation* is the separation of blues from the contemporary social and political struggles of African Americans in 1960.[77] Indeed, in his introduction he argued:

> Blues is not the music of the black leaders, of the black intelligentsia. The active militant members of CORE or the NAACP seldom show interest in blues; the music does not feature in the black periodicals except as an occasional success story.[78]

As W. G. Roy has recently observed, it is clearly the case that blues songs did not feature prominently in civil rights protests, as black activists from the groups mentioned above favored the freedom songs of the thirties in order to build group cohesion.[79] It was also true that black audiences for the blues, particularly the music of the interwar years that was deemed "country" or "down-home," were on the wane in this period. But there is an inherent paradoxical quality in the separation of blues from the social and political milieu. In the introduction Oliver begins by presenting his experience of witnessing a black protest against the job discrimination of a store. The person he interviews, whom he had originally believed to be the singer Alice Moore, was in fact a member of the NAACP who reacted strongly to being stereotyped as a blues singer only because she was a black woman from the South. Another protestor, Marion Oldham, argued that the blues represented a step backward for African Americans, and that she was unaware of anyone who actually liked that musical form.[80] While Oliver regarded this as a clear indication that blues belonged to a different generation, the situation also demonstrates that the people he would interview during his trip were experiencing very turbulent times.

It is important to stress that in the few years prior to Oliver's visit to the United States, there was a large increase in grassroots black activism, as exemplified by the Montgomery bus boycotts of 1955 in Alabama, in which local black residents boycotted the use of segregated public transport for over a year. In the months preceding Oliver's trip, students had begun the sit-ins and protests of civil disobedience in public spaces that would spread across the southern states. These protests, which had begun in Greensboro, North Carolina, in February 1960, would eventually see over 70,000 people involved, leading to over 3,600 arrests. The fact that these demonstrations are often portrayed as a student-based phenomenon may have influenced Oliver's generational divide between older blues people and young civil rights activists. According to Adam Fairclough, however, older generations of African Americans, although slow to react initially, eventually rallied behind the protest and took part in boycotts and sit-ins.[81] While this does not mean blues singers were personally involved in demonstrations, they nonetheless existed in a society and in communities where demonstrations were becoming common and attracting significant media attention.

Nonetheless, this was not the society the British author believed had produced the blues, but one that had rather turned its back on it; hence his decision to omit some of his experiences of the racial struggles from *Conversation*. For instance, due to the fact that it was illegal for a black man and a white woman to be in the same vehicle, when driving around with Wade Walton in Clarksdale, Mississippi, Oliver's wife Valerie was forced to hide in the back of the car to avoid being seen and possibly arrested. He also recalls being "run out of town" by police in Texas, and also being escorted out of Clarksdale. In another episode, Oliver entered a club looking for Alex Moore. Upon hearing that a white man was looking for him, the singer proceeded to hide outside under a large pile of dirty clothes, where Oliver eventually found him.[82] This experience or others similar to it are not present in *Conversation*, suggestive of the book's intentional disconnection from some of realities of life in the segregated South. The omission of these events from the book is partly explained by Oliver's deliberate downplaying of their importance. As his experience in Harlem shows, Oliver believed that racial tensions did not affect his field trip in a major way:

> I thought there would be far more [issues of racial tension]. I mean, really it was not a serious problem; the only thing was that there often were signs of discrimination and you had to be aware of them. For example, I was in Dallas, Texas, in a saloon and was looking for a particular pianist and guitarist who played both, Joey Long, and eventually I'd seen a photograph of him and I spotted him. So I said, "I'm just going to go over," and they said, "Oh no, no, don't," but I didn't know why and it was because there was just a little piece of string which was suspended across the room and that was dividing the white area from the black area. . . . It was absolutely bizarre really. I think they were afraid that if I was deliberately undoing the rope and going through and so on it may cause a real problem.[83]

Thus, while Oliver saw protests, was run out of town by police, and experienced the tensions of segregation, he did not believe that he had experienced the overt racism that the English singer Shirley Collins had witnessed just a year earlier with Alan Lomax. Collins recalls seeing vivid signs of the Klu Klux Klan in southern towns and hearing statements such as "We don't like niggers here and won't allow 'em."[84]

Conversation has numerous examples where interviewees make reference to the social conditions that gave rise to the protests of the civil rights movement, but importantly, there are no traces of a sense of protest, activism, or even anger in their responses. For instance, Sam Price talked of a man being lynched near his hometown in Texas when he was a boy, but after acknowledging what things were like, he moved on to talk about the typical work patterns of picking cotton in the fall and fruit in the summer; Sam Chatman sang a song that referred to the negative associations of being "kin to that Ethiopian race," but aside from stating that "it was real hard for colored folks," his excerpt continues by describing his upbringing as a "yard boy."[85] Instead, as Lil' Son Jackson's example given earlier suggests, there is often a resigned acceptance of the harsh realities affecting the lives of the interviewees. In describing the exploitation by white plantation owners, the singer simply states that "you can't argue."[86] Oliver claims that he edited out some references to the demonstrations or civil rights as he didn't want to anger anyone, and this probably referred to the U.S. State Department, which had funded his trip. Oliver's reproduction of black speech in the oral responses is also another way in which he separates the "black intelligentsia" from the folk culture of the South. However, the apparent lack of anger or desire to react in the responses could be explained by reasons other than Oliver's editing. For instance, the respondents may have had little interest or not known about black grassroots activism, although this seems unlikely. Alternatively, the singers may have refrained from talking about this subject with whites. Whatever the reasons, the absence of protest or reference to the social upheavals of the late fifties and early sixties in the excerpts furthers the cause of distancing the blues from the present sociopolitical circumstances of ordinary African Americans.[87]

What makes *Conversation* even more problematic in this regard is the fact that by the time it was published in 1965, the African American struggle for civil rights had become far more visible internationally through the television exposure of high-profile events such as James Meredith's enrollment at the University of Mississippi in 1962 and the resulting riots, the scenes of civil rights activists being hosed down by police in Birmingham, Alabama, in 1963, the March on Washington and the "I Have a Dream" speech given by Martin Luther King Jr. in the same year, the signing of the Civil Rights Act in 1964, and the assassination of Malcolm X in February 1965. To produce a book following these events, which included African American memories of hardship, exploitation, and poverty, points to the nature of transatlantic scholarship on the subject. Oliver seems to have felt unequipped to challenge large political issues such as civil rights from such a social and cultural distance. He may have even felt uncomfortable challenging America's racial issues given the State Department's backing for his project. Officials in the State Department had exhibited some ambiguous conceptions toward African American culture. For instance, Oliver recalled that in Detroit their involvement in trying to arrange his visit was "embarrassing." Oliver was determined to make his own arrangements:

> We compromised, with my agreeing to attend a performance by a black dancer of Wayne [State] University, which [the State Department representative] had put on especially for me. The dancer was named LaRogue Wright, and when the curtains parted he came prancing on stage in leopard skin and brandishing a spear. I found it excruciating and asked if he could stop.[88]

The State Department had probably misunderstood the objectives of Oliver's trip, and combined this with dated perceptions of African American folk culture, as opposed to a more modern conception of jazz. Subsequently,

Oliver refused all future State Department invitations, preferring to make his own arrangements.

His primary objective was to understand and learn about the social and cultural contexts that produced the blues, rather than to investigate the circumstances that made civil rights an urgent necessity. While he may have consciously opted to avoid discussing these issues with his respondents, or the interviewees may have decided not to comment, directly or indirectly, civil rights issues did affect the lives of the people he recorded and photographed. As Oliver's language indicates, unearthing the story of the blues "from the lips of those who made it" was a quest to discover the origins and nature of a folk music that had survived in "semi-isolation" from the mainstream.[89] For the music be "folk" in the sense that folkloristic scholarship of the postwar era believed, the blues had to exist at the margins of society. The disconnection of the blues from contemporary and more importantly mainstream social struggles of ordinary African Americans was thus also a necessity if the blues was be appreciated as folk music. In addition to recording blues singers' memories of the past, which helped to distance the blues from the present day, the other means of capturing this world was by using photography. Images of the musicians and where they lived would provide a visual reference of the blues existing on the fringes of modern society.

Photography and the Blues

The eighty-seven images that accompany the oral responses were also the basis for Oliver's exhibition at the American embassy in London in 1964 entitled "The Story of the Blues," an event that was attended by blues musicians such as the guitarist Lightnin' Hopkins and harmonicist Little Walter, as well as African American author Langston Hughes.[90] Some of Oliver's photographs also became record covers for some of the rediscovered singers who went on to record in the sixties.[91] Despite this appreciation for the images from the trip, *Conversation* has been critiqued primarily as an oral history. It is remarkable that the role of images and photography has received no attention from revisionist scholarship that has considered how blues music has been "invented" over the last fifty years. This omission is surprising not only due to powerful role that images can play in the process of constructing visual symbols for cultures and cultural objects, but also because images of singers were prevalent in music magazines from the late fifties. The trips across the South that produced *Been Here and Gone* (1960), Frederic Ramsey Jr.'s photographic essay on African American life in the

South, also produced numerous photographs of African American musicians and their surroundings in British periodicals such as *Jazz Journal*.[92] Again, despite the fact that during the fifties blues appreciation was the pastime of a small nucleus of collectors and folklorists, the presence of Ramsey's photographs in British periodicals demonstrates the transatlantic links in early blues scholarship, and also how images of "real" blues musicians in their milieu were highly valued. Nonetheless, criticism has tended to concentrate on the written element, failing to acknowledge the range of representative mediums that characterized the reception of the blues. The photographs and the oral accounts in *Conversation* are intricately interwoven and thus instrumental in creating an idea of the blues rooted in the ideology of folkloristic scholasticism and romanticism.

What differentiates the images from the oral responses, however, is their overwhelming ambiguity, which is created by the author's failure to outline their purpose, thereby giving priority to the interviews. The photographs, all taken by the author, can be divided into three main categories: portraits; singers in the act of performing; and environmental images of landscapes and architecture. The high level of variation in their content, from smiling portraits, shots of squalid wooden shacks, and decaying urban buildings to images of singers performing in urban clubs, further confuses the purpose of their inclusion. If we judge by the book's positive reviews, which welcomed its exposure of the harsh realities that singers had experienced and that helped to produce the music, it seems to have been taken for granted that the photographs conveyed the world as it really was for black Americans. This is supported by one of the rare references to Oliver's photographs, in which David Breeden argued they "prove that poverty breeds a need for creative outlet, and that it is in such conditions that blues music frequently, if not always, comes to play an essential role in people's lives."[93] It seems likely that Oliver shared this view and believed the photographs required no explanation: "I didn't want to just be focusing only on the singer or musician or the record company but more of the environment in which they worked or what they reflected." In other words, in a way very similar to the oral responses, the images *spoke* for themselves. They represented the physical reality of the African American experience in which the blues had emerged.[94]

In many ways, this is unsurprising, as photography has always possessed a great seductive power as a medium that reproduces the *real*, as Alan Tratchenberg explains:

> The camera offered what seemed a new relation to the physical world, especially to its transitory nature and the illusory character of its sur-

> faces. The photograph's mirror-like ability to capture the moment and preserve its uniqueness made the camera seem (as it still does) a near-magical device for defeating time, for endowing the past with a presence it had previously had only in memory.[95]

The act of "defeating time" seems perfectly congruous with the folkloristic aims of capturing the social and geographical conditions of the blues before it was too late, and the last exponents of the real blues vanished forever. Much as recording could preserve the sound of the blues, photographic images could provide a visual reference for the memories given by the respondents. However, as Lawrence Levine points out, "Photographic images, like statistics, do not lie, but like statistics the truths they communicate are elusive and incomplete."[96] Thus images that appear to freeze time and capture a transparent moment of reality "as it was" are much more relative and constructed. As the deconstructionist approach to history argues, the meaning derived from the object from the past is dependent on a negotiation between the historical object and the interpreter in the "here and now." In other words, while photographs offer the illusion of faithfully representing a real moment in time, what is captured in the image is a combination of two main processes: first, the aestheticizing process of the photographer taking the picture and then selecting and/or editing it; and, second, the processes involved in the viewer looking at the image and interpreting the object in the present.

With regards to the former, Susan Sontag's seminal work on the nature of photography suggests that there is an inevitable sense of appropriation in taking photographs (as exemplified by the verb used to describe the action, "take'), which ultimately leads to a transformation, rather than a representation of reality:

> To photograph is to appropriate the thing photographed . . . photographic images now provide most of the knowledge people have about the look of the past and the reach of the present. . . . Photographed images do not seem to be statements about the world so much as pieces of it, miniatures of reality that anyone can make or acquire.[97]

Transformation implies that in capturing the photographic image, the photographer's choice of when to take the photo, what to include or exclude, the angle, the lighting, all contribute to manipulating and creating a version of reality, heightening a mood, or attempting to elicit a certain response. Sontag also observes that despite photographs' apparently objective presentation of a real moment in time, the production of the photographic image is "still haunted by the tacit imperatives of taste and conscience."[98] This also occurs in the process of editing photographs for effect. Nicholas Natanson provides a useful example by describing Edwin Rosskam's editing of the Interior of "Kitchenette" photograph for Richard Wright's *12 Million Black Voices* (1941).[99] In the original photograph taken by Russell Lee under the auspices of the Farm Security Administration (FSA), one of the young girls was shown with her tongue out, as a child would normally behave. This was edited for publication in Wright's book by removing the tongue, having the effect of creating another subject altogether.[100] Oliver recalls that his photographs were mostly taken "spontaneously," but this, however, does not eliminate the fact that each shot represented a choice, and every photograph was selected and organized into a sequence and may have been enlarged or cropped for publication.[101]

The meaning of photographs, however, is also created at the interpretive stage. As Tratchenberg makes the case, meanings constantly change depending on "how and where and when, and by whom" the photograph is seen.[102] The consequence of the "transitory" meanings conveyed by images is that the photos of the singers, their homes, and landscapes are both the representation of a fragmentary reality and the basis for the construction of multiple realities dependent on the interpretation of the audience. A means of conceptualizing this process is given by Roland Barthes's thesis that meanings in photographs are always constructed by a "connoted message," that is, by culture that has a preexisting set of codes and stereotypes that are superimposed on the image.[103] Derrick Price took this further by adopting a Foucauldian conception of power systems to argue that rather than mirroring the real, photographs construct a form of reality shaped within discourses of the dominant social system.[104] Applying this to the theme of blues scholarship would be to equate the "dominant social system" with the pervading folkloristic approach toward the study of popular music that tended to romanticize the "folk" in opposition to commercial and more popular cultures.

What is interesting however, is that Oliver's black-and-white photographs of mainly economically deprived African Americans, combined with the author's unstated faith in the photograph's ability to mirror reality and the era's interest in social history (particularly that of the Depression), invite a comparison with the FSA documentary photography of the late thirties and early forties. As already mentioned, *Conversation* followed the reissue of some of the major photographic works that had been originally produced with the sponsorship of the New Deal. Also, Oliver had come across many of the images from this era through the USIS at the American embassy in London. Notable FSA photographers such as Dorothea Lange, Walker Evans,

Jack Delano, and Ben Shahn had focused on representing the poor and creating stories of real Americans struggling with the effects of the Depression. Recalling his experiences of meeting African Americans in his trips to the South, Ben Shahn recalled that "I came to know well so many people of all kinds of belief and temperament, which they maintained with a transcendent indifference to their lot in life."[105] This experience seems to resemble Oliver's in 1960, particularly in his descriptions of the overwhelming generosity of the people he met, and the "innate dignity" that characterized their oral responses despite their bitter experiences of segregation.[106] A distinctive similarity between Oliver's photographs and those of the FSA photographers can also be seen in Oliver's images of rural and urban landscapes, particularly in the images of homes, towns, and buildings. For instance, the image of the railway tracks running through Richmond in East Texas, and the photo of Nelson Street in Greenville are highly reminiscent of photos by Walker Evans in *Let Us Now Praise Famous Men.*

William Stott's analysis of photo-documentary expression highlights the manner in which a considerable proportion of the photographic works of the FSA photographs equated to a populist form of propaganda.[107] This was also the focus of Lili Corbus Bezner, who demonstrated that the FSA photographers often sought out "truth" and "honesty" in their images in order to arouse a sympathetic response in viewers. The spirit of many of the photographic works of the time was to incite social change through the provocation of feelings of sympathy for the dispossessed, an emotion that was carefully "guided into the safe waters of human tragedy and national populism."[108] The key to evoking feelings of sympathy, according to Roy Stryker, the head of the FSA's Historical Section, was to faithfully reproduce the realities of ordinary Americans at the bottom of the social order. This was exemplified by James Agee, author of *Let Us Now Praise Famous Men* (1941), who firmly believed that the photograph could capture the "absolute, dry truth."[109] The emphasis on truth and honesty that seemed to motivate the FSA photographers is reflected in many instances in *Conversation*, particularly in Oliver's desire to capture the direct voices of singers and in the emphasis on the blues as sincere expression.

However, photography, as oral history, cannot portray the real in unproblematic terms. Stott argues that most often FSA photographers would purposely present their subjects as "never vicious, never depraved, never responsible for their own misery." He provides the fascinating example of how Margaret Bourke-White and Erskine Caldwell actively sought out facial expressions *they* desired for *You Have Seen Their Faces* (1937). They would often time their shots to capture facial expressions that expressed "the *look*: mournful, plaintive, nakedly near tears," an image perfectly epitomized in Dorothea Lange's famous Migrant Mother.[110] While Oliver concentrates on African Americans and some photographs capture people with the "look," the purpose of *Conversation* was not to inspire social change or to evoke feelings of sympathy, despite the fact that the latter may have well occurred in viewer responses. While Oliver focused on images of African Americans, the photographs were not aimed at inspiring change, such as in Richard Wright's *12 Million Black Voices*. Wright's photo-documentary portrayal of black life used more powerful and overtly challenging images, such as that of a lynching in Georgia in order to promote the antisegregationist message.[111]

The ambiguous nature of Oliver's photographs and the lack of a political motivation complicate the wholehearted comparison with FSA photography. In breaking down the nature of the term "documentary," Stott defines the photographic works of the FSA era as "social" documents, which strive to evoke emotional responses to incite participation in social change. It is doubtful whether the entirety of Oliver's photographs could be grouped in this category. Some of the images in *Conversation* could be categorized as what Stott terms "historical" and even "human" documents, which require intellectual and emotional responses respectively.[112] While the images may not have the stated purpose of promoting social change, they do represent the manner in which Oliver attempted to portray the culture of the blues.

The Photographs in *Conversation with the Blues*

In the same way the oral history represented a means of connecting the blues to the source of its creators, the photographs in *Conversation* function largely as a means of rooting the music in a specific geographic location. The images function as a visual progression from the rural South to the urban North of Chicago and Detroit. This could be interpreted as an attempt to mimic the Great Migrations of the early and mid-twentieth century, or perhaps the journey northward undertaken by many blues singers such as Muddy Waters (the example given by Robert Palmer in *Deep Blues*).[113] Interestingly, this progression is the opposite of the route Oliver took in 1960, which began in New York, went on to Chicago and Detroit, was followed by the rendezvous with Strachwitz in Memphis and across the South, and ended in Washington.[114] In addition, the photographs gradually become more populated, beginning with portraits of individuals in rural areas to group photos of blues singers living together in Chicago, from photos of single farms or sharecropper homes to aerial shots of large cities, from desolate country barrelhouses to crowded city blues clubs. The arrangement therefore appears as a representation of the African American journey of the twentieth century, from rurality to urbanity, from South to North. While this seems a fairly accurate reference to the prevailing migratory patterns of African Americans, it was also an attempt on Oliver's part to make *Conversation* "a bit more readable," demonstrating the way in which the author made his findings conform to a narrative style, or in other words, working toward "the story of the blues."[115] The general arrangement of the photographs also indicates the presence of Barthes's "connoted meaning," that is, meaning imposed by a preexisting set of assumptions. The photographic sequence is made to conform to a prevailing notion of the African American experience.

The book therefore begins in the rural areas, opening with a picture of a wooden and seemingly vacated sharecropper's home (fig. 10). The image is accompanied with the caption "Blues Standing in My Door," which instantly establishes a link between the small home and the blues, or in other words, this is where the blues "lives." The intentions of the photograph can be automatically detected by the desire to physically place the music in specific geographical space—the home of a sharecropper, the black manual laborer or the rural South, or even the image cultivated by Big Bill Broonzy in his European tours. The angle of the photograph, taken from higher position to the side of the shack, is also suggestive of a disconnection between photographer and object. A full frontal view of the home was not given, as if to suggest that it was not accessible to an outsider. A similar effect is achieved in an urban context, with the image of black housing in Chicago's South Side (fig. 11). This image, highly reminiscent of Russell Lee's photographs of housing used in *12 Million Black Voices*, reinforces the connection between the subordinate social standing of African Americans and the blues.[116] Chicago, where the black population had increased from 277,731 in 1940 to 812,637 in 1960, was also the city that had experienced more housing-related violence as a result of migratory pressures and racial discrimination.[117] However, the image does not draw attention to issues of overcrowding. While the rubble piled up in front of seemingly unstable buildings points to the condition of black housing in the city, a wide-angle frame creates a sense of isolation and distance from the object similar to that seen in the wooden sharecropper's home. Importantly, these images need to be considered in the context of their publication in 1965, which sets up a contrast with the commercial success of white groups playing African American music during the blues revival, or even the burgeoning soul culture of the sixties. This emerging culture was more centered on celebrating blackness, and figures such as Marvin Gaye, James

Brown, and even Aretha Franklin began to symbolize the fact that for many African Americans culture was an arena for political assertiveness and agency. Nor was commercial success antithetical. Franklin's reworked version of Otis Redding's "Respect" topped the charts in 1967, and Brown's "Say It Loud, I'm Black and I'm Proud" went to number ten in the charts in 1968, and still became an anthem for the Black Power movement.[118]

The "real" home of the blues that Oliver presents, on the other hand, is anything but glamorous or commercial. It is harsh and, as the photographs indicate, it is real, isolated and perhaps impenetrable. Importantly, the image conforms to the folkloristic approach to blues scholarship that exalted anticommercialism as the purest element of the folk. Nothing seemed more anticommercial than a sharecropper's small wooden shack, or the squalid housing of African Americans living in Chicago's South Side.

A number of photographs serve to illustrate the seemingly anticommercial nature of the blues. For instance, the image of a smiling Blind Arvella Gray playing with a tin cup pinned to his jacket on the streets of Chicago, also used as the front cover for the 1997 edition, is suggestive of the commercial decline of the blues, with singers reduced to street performances for pennies (fig. 13). What is significant, however, is that the singer does not inspire sympathy and is not made to seem overly downtrodden or defeated. In the quaint grin toward the camera, he appears with a certain dignified acceptance of his circumstances. Many other portraits in *Conversation* share this quality by presenting singers smiling at the camera, whether posing for the shot or while playing a song.[119] Similarly, the image of Butch Cage and Willie Thomas playing outdoors under a tree, with no sign of an audience, and with the musicians not looking at the camera, is captioned "What We Played Is Just All We Know" (fig. 12).[120] This image seems to reaffirm that the music has its roots in this rural setting, while the captioning of a quote from the musicians as a title plays on the directness and honesty of the music, again an important criterion of folk and anticommercial music.

The image of Cage and Thomas highlights one of the more striking features of a large proportion of the photographs. At first glance, the camera seems to subtract itself from the process, giving the impression that Oliver is almost "not there" taking the photograph. This impression is created by a number of images in which the people photographed are not looking into the camera, but instead either focused on something else or gazing into the distance. This characteristic immediately reminds of well-known FSA images such as Dorothea Lange's "Migrant Mother," or even Russell Lee's church service photograph used in Wright's *12 Million Black Voices*, that show their main subject looking away and past the camera. In Oliver's photos, this characteristic helps to create a fly-on-the-wall mood that adds a certain sense of naturalness, as if the images were not the product of Oliver's presence.[121]

This is particularly the case in the photographs taken of musicians performing. One photo of Maxwell Street Jimmy shows the guitarist playing on a busy street in Chicago, and no one gazes at the camera or seems to acknowledge its presence. A similar impression is created by the photos of Daddy Stovepipe playing on Nelson Street, of Eddie Hines and Tom Stewart, and of Boogie Woogie Red and Little Eddie Kirkland around a piano (fig. 14). In the latter image especially, the angle from which the shot was taken, behind the two musicians, creates the feeling that the photographer has stumbled upon a performance, giving the impression that the image is merely capturing what is happening, rather than the situation being organized for the photograph. Consequently, these images suggest a certain photographic anonymity, with Oliver almost becoming absent in the process of production. This anonymity complements and reinforces the ideology behind the use of oral history, that is, to let the people concerned have their say. These images provide an illusion of the real, suggesting that what is occurring in the image is a natural occurrence, rather than having been arranged for the interviews and the photographs.

While the photos discussed would appear to have a spontaneous and natural quality, the inclusion of these images in *Conversation* serves to reinforce an idea of the blues being shaped by the contemporary cultural norms of the time. Oliver, as acknowledged earlier, was determined to seek out the music's "natural context."[122] The pictures of the singers playing on the streets force a strong bond in the reader between the music and a specific geographical time and place. The street corners represent one of these "natural contexts." They suggest marginality rather than success or a central position within society, with people walking by and the absence of a dedicated audience, that would conform to the folkloristic view that true folk music was anticommercial.

The fact that an outsider is looking into the world of the blues, which has been highly influenced by a preexisting body of knowledge, is demonstrated by the emphasis on images that produce a sense of nostalgia for the past. For the most part, the effect of the photographs is directed by Oliver's captions, which seem to impose meaning on the images. For example, a picture of a Beale Street signpost on a street corner is accompanied by the caption that states, "Where Highway 51 meets Beale Street was a goal for migrants from Mississippi"; and a picture of Hastings Street in Chicago is entitled "Hastings near Brown's Club where Big Maceo worked has been destroyed to make room for an expressway."[123] A notable example is the image of a disused warehouse in Terrell, Texas (fig. 15). The caption imposes nostalgic responses on the interpretation of the image, by forcing the viewer to acknowledge that the music that used to fill the warehouse, is no longer present. In this sense, Oliver's photography contains an element of tourism. The photographs captured historically significant locations that the natives had taken for granted. Oliver's captioning narrows the process of interpreting the images, by directing the viewer toward a nostalgic attachment to the past, which is also generated by the backward-looking focus of the oral excerpts. Importantly, Oliver's captions have a similar imposing function to Bourke-White and Caldwell's *You Have Seen Their Faces*. Their use of captions for the images revealed their own views of the photographs, rather being more faithful to the perceptions of their subjects, as Dorothea Lange and Paul Taylor were in *An American Exodus* (1939).[124]

Portraits of the singers also manage to convey the idea that the blues Oliver went looking for had been lost to history. The photograph of Bo Carter (fig. 16), captioned as "I Used To Play for Doctors," is followed by Oliver's comment, "Once a 'medicine show' guitarist, Bo Carter became sick and blind, scarcely able to play his old 'National' steel guitar."[125] A tired-looking Carter faces away from his instrument, looks down toward the floor, and holds up his guitar as if not to play any more. The combination of these factors creates a sense of loss, the feeling that Carter could once play the blues, but now time and illness converge to prevent that from happening. Two images of Mance Lipscomb evoke similar responses, but also highlight a sense of disconnection between photographer and subject (figs. 17 and 19). In the first, Lipscomb is shown playing inside his two-room cabin, backed by his young children on beds, looking at Oliver's camera and apparently indifferent to the performance. The presence of the microphone also signals the artifice and arrangement of this situation for the purpose of recording. The situation is repeated in slightly different circumstances in the second photograph. Lipscomb is now seen playing on his outer doorstep, while looking into the distance across and away from the camera, as if he were gazing into the past. Behind the singer, a young grinning child peeks through the door to look at the camera. In both images, there is a generational disconnection in the fact the young seem uninterested in the music, and are more interested in Oliver's presence. In turn, Oliver's focus is on the singer, while the singer gazes out into the distance. While Lipscomb's lack of eye contact with the camera reinforces the feeling that Oliver has instead stumbled upon a natural occurrence of an aging man singing a blues for his own purposes, the children's gaze at the lens reveals the artifice of the situation. Again, the overall mood of the two pictures is that the blues belongs to an older generation, and that the only other people who are interested in this music are the photographer and those looking at the images.

Interestingly, these images and many others in *Conversation* are also representative of the social and economic circumstances of many African Americans in 1960. It is in these images that Oliver's photography is most reminiscent of the FSA photographs. For instance, the cramped and squalid condition of Lipscomb's home is accompanied by that of an adolescent barefoot boy outside a corrugate iron store, looking directly at the camera with dejected body language (fig. 18).[126] While this photograph may have proved useful in the promotion of social and economic improvement for African Americans in 1960, the caption of the image, combined with the lack of protest in the oral excerpts serves to marginalize the racial and political battles of the period. Two additional photographs create a similar effect. The first example shows Percy Thomas and Bill Johnson playing together (fig. 20). In the background, a younger black man with a bandage around his swollen face looks intently at the camera. The viewer is left to assume the reasons for his injuries based on his intense and unsettling stare at the lens and on the fact that the injuries have affected his face. Considering the visibility of the civil rights protests and the violent reactions of white authorities in southern states by the mid-sixties, it would have been easy for observers at the time to conclude that the individual suffered the injuries at the hands of white racism or prejudice.

An image of a black café that stands alone alongside a road may have aided this conclusion (fig. 21). What makes this photograph significant is that it is the only image in the book that displays an overt sign of segregation, here present in the "Colored Café" sign above the doorway. In addition, the caption highlights the fact that the white café is on the other side of the road and out of sight. At first, this photograph reminds us of the work of photographers such as Marion Palfi and Dan Weiner, who were more explicit in their attempts to portray the injustices of racial segregation by focusing on similar symbols of Jim Crow.[127] However, the effect here is contradictory. While segregation is evident in the photograph, the viewer is forced to interpret black life in isolation from the outside world of the South. Oliver may have evaded the comparison of the two buildings to avoid confronting the visibility of segregation head-on. This seems to represent the author's timidity on wider racial and political issues that affected the lives of African Americans during his field trip. Overall, the combined effect of these images serves to aestheticize the harsh social and economic realities of black Americans and to relate these realities to conditions that produced the blues, rather than to reveal the injustices that continued to pervade African American life in 1960. Therefore, the subjectivity of these images, combined with Oliver's captioning, indicates that the photographs in *Conversation* are as revealing of a world that Oliver imagined, than they are of the African American experience.

In *American Photographs* Walker Evans had opened up the possibilities of his photographs by omitting names, dates, and places. According to Tratchenberg, "The book invites its readers to discover meanings for themselves, to puzzle over the arrangement of pictures and figure out how and why they appear as they do."[128] By complete contrast, the visual aspect of *Conversation* reduces the possibility for open interpretations. The photos place the blues within the poverty of the rural South and the urban ghettoes of the North, which means that the music is portrayed as belonging firmly within these deterministic social and geographical categories. Consequently, what is excluded is the affluent side of African American music, the commercially successful or popular. The people are presented in their disadvantaged socioeconomic circumstances, but importantly, as in many FSA photographs, the subjects are rarely made to look pitiable. In the context of revivalist blues scholarship, this representation acts as an identification of the music as a folk form, rather than a documentary report on the conditions in which African Americans were living in 1960. *Conversation* indicates that there is an innate dignity in African American culture that transcends social, economic, and racial strife.

For the author, the 1960 trip confirmed that the world and society he had been describing during the fifties and in *Blues Fell This Morning* "were all too painfully accurate."[129] *Conversation with the Blues* was thus a representation of what Oliver regarded as the reality of the African American experience that had produced the music. While the approach of using oral responses and photographs was employed in the hope of the world of the blues speaking for itself, the effect was to create a reality that was forced to conform to an idea, constructed by "connoted meanings" that had been developed in the previous decade of scholarship on African American culture. Oliver aimed to let the creators of the blues have their say, and the voices that echoed through the excerpts were regarded as beckoning directly from the source. However, the scattering of his interviews into small segments, framed within a distinctive pronunciation, and which focused on the past, helped to create an idea of the blues as a cultural expression that belonged to history, was the voice of people who had struggled through harsh manual labor, violence, and poverty. It also emphasized that the music's true origins remained within the memories of old and relatively unknown blues singers, and was thus in the process of dying out. Importantly, these fragmentary memories presented in excerpt format were not transparent historical facts, but rather signified what the singers thought of themselves, their history, and the interviews. In turn, Oliver's selection of the responses combines with their content to separate the blues from the present, the world of the 1960.

The images add a visual dimension to the separation of the past and the present. While they capture moments of Oliver's experiences and put faces and places to names, they are also indicative of a choice, of a selective vision that carves out a version of reality. The meanings imposed on the photographs by Oliver's captions direct the gaze of the viewer toward a visual construction. This world is, as can be expected, poor and black, but most importantly, it is vanishing, its people are dying, and its places are disappearing. Moreover, these people and places are isolated from the mainstream, whether the mainstream is the popular culture of 1960, the blues revival, or the civil rights movement. Combined with reminiscences of days gone by, the photographs testify to *Conversation*'s ability to physically root the blues within a distant historical past created by selected African American memories.

The idea of the blues as belonging to a bygone era was largely shaped by the author's attitudes toward the growing popularity of African American music among young white audiences and musicians in the sixties. White British bands had popularized the music with their commercial success, and this derivative enterprise had made Oliver "shudder" with revulsion.[130] Black singers had visited Europeans shores and toured extensively, appeared on television and entertained large audiences. In a sense, these large uninitiated audiences had to be "educated" as to what the blues was and where it came from. In this context, the book was extremely important in blues scholarship, for it played a fundamental part in constructing the idea that the blues was the music of the unknown, aging, black singers of the South, and that it emerged from their toil and exploitation in the rural South and had traveled with those who had been part of the Great Migration. It helped to strengthen the boundaries of the genre that isolated it from any notion of popularity or commercial success. Most importantly, it claimed to communicate this message from the voices of its creators and the expressions in their faces. However, the oral responses and the images were the product of a mixture of memories and history, facts and fiction, the real and the imagined. In the disconnection with the contemporary experiences of African Americans in 1960 in particular, *Conversation* is revealing of the way the African American world was nostalgically imagined by the author and by readers who championed his efforts. The emphasis on the rapidly vanishing past would drive his next enterprise in blues scholarship, *Screening the Blues: Aspects of the Blues Tradition* (1968), which reified the blues presented in *Conversation* by tracing the continuities and discontinuities of the music as a tradition.

Figure 10. Oliver's caption read: "Blues Standing in My Door—Clarksdale, Mississippi: sharecropper's home." Photo by Paul Oliver, 1960.

Figure 11. The caption read: "Very Poor on the South Side—Black housing behind South State Street, Chicago." Photo by Paul Oliver, 1960.

Figure 12. Oliver's caption read: "What we Played Is Just All We Know: Butch Cage (fiddle) and Willie Thomas (guitar) playing on the Old Slaughter Road, Zachary, Louisiana." Photo by Paul Oliver, 1960.

Figure 13. Oliver's caption read: "A Quarter in a Tin Cup—Blind Arvella Gray on the corner of Halsted and Maxwell in Chicago."

Figure 14. Oliver's caption read: "Boogie and Blues—Boogie Woogie Red and Little Eddie Kirkland." Photo by Paul Oliver, 1960.

Figure 15. Oliver's caption read: "To Catch the Cotton Crop: In such barns and warehouses travelling shows played. Outside, Cola sells on work incentive. Terrell, Texas." Photo by Paul Oliver, 1960.

Figure 16. Original caption read: "'*I Used To Play for Doctors*'—Once a 'medicine show' guitarist, Bo Carter became sick and blind, scarcely able to play his old 'National' guitar." Photo by Paul Oliver, 1960.

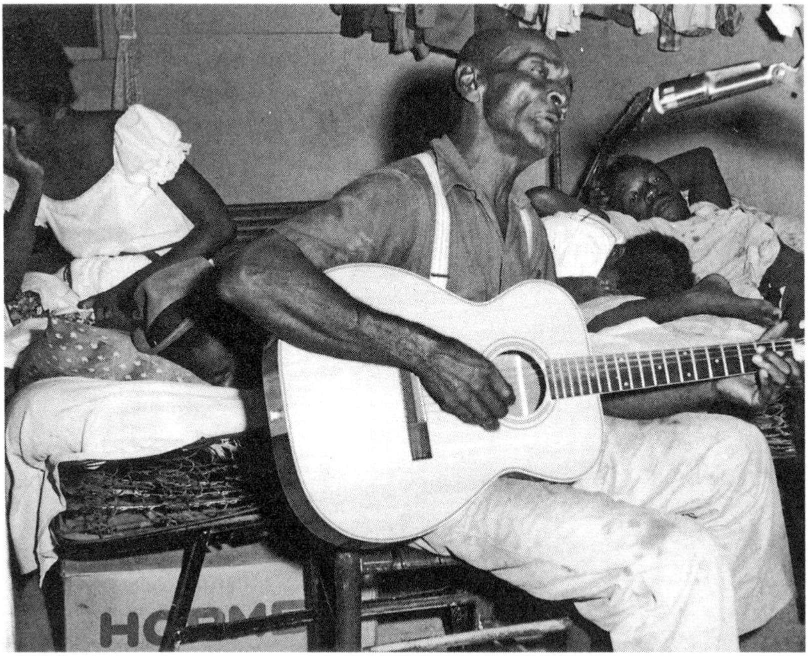

Figure 17. Original caption: "Farmed Mostly All My Life: Mance Lipscomb sings in his two-room cabin while his grandchildren listen." Photo by Paul Oliver, 1960.

Figure 18. Original caption: "When Final Settlement Comes: pause for refreshment at the corrugated iron grocery at Luisa, Mississippi. The mules wait by the cotton gin." Photo by Paul Oliver, 1960.

Figure 19. Original caption: "An Open Player: Mance Lipscomb is proud that he has 'got it in the fingers.'" Photo by Paul Oliver, 1960.

Figure 20. Oliver's caption read: "*We Played for Shuckin–Bees*: Percy Thomas on guitar, and Bill Johnson on fiddle, with the bandaged man behind them." Photo by Paul Oliver, 1960.

Figure 21. Oliver's caption read: "'*Colored Folk's Juke*': Across the road from the juke at Rome, Mississippi, in Sunflower County, is the cafe for white patrons." Photo by Paul Oliver, 1960.

4 • Tracing the Tradition

History and "Invention"

In *Screening the Blues: Aspects of the Blues Tradition* (1968), Oliver returned to the methods of *Blues Fell This Morning* by analyzing the lyrics of blues songs. However, this time the focus was on the use and adaptation of themes by singers over different generations, and how continuities revealed the existence of a blues tradition. The book examined some of the previously unexplored and more obscure aspects of the music, such as blues about sex, to further emphasize that the music belonged to a culture far removed from the contemporary scene of the pop industry. It would act as a lengthy introduction to the seminal book published the following year, *The Story of the Blues*, which was one of the first major attempts to narrate a comprehensive history of the music (chapter 5). The late sixties were therefore characterized by the historical exploration into the origins of the blues and its evolution up to the end of the revival.

While Oliver maintains his typical conscientious approach by acknowledging the limits of his scholarship in *Screening the Blues*, the process of historicizing and effectively canonizing the music through the identification of a "tradition" reveals a highly subjective process of categorization based on an often romanticized, but also restrictive, interpretation of African American culture. This chapter will consider the problems involved in tracing the blues tradition, and will demonstrate the manner in which this canonization served to strengthen the categorical boundaries that made the blues a distinctive and authentic culture in the eyes of the blues writer in the late sixties. However, it must be remembered that the aim of this analysis is not to identify areas of historical inaccuracy in Oliver's work, or to deny the existence of a blues tradition. There are distinctive and unique aspects that characterize the development of African American music in the first half of the twentieth century, such as in the borrowing and adaptation of traditional themes, the hybridization of a number of musical styles and influences, lyrics, and stylistic approaches. As in the rest of this endeavor, the emphasis here is to draw attention to how blues writers of the late sixties understood and interpreted these elements, and how these interpretations helped to form certain ideas about the blues that have come to be questioned in recent years. The process of identifying the "blues tradition" allows us to consider how blues scholarship developed particular interpretations of African American history.

In examining certain aspects of black culture that were regarded as traditional, authors such as Oliver were also susceptible to romanticizing their nature, and sometimes relying on stereotypical assumptions of the differences between a supposed "folk" African American and a commercial white mainstream culture. What arises is an increased sense of nostalgia for a vibrant world of unmediated expression, deeply rooted in the traditions of an imagined African American past. The language used to describe this culture serves to highlight the attitudes of the writer as much as it illuminates the subject matter. As Oliver traced and defined the characteristics of the tradition, he was also able to discern when that tradition was no longer being respected, a trend that was becoming much more commonplace in postrevival world of the sixties. *Screening* is permeated with categorical boundaries imposed by the binary vision of authentic folk and commercial pop culture. While Oliver argues in many instances that the difference between blues and pop is purely cultural, the writing contains a timid but nonetheless significant racialized tone, which is part of the response to the white discovery and appropriation of African American music in the sixties. Oliver had now to contend with the fact that music labeled blues had reached much larger audiences on both sides of the Atlantic through the interpretations of white groups, and the rediscovery of older bluesmen, which had generated increased interest among enthusiasts and collectors to discover more about the origins and nature of the blues. The act of "screening" the blues was therefore representative of the bolder steps Oliver took toward the end of the sixties to fix definitions and conceptions of the blues as the music of an imagined African American world in the pre–World War II era.

Blues Scholarship in the Middle and Late Sixties

It was evident that there had been a marked increase in the number of people interested in the background and history of the blues after 1965. This was in clear contrast to the changes occurring in the world of popular music. Schwartz notes that British musicians and audiences had begun to tire of repertoires heavily dependent on 1950s rhythm and blues, with many turning to the more contemporary sounds of soul. British audiences at the American Folk Blues Festivals had also begun to drop as a growing sense of "discovery fatigue" emerged following the repeated appearance of the same visiting blues musicians.[1] However, a number of factors helped to create a new generation of enthusiasts for the blues by the mid-sixties, particularly the music of the interwar years. The "rediscoveries" in the early 1960s of musicians long thought to have been lost, such as Son House, Mississippi John Hurt, Skip James, and Sleepy John Estes, as well as previously unrecorded singers, such as Mance Lipscomb and Mississippi Fred McDowell, were akin to great archaeological discoveries, promoting the idea that the creators of the music could still be found, that the music was still alive, still significant, and that much of the music's history could be learned from them.[2] McDowell had been "discovered" by Alan Lomax on his journey across the South in 1959 and was subsequently involved in the American Folk Blues Festival in London in 1965. In Oliver's description of the singer, which anticipated his imminent arrival and performance, it is possible to discern the ideal these rediscovered musicians represented:

> Fred McDowell represents the purest form of Mississippi blues; influenced, of course, by the work of other blues singers including the great names of the Delta, and by the records that he heard, but playing today, as he has all his life, the music of the country and the cotton patch.[3]

The appreciation for these rediscoveries was accompanied by a sense of caution on the treatment and exploitation of aging singers. Oliver argued: "Let those of the Anglo-Saxon intelligentsia who take such an interest in the Negro people of America never forget the responsibility they have for the changes they have wrought in those lives." While such a comment may appear to echo some remnant shred of paternalism, Oliver was concerned by the fact that aging blues singers may have been ill-prepared to face the demanding nature of transatlantic tours, and were thus easily exploitable. This mixed attitude of anticipation and caution reveals some of the inherent tensions Oliver felt toward the popularization of the blues in the sixties, fearing the effect of white audiences on the music, but also worrying that "the Negro musician may be playing his old role of entertaining the white folks."[4]

In this period the pages of *Blues Unlimited* became filled with notices by readers seeking other individuals with which to share record collections and information. The contributors of these new blues magazines were also representative of the transatlantic scope of blues writing and criticism by the mid-sixties, with numerous articles by emerging American blues writers such as Pete Welding, David Evans, Bob Koester, Paul Garon, and Gayle Dean Wardlow.[5] As a result, blues clubs and societies began to form all over England and Scotland in the middle and late sixties.[6] Oliver was also in the business of advising budding record collectors on forming a reputable discography of blues recordings, which included pointing readers of *Jazz Beat* to the discography of *Blues Fell This Morning*.[7] This expanding group of blues acolytes across Britain sought detailed knowledge on the history of the music, the lives of the singers, the significance of the blues vernacular and, more fervently than ever, sought to differentiate authentic blues from the inauthentic. This growth in interest also saw the formation of the National Blues Federation, which organized two conventions, the first of which was held in September 1968 in London. Over the two-day conference there were talks, recitals, performances, workshops, and films. An advertisement clearly displays Oliver's name at the top of the bill as one of the keynote speakers, demonstrating the writer's reputation. In a review of the convention, Oliver was described at the "doyen of blues writers" and was applauded for the fact that he "gave the most professional lecture seen throughout the whole convention."[8]

The musical landscape had changed dramatically over the preceding decade. While in the fifties blues enthusiasts desired the recognition of the blues as a musical culture separate from jazz, in the sixties the picture had been complicated by the mass exposure given to the music by blues revival. The efforts of British bands to turn young audiences onto the blues "masters" seemed to have worked very well. Bands such as The Rolling Stones, The Yardbirds, and The Animals and people such as John Mayall and Eric Clapton had all been hugely successful playing blues covers and blues-inspired material, and it was evident that this popularity had caused some major shifts. In popular music in general, the likes of Cream, Janis Joplin, and Jimi Hendrix had also made use of the blues to experiment and fuse a number of styles. Adelt has commented that many of these musicians had produced highly innovative music by using the blues as a basis.[9] By contrast Oliver was arguing that by the mid-sixties "some forms of blues ha[d] moved away from the Negro world to that of the white folk world; many successful white singers are successfully imitating the blues." For Bob Dawbarn the idea that whites were trying to commercialize the blues was "ridiculous."[10] Evidently, the blues intelligentsia were highly cynical of the musical miscegenation that the sixties blues revival had produced. The appropriation of the music by young, white, and often British musicians strengthened the resolve to distinguish what was authentic from imitation, which required a reliance upon the now firmly established folkloristic interpretation of music. This helps to explain the growing interest of blues within the folk world, as exemplified by Oliver's presentations at the English Folk Dance and Song Society (EFDSS) at Cecil Sharp House in London in 1965. The author was surprised by this shift, arguing that ten years earlier the performance of a singer such as Blind Gary Davis at Cecil Sharp House would have been "unthinkable." Oliver described Davis as being "part of the authentic tradition," in contrast to "professional" folk singers like Harry Belafonte who had "little or no connection to the tradition."[11] The entrance into the folk world was also in contrast to other European conceptualizations of the blues. Adelt has noted that the German organizers of the American Folk Blues Festivals, Horst Lippmann and Fritz Rau, had always espoused a more primitivist idea of the blues, based on a nostalgic attachment to an idea of the blues from the past, in a way very similar to Oliver's scholarship. However, by the late sixties and with the changes in popular music, the festival organizers had become much more willing to incorporate the links between the blues and the modern phenomenon that was rock.[12] By contrast, Oliver's emphasis on the "tradition" in this period demonstrates that his efforts became focused on the music's historical and cultural roots, which would help to differentiate the real from the ersatz, effectively "screening" the real thing from the imitation by giving the music historical legitimacy. His method was to establish the traits of the blues tradition and to demonstrate ways in which this tradition had been maintained and developed by subsequent generations of musicians. His approach in *Screening* was appreciated by Derek Jewell of the *Guardian*, who stated that Oliver was "an invaluable guide, especially in a decade when the blues [had been] massively intermixed with the mainstream of Western popular music."[13] The appropriation of the blues in the popular music of the sixties served to strengthen the conviction of blues enthusiasts that "authentic" blues lay firmly within the African American experience of the early twentieth century, and was separate from the mainstream of white popular music.

Identifying and Constructing the Blues Tradition

In *Blues Fell This Morning* and *Conversation with the Blues*, Oliver had been less direct than suggestive about the blues' links to the past. However, in *Screening the Blues* and *The Story of the Blues*, the author's writing became distinctly historical in nature. The fact that the blues is referred to as a "tradition" in *Screening* is demonstrative of the historical emphasis in Oliver's writing in this period. This book saw Oliver returning to the analysis of blues on records primarily from the interwar years, and focused on the themes of traditional verses and their relevance to the African American culture of the South in the first half of the twentieth century. The main themes that Oliver examined were blues on the subject of Christmas, religion and the church, gambling, heroic figures, and sex. The book concentrated on the manner in which subsequent generations of blues musicians made use of these themes to continue in the tradition. By finding continuities in the music and the lyric content, the blues could be linked to the past, or more specifically, the African American past he had been describing for two decades. Interestingly, a considerable proportion of the writing was taken from previously published material. A large part of the book is based on articles that Oliver had written for the English periodical *Jazz Monthly* between 1960 and 1961 under the title "Screening the Blues"; the chapters entitled "The Santy Claus Crave" and "The Forty-Fours" are both expanded versions of articles that appeared in *Music Mirror* even earlier in 1955; and the chapter on sexual blues themes, "The Blue Blues," was also developed from an article that appeared in a 1963 edition of the periodical named *Jazz*. While the older material offered Oliver a chance to further explore the themes of the originally shorter articles, their use indicates that rather than challenging assumptions on the nature of the blues or of popular culture itself, his fieldwork experiences and the blues revival of that decade strengthened the binarism that saw folk blues in opposition to commercial popular music.

The traditional aspects of the blues, that is, material and practice rooted in the cultural past, are of paramount importance to the folkloric interpretation:

> For blues has a tradition. Perhaps the music is now in decline but it has enjoyed a life-span long enough to establish a tradition of its own, comparable with that of say, the Dutch school of painting, whose artists, from the generation of the 1590s to the generation of the 1620s anticipated those of the blues by exactly three hundred years. In a period of unprecedented acceleration of social, technological, economic and cultural changes, the blues has changed too. But though it has been altered by the differing environments which gave it birth and modified by the social climates in which it has flourished, those constants, the elements of tradition within the music, relate it to the folk forms that preceded it and establish links between the various categories that have been discerned in its development.[14]

Demonstrating once again his artistic background in the likening of the blues to Dutch art of the Renaissance, Oliver identifies the "constants" that make up the blues tradition: the three-line stanza, common stock verses and themes, and the influence of pre-blues styles such as minstrel songs, work songs, spirituals, and the ballad tradition. The repetition of these "constants" forms the basis of a tradition that links the practice of blues musicians with a shared cultural past. Oliver's focus on the tradition can therefore be interpreted as an attempt to confront the changes wrought on the music by the "unprecedented acceleration of social, technological, economic and cultural changes." As the blues was "in decline" at the time of the book, by establishing the tradition the author would use the past to form the canon that defined the qualities making the music unique and distinctive, thereby rescuing it from the demise that the revival of the sixties had caused. However, Oliver's declaration that the blues was in its final days is suggestive of the subjective adherence to an ideal of the blues, which was not shared by all other blues writers. Keil, for instance, had already challenged the "moldy fig" mentality that was particularly strong among English blues writers. He maintained that the African American tradition of expressing the condition of ordinary blacks was alive and well in the newer urban and more "soul"-influenced sounds of musicians such as B. B. King, Bobby Bland, and Ray Charles, but had been marginalized by writers such as Oliver due to their aversion to the contemporary decadence of the entertainment industry.[15]

Thus, Oliver's search for the tradition became as much an exercise in highlighting continuities among generations of musicians as it was about defining and maintaining an idealized conception of the music. As was common in his work, Oliver demonstrates an incomparably detailed knowledge of blues recordings that allows him to discuss the continuities and adaptations made to traditional themes in lyrics and in musical terms. Examples are numerous in the book, and one such instance is the discussion on songs that use the Santa Claus theme. Oliver suggests that Jack Dupree's version of "The Santy Claus Crave" borrowed aspects from Peetie Wheatstraw's "Santa Claus Blues" and Elzadie Robinson's "The Santy Claus Crave," but rather than being derivative, "he creates a new blues from the raw material of two rich seams within the idiom."[16] Another method employed by Oliver analyzes the general treatment of a subject in songs, such as the church or religion. Oliver argues that a survey of recorded songs over a number of decades indicates a cautious approach to religion or the authority of the church in the blues, and appreciates that this may have been caused by some form of censorship by record companies, or even that many singers may have felt inhibited by their own connections with religious life.[17]

In a musical sense, the author also traces the evolution of a melodic theme, such as in the chapter "The Forty-Fours." In this chapter, Oliver becomes much more technical in his analysis of continuities by including musical notation. This is perhaps a sign of the more specialized language that blues scholarship had begun to develop in the late sixties, a period when ethnomusicology was turning its relatively young eye upon the blues with people such as Keil, David Evans, and Jeff Titon. Oliver presents the notation for Little Brother Montgomery's version, to then show the variance among other blues musicians who recorded the song. He argues,

> *The Forty-Fours* . . . demonstrate the complex family-tree of the blues. Its basic instrumental theme provides the groundwork for two major vocal tunes and a number of subsidiary ones; the instrumental theme itself is also subject to many variations. The blues shows the degree to which a singer's individual style may influence the way in which a tune is interpreted by others; it exemplifies the passing on of traditional verses and lines, the dropping of some and the grafting of others in the process of evolution.[18]

In this manner Oliver traces the genealogy of some of the main themes of the blues tradition, and how they have been modified and adapted to the requirements of each singer. What is particularly significant is that the "process of evolution" gives a sense of coherence to the blues as a clear and identifiable category, an organism with a story of its own. However, the interpretation and description of the blues as a tradition in *Screening* raises a number of analytical problems.

First, as is the case with most music styles, there had been no official definition or general agreement by writers as to what the blues actually was by the end of the sixties. A broad number of familiar categories such as classic, country, "down-home," Chicago, East Coast (Piedmont), and urban blues had been used by various blues writers in different ways. For American revivalists that produced the Origins Jazz Library, singers who sailed closest to the gritty aesthetic of the Delta, such as Charley Patton and Son House, were held in the highest esteem.[19] By contrast, Samuel Charters had paid more attention to audiences by placing emphasis where African Americans had spent their money, and thus revealed a wide range of styles in *The Country Blues*, from Leroy Carr to Big Bill Broonzy. As previously acknowledged, Keil challenged the privileging of the oldest and most obscure rural singers as more emblematic of the blues genre, by highlighting the importance of newer forms of electrified urban blues to African American popular culture.[20] Consequently, what the blues *is* depends almost entirely on each writer's subjective interpretation. The identification of the tradition's characteristics, traits, and continuities would therefore conform to a highly personal reading of the blues.

This opens up the possibilities for invention, which is the second problem with defining a cultural performance as a tradition. As Hobsbawm argues, "'Traditions' which appear or claim to be old are often quite recent in origin and sometimes invented." The basis for Hobsbawm's idea of invention is in the sense of crisis that arises from rapid changes in the social, economic, and cultural climate"

> Inventing traditions, it is assumed here, is essentially a process of formalization and ritualization, characterized by reference to the past, if only by imposing repetition. . . . we should expect it to occur more frequently when a rapid transformation of society weakens or destroys the social patterns for which "old" traditions had been designed, producing new ones to which they were not applicable.[21]

Hobsbawm's suggestion that traditions are invented in times of significant social crisis would seem to concur with Oliver's description of "unprecedented" social and cultural change mentioned earlier. This is combined with the sense of disillusionment with the world of contemporary pop music, and the nostalgic sense of loss for an African American way of life prior to the postwar era that was so prominent in his writing. Fueling this nostalgia was a growing sense that the blues was close to its demise, primarily due to the white "discovery" of the music:

> Facile but skilful imitation by young white singers has further obscured the individuality of the blues and it seems likely that the future of the blues as "the song of the folk," as a "spontaneous utterance, filled with characteristics of rhythm, form and melody" is likely to be a brief one. No longer "without the influence of conscious art" the blues may become a self-conscious art music and as such survive in a new form, but its days as a folk music may be numbered.[22]

If the blues as "the song of the folk" had little chance of survival, then the presence of a tradition would help to solidify the music's place in the past. Importantly, however, the tradition would also act as a process of boundary formation, helping to establish the blues as Oliver represented it, as a definable category, and traceable to a definite set of characteristics that conform to the tradition that set it apart from other forms of music.

The examination of the process involved in the construction of a tradition has precedents in musical historiography, as in Scott DeVeaux's analysis of jazz scholarship:

> The "jazz tradition" reifies the music, insisting that there is an overarching category called jazz, encompassing musics of divergent styles and sensibilities. . . . Jazz is what it is because it is a culmination of all that has come before. Without the sense of depth that only a narrative can provide, jazz would be literally rootless, indistinguishable from a variety of other "popular" genres that combine virtuosity and craftsmanship with dance rhythms. Its claim to being not only distinct, but elevated above other indigenous forms ("America's classical music"), is in large part dependent on the idea of an evolutionary progression reaching back to the beginning of the century.[23]

The function of the tradition, therefore, is to establish roots that legitimate the blues' place apart from other music styles. As highlighted previously, Oliver sought to "relate [the blues] to the folk forms that preceded it." By tracing themes, imagery, expressions, and tunes back to the earliest available records, the blues could be linked to that place in the past which was echoed in the lyrics examined in *Blues Fell This Morning* and the memories of *Conversation*. It was in the latter that the Detroit-based pianist Boogie Woogie Red stated that the "blues have been goin' on for centuries and centuries, and the blues was written years and centuries ago."[24] Oliver reemploys this quote in *Screening* in order to create a sense of the history and continuity justifying his analysis of the music's genealogy, but it also highlights that more importance is placed on the music's past than on its "present." The categorical boundaries drawn up by a tradition allowed the author to expose how traditional elements were lacking in the more commercial and white interpretations of the blues in the sixties. DeVeaux describes scholars who prioritized New Orleans and "trad" jazz above the newer styles of bebop and free jazz as "neo-classicists." These, he argues, attempted to "regulate the music of the present through an idealized representation of the past."[25] Similarly, through the concentrated analysis of records from the interwar years, and the backward-looking focus of *Conversation with the Blues*, it is to the blues of the past that Oliver looks in his writing. In *Screening* he reiterates that the blues is "one of the last great bodies of folk-song," which simultaneously hints at a glorious past and a pessimistic present. Importantly, defining the tradition and the link to historical origins would pave the way for discovering and narrating the history of the music in *The Story of the Blues*, which became Oliver's next publication following *Screening*, and would complement the process of reifying the blues as a definable and identifiable category worthy of its own unique story.

Folk Origins and the Role of the Recording Industry

Inherent in this nostalgic notion of the past is the appeal of the mysterious nature of the music's genesis. This is exemplified by Oliver's questioning of the origin of the some of the traditional images and phrases employed by blues singers:

> And who was the source of:
> I'm goin' to the river, take my rocker chair, (2)
> If the blues overtake me, gonna rock away from here,
> which has had a life of more than fifty years? [26]

The murky origins of these expressions and common blues phrases evoke the image of the anonymous songwriters of traditional folk songs, indicating that the blues has developed from deep within a now practically impenetrable and vanishing African American oral culture. In the chapter relating to the *Forty-Fours*, he states, "These words come from no special blues, but from a hundred, or a thousand."[27] The mysterious origins of the expressions therefore appear to go far back enough to establish the roots of the blues deep within the African American past, with the blues phrases emanating from the collective experience of the African American community. Making these verses traditional is their reuse and adaptation by subsequent generations of singers. Oliver refers to stock expressions that transfer from one theme to another as "maverick lines," which singers adapt to different themes based on individual preference and style.[28] The use, development, or modification of these lines by newer generations establishes what Oliver interprets as the blues tradition:

> It is the strength of the blues that as an art it regenerates itself; the singers continually draw from traditional resources to create anew and they invest in old and familiar themes fragments of their own experience which impart to them a refreshing individuality.[29]

Fundamental to Oliver's idea of the blues tradition and its origins is the early twentieth-century conception of folk music, which in *Screening* becomes much more explicitly pronounced through the adoption of the early twentieth-century definition of the American musicologist Henry Edward Krehbiel:

> Folksong is not popular song in the sense in which the word is most frequently used, but the song of the folk; not only the song of the people but, in a strict sense, the song created by the people. It is a body of poetry and music which has come into existence without the influence of conscious art, or a spontaneous utterance, filled with characteristics of rhythm, form and melody which are traceable, more or less clearly, to racial (or national) temperament, modes of life, climatic and political conditions, geographical environment and language. Some of these elements, the spiritual, are elusive, but others can be determined and classified.[30]

As was demonstrated in previous chapters, Oliver was a close adherent of the folkloric paradigm in the binary interpretation of folk and popular music. In *Screening*, Krehbiel's definition of folk song represents the ideal to which the blues must conform, and to regard the blues as such meant that "the influence of conscious art" was absent, but also that it was, as Oliver had indicated in his view of the white appropriation of the blues, a folk song on the verge of extinction. Interestingly, Oliver also adheres to Krehbiel's notion of identifiable "racial temperament," a problematic idea that shapes a racialized representation of the blues. However, Oliver's polarized view of the blues tradition existing as a distinct category from any forms of commercialism and "conscious art" deserves attention.

In his typical considered manner, Oliver was appreciative of the blues' exceptional circumstances as a folk genre, demonstrating that he was perhaps more open to the contradictions inherent in the folk label than other purists. He describes how the music occupied a foot within the marginalized circumstances of the African American experience of Jim Crow, and the other within the race records industry of the interwar years. Interestingly, however, the music is never seen as dependent on the recording industry. Instead, it was a pure "accident of history" that saw the blues' "simultaneous evolution with the perfection of recording techniques." This is despite the fact that by the mid-twenties between five and six million race records were sold per year. And yet for Oliver the blues remained a folk music. So rather than simply considering technological progress as a poisonous influence, he acknowledged how mass media, radio, recordings and jukeboxes played an important, but not an essential, role in the development of the tradition:

> If, as a result of recording, there was an inevitable "influence of conscious art," there was also within the various types of Race music, a cross-fertilization of traditions and ideas, of lyrics and music which have been continually enriched by the creative inventiveness of individual singers and musicians.[31]

Here the negative influence of mass media on the blues as a folk idiom is balanced with the positive effects on the music. In the chapter that considers sexual themes in blues songs, Oliver argues that the censorship that recording may have imposed (either by record companies or the singers themselves) "may have enriched Race music rather than impoverished it," inspiring singers to come up with new ways of communicating familiar themes.[32] It is not until the advent of postwar era and the sixties in particular that Oliver forecasts the negative effects of modern technology,

> It must be conceded that in the long run blues suffered from the levelling-out of character of which recording and radio were the primary causes. Whatever the outcome of the present confused state of the music, it is clear that mass media and the commercial interests that have inspired their exploitation of the blues, will have played a large part in determining its fate.[33]

The impact of recording on the music is therefore interpreted as having had different effects in different time periods. Given the condescension with which white blues musicians are often described, the main reasoning behind this interpretation lies in the fact that in the sixties, mass media diffusion permitted white listeners to appropriate and ultimately corrupt the music. The major consequence was that Oliver regarded the white discovery of the blues as the cause of the "diminution in importance of the lyrics."[34] In other words, the texts of blues songs no longer performed the function for African American society that *Blues Fell This Morning* had described. In the 1920s, by contrast, the race records industry, which was primarily produced by and for African Americans, worked to keep the music within the black community despite its standardizing effects, even though this industry was very much run by corporate whites who were not folklorists. Nonetheless, the music was able to retain its functionality as a folk idiom within African American society, fostering racial solidarity and acting as a "safety valve," a method by which to sidestep real-life issues and anxiety built up from the experience of marginalization in American society.

There are numerous examples of this in *Screening*. For instance, Oliver argues that while the "policy blues" (on the subject of illegal gambling, or "playing the numbers") may have baffled white listeners in the thirties and forties, "their very obscurantism had its value for the Negro who bought the blues records. They helped to give him the security of being part of a tightly knit community and afforded him a sense of racial solidarity."[35] Here, the popularity of the blues on the subject of playing the numbers is equated directly with the sense of community and the fostering of group cohesion, with little possibility for the fact that the songs make light of a serious problem in black society, or that listeners simply enjoyed the tunes. Another important (and somewhat ironic) consideration is that there is no acknowledgment that record companies may have been more in tune with African American culture and society than blues scholars were willing to acknowledge.

The underlying assumption is that blues artists were able to use the race records industry to their advantage, and for the main purpose of preserving their own culture. Indeed, Oliver loosens his tight grip on the Adorno-esque vision of the music industry to consider the process by which black audiences actually *consumed* blues records: "Though listening to records is not as active a form of participation as singing songs with a group, it does demand participation of a kind." The acts of selecting, purchasing, and listening to records are seen as an extension of the processes that sustain the folk tradition, rather than a threat to the traditional processes of active participation.[36] What appears here is an uneven perception of the effects of consumerism in interwar African American culture and in postwar transatlantic culture. The record industry and purchase of records was a means of maintaining and strengthening the status quo for American Americans, who could hear themselves and their issues on record, and furthermore, musicians could resist the temptations of the recording industry and the lure of financial reward. As Oliver highlights, "Blues is not the music of recorded singers only. It originated without the benefit of the phonograph and would probably have continued to evolve without it."[37] In the postwar era, by contrast, commercialism had taken over, and the culture that the race industry had helped to maintain had vanished. The representation of blues musicians indifferent to material wealth possible through a successful recording career would become particularly complicated in *The Story of the Blues*. The ideal of musicians unconcerned with commercial success would conflict with the numerous photographs of musicians in sharp suits that are much more suggestive of mainstream aspirations of respectability than the adherence to an "unconscious art."

Tracing Continuities and Restricting the African American World

The manner in which Oliver traces the continuities of traditional traits in *Screening* is demonstrative of the imagined vision of blues musicians as keepers of the tradition. When indicating where singers have borrowed from others, the author relies on the ideal that this was a means of staying within the boundaries of the tradition, rather than an attempting to replicate a previous commercial success and obtain recognition through a popular motif. This can be seen in Oliver's analysis of the use of the automobile image in songs:

> It is superfluous to examine in detail the innumerable blues and blues songs which extend the automobile theme further, from the many variants of Sonny Boy Williamson's *My Little Machine,* which has become a traditional blues, to the versions of *Auto-Mechanic blues*; their existence, their frequency of use, are evidence of the appeal of a powerful sexual symbol in the blues.[38]

The repetition of the automobile theme is taken as a signifier of its presence within the tradition, albeit only by virtue of being a popular "sexual symbol." It does not allow for the song's commercial success to influence the recording of subsequent numbers on similar themes. Interestingly, the use of automobiles as sexual metaphors in the blues provides a vivid example of the manner in which Oliver imposes restricted aspirational levels on African Americans. Initially, Oliver suggests that the car is more attractive as a metaphor than other objects such as the train, as it lent itself more easily to use by the individual. Also, as "the images are most affective when they come within the immediate world of the Negro," it is assumed that objects outside the immediate reach and the manual operation of ordinary African Americans would fail to strike a chord among listeners. For this reason, Oliver argues that the automobile became a powerful and recurrent theme due to the mass availability of secondhand Model-T Fords:

> When Ford changed his policy in 1927 and commenced making more luxurious models, second-hand Model-Ts came on the market at sensationally low prices and the vehicle was widely popular among Negroes. Its near-indestructability, its dependability, its lack of glamour, reflected virtues that the Negro liked to see in himself.[39]

What is notable here is that, rather than attempting to assert some form of citizenship, economic self-assertion, or make his life easier by owning a vehicle, the African American is assumed to revel in his "lack of glamour" by equating himself with a used car that is now only available because wealthier whites can buy more luxurious ones.

The automobile theme demonstrates the manner in which the investigation into the blues tradition permits Oliver to make assumptions about the condition of the African American psyche in the early twentieth century. This is not to say that there was not a historical case for Oliver's suggestions, but that the author tended to generalize on specific instances to produce an image of the African American world that conformed to the idealized vision of the blues singer. A case in point is the chapter that examines blues singers' treatment of heroic and successful figures in the thirties, such as the athlete Jesse Owens and the boxer Joe Louis. Oliver argued that while this decade witnessed events such as the brutal invasion of Ethiopia by Mussolini's armed forces in 1935, the blues singer's realm of experience was too marginal to consider such issues for his songs. This is in contrast to the general African American population and press, who shared a "strong feeling of association with Emperor Haile Selassie and his tribesmen" and were "overjoyed" by the achievements of African American athletes such as Jesse Owens and Marc Robinson at the 1936 Berlin Olympic Games. The exception to these shared sentiments was the blues singer: "The events [of the Ethiopian invasion] were too far away for a clear conception of them to be in the experience of blues singers." Not even the triumphs of Jesse Owens could inspire them to song: "Perhaps these events were also too remote for most Negroes for whom the events on American soil before the eyes of watching white Americans would have been more immediate."[40] Oliver equated the absence of recorded blues songs on these topics as directly indicative of the blues singer's lack of interest in them, and as a result of the interpretation that song themes reflect reality, he also assumed that blues singers were unconcerned with that which lay beyond their daily experiences. This analysis serves to promote the idea of the bluesman espoused by the Beat-inspired "male flight from commitment," as suggested by Hamilton.[41] Oliver promotes the myth of the blues singer as a figure who is marginalized by both American society and his own community for leading an immoral lifestyle, but importantly also withdraws himself from issues that have wider influences in society. For this reason, the separation of the blues from the social and political condition of African Americans in the postwar era is cemented in *Screening*: "Of the Civil Rights movement, of Freedom marches, of anti-segregation demonstrations and lunch-counter sit-ins, Black Muslims and Black Power, the blues says nothing."[42] As previously acknowledged, while blues songs on these subjects were lacking, this is not to say that blues singers withdrew themselves from such debates. Such a statement is demonstrative of Oliver's reification of the blues as not only a form of music, but also an aesthetic philosophy that sought to withdraw from the mainstream of popular culture.

What is evident here is that while Oliver attempted to describe a form of collective black consciousness, he also imposed limits and restrictions:

> For all his extraordinary successes Jesse Owens was a member of a team, a team which was an American one which fought for America first. This was as it should be, but the state of mind of the Negro in America at the time was not one to moralize on such issues; the pains of the Depression, the injustices of job discrimination were too close.[43]

There is an inherent disconnection between the successes of black athletes at the 1936 Olympics with the daily struggles of ordinary African Americans, exemplified by the blues singer's refusal to comment on them. Therefore, while adherents of the blues tradition are unconcerned with a "conscious art," they are at same time largely unmoved by the significance of racial discourses during the thirties. Importantly, Oliver seems to have been keen to emphasize that the African American "state of mind" was represented by the "dispirited blues" at a time when "the Depression hit the Negro hardest and civil rights was a meaningless phrase."[44] The lack of a significant number of recorded blues on issues of segregation, politics, or Jim Crow is associated with a sense of apathy toward social change in the consciousness of ordinary African Americans in the pre–World War II years. This view sustains an accommodative vision of the blues. While the music may have "bolstered a sense of racial solidarity . . . [the blues] also diverted repressed hostilities that may otherwise have found more immediate expression."[45]

The lack of protest in the blues or association with the postwar civil rights movement is convenient for the folkloric stance on the blues, as it associated the music with earlier African American forms of cultural expression, such as the spirituals and folktales such as Br'er Rabbit and Uncle Remus. Oliver equates the sense of protest in the creative storytelling found in the latter by Kardiner and Ovesey's *The Mark of Oppression* (1962) to the emotional release that the blues permitted.[46] A poetic description of sacred and secular black culture coexisting on West Lake Street in Chicago highlights the similarities seen in the role of both musical forms:

> At night the paint-starved woodwork, the bug-infested cracks, the thick layers of smuts and dust, are less evident; the lights from the joints glow and the neon crucifixes shine pink in the shop-front windows of the store-front churches. A door swings open and one may hear the shouts of laughter of a jostling crowd packed solid to the far end of the smoke-filled interior, where a dimly perceived blues band thunders with amplifiers turned up to maximum volume and the lead singer roars hoarsely into a hand-held microphone, mere inches from his closest listeners. Another door may open on a scene no less intense, as a gospel quartet, with frenzied gestures and heads thrown back, stir a small but exultant congregation into irrational ecstasy. Sacred and secular are found side by side on West Lake and however different the avowed purposes of the church and the blues joint, to the observer the heady mixture of music and emotion to be found in each has much in common. Exhilarating and elemental, the music transports the gathering from the meanness and poverty beyond the doors.[47]

This passionate vision of a street scene in Chicago, ambiguous in terms of when and how it was observed (whether eyewitnessed or invented), offers a concentrated view of the interpretation and representation of African American culture. A distance is created between the observer (a white, blues enthusiast perhaps) and the blues joint and church interiors, adding to the sense that the blues belongs to a distant other world, one of that white observers can only occasionally glimpse through an open door. In addition, both gospel and blues are seen to perform similar functions in black society, allowing participants of this culture to transcend the physical reality of "paint-starved woodwork and bug-infested cracks," rather than directing protest against the causes of those conditions.

Instead, Oliver argued that direct protest was most often substituted by a release of sexual repression through music. Even in the largely female-attended churches, the ecstatic and feverish reactions of the congregation are seen as "sublimated expressions of sexual ecstasy" created from the "inhibitions that the strictures of the church demand in their private lives."[48] Similarly the blues "provide the same catalyst; they sublimate hostility and canalize aggressive instincts against a mythical common enemy, the 'cheater.'"[49] The creative manner in which sex and relationships are treated in the blues allow "the realities of racial oppression [to be] side-stepped."[50] For Oliver, the channeling of bottled-up energy through sexual metaphor points to one of the psychological consequences of segregation. An example is provided in the analysis of sexual violence expressed in Uncle Skipper's "Cutting My ABCs" and Lightnin' Hopkins's "The Dirty Dozens":

> *Cutting My ABCs* casts a thin veil of humour over a brutal theme; *The Dozens* obscures in the recordings a fathomless well of bitterness, humiliation and anger, which the uncensored version by Lightnin' Hopkins openly reveals. The anal-eroticism of the song may be exemplary of arrested adolescence, but it is the stunted development of a racial minority which has not been permitted its full maturity.[51]

Whatever one may make of the psychological significance of these more sexually violent blues lyrics, Oliver's interpretation is used here to demonstrate the manner in which his scholarship represented African Americans through the language of the blues. It could be argued that the emphasis on the release of sexual tension in church and through blues themes relies somewhat on the stereotype of promiscuity among African Americans. Indeed, Spencer argued that it was the white blues scholars' obsession with the sexual content of the music, which "teased [their] Victorian sensibilities," that helped to lay the foundations for the "Oliverian tradition" of blues scholarship.[52] More significant, however, is that the stigma of the racial minority dominates every aspect of the analysis of black consciousness and culture, forcing African Americans to be confined in psychological, physical, and expressive terms, within the prison of segregation. Blues songs about cars are not indicative of the tendency toward modernization and economic self-determination, but instead are mainly a metaphor mechanics of sexual interaction; sexual imagery, metaphor, and violence are repressed feelings of frustration and in no way representative of attempts at creating controversy or generating commercial interest. Importantly, however, in linking blues to earlier forms of cultural expression that emanated from slavery, Oliver was solidifying the music's position as the cultural expression of a people sharing a particular experience in the past. It is in this sense that the blues was more emblematic of historical folk expression and thus more distant from the more contemporary African American political activism and militancy of the sixties.

Ordinary African Americans and blues singers are represented in a fairly confined cultural and political context, and this is part of the "screening" process that filters the blues from other genres. The idea that the music functioned to foster sentiments of belonging to a tightly knit community, a people that shared a disadvantaged position in American society and therefore shared cultural expression, reinforced the "folk" function of the blues. However, what is significant in Oliver's writing is that while the emphasis is on the seeming accommodationism toward racial segregation, through the lyrics of the blues the singer is to some extent seen as having made the choice to remain marginal:

> He accepts his position in the social sub-stratum on, as George Schyler termed it, "the mud-sill of America" in numerous self-abasing metaphors and then rejoices in them: "I'm ragged but right"; "it's dirty but it's good," "I'm blue, black and evil and I did not make myself."[53]

This quote is similar to the interpretation of the automobile image, where the blues singer is depicted as embracing his lower social status, and it is this sense of pride in poverty that seems most admirable to Oliver. In this sense, he is akin to Cecil Sharp who, as Filene argues, made the poverty of Appalachian songsters appear as an "ascetic philosophy."[54] The subtle manner in which poverty is aestheticized in blues scholarship demonstrates the imposition of antimodern ideals on blues singers, despite the fact that in reality blues singers it was often the opposite. The singer and guitarist Brownie McGhee was astounded at the success of Josh White in the white folk circles of New York in the early forties: "when I saw how much money he was making, I said, 'Hey, show me how to go white, too.'"[55] Instead, Oliver borrowed from Kardiner and Ovesey's study on spirituals and folk-tales that argued that it was African Americans at the bottom of the social order that carried "the greatest amount of self-preservation anxiety."[56] Therefore, while there may not have been a sense of "conscious art" for the blues singer, there nonetheless existed a sense of conscious cultural agency to preserve the tradition.

The Language of *Screening the Blues*

Oliver conveys this sense of racial solidarity by employing a highly personalized language to describe the sentiments and choices of blues singers and audiences:

> As a member of a victimized minority rather than as an individual victim of prejudice, [the blues singer] shares with other Negroes the common frustration that a repressive social system has provoked. Through the blues songs and traditional songs, through the ebullient reiterations of time-worn themes, he bolsters his ego with sexual fantasies and shares them with the listeners for whom he sings and whose repressions are his own. Through them he asserts his masculinity, and

> achieves the power that the system denies him; through them he, or she, brags of his prowess, asserts his superiority and challenges all comers. Listening to the records and purchasing more, the Negro joins the singer in a shared experience, feels with him a sense of racial solidarity.[57]

The personalized language that Oliver uses here in "his masculinity," "his own," "he bolsters his ego," and "he joins and feels" creates an intimate connection between singer and audience, but also between writer and subject matter. The writing goes beyond mere description and evokes a sense of admiration. By personalizing his narrative, Oliver gives a human face to the connections and relationships that maintain the folk community. However, another example of Oliver's personalized language demonstrates how susceptible the categorization of folk music is to contradiction. Here, the blues singer is depicted as predominantly individualistic and egocentric, a trait momentarily abandoned when taking on the role of balladeer in telling the story of the boxer Joe Louis, "forgetting for a moment his preoccupation with himself, the blues singer spoke briefly for his racial group as a whole, giving voice to its exultation over the hero's winning bouts."[58] This contrasts the previous example in which Oliver represented the blues singer as singing for his listeners with whom he also shares repressions. The individualism of the blues singer is difficult to reconcile with the idea of the African Americans' sense of shared cultural self-preservation. What this demonstrates is that Oliver's representation of the blues as folk music serves to highlight the unstable nature of the folk concept in blues scholarship overall. That the blues—despite being recorded commercially en masse—is persistently represented as being a product of an authentic folk African American culture and functions as a cohesive agent in maintaining that culture says much more about the attitudes of the analyst than of the culture itself.

The manner in which the author describes musicians is typical of the folkloric paradigm that dominates the concept of the blues tradition. For instance, Oliver presented his view on the recurrent debate between the natural folk as opposed to the schooled Western approach to music:

> It is one of the strengths, but also one of the weaknesses of the blues that it offers to the singer or the instrumentalist of very little accomplishment a means whereby he can give some expression to his ideas. Many blues guitarists never learn to form a chord—John Lee Hooker is one who has achieved wide fame in the blues without even this degree of musical knowledge. Often it is better so; unorthodox fingering

> and the trial-and-error process of finding his way along the fingerboard of his guitar has given to many a blues musician a sound quality which is his own.[59]

The improvised and instinctive is repeatedly placed above the dedication to technical skill and artistry. Again, the view that the blues is characterized by more intuitive didacticism and that "often it is better so," supports the vision of the blues as an unconscious art. It also separates the music of musicians such as Hooker from the young white generation of guitarists claiming to be playing the blues such Eric Clapton (i.e., "Clapton is God'), who by the late sixties were very much, according to Oliver, "applauded and lauded."[60] To be sincere, the instrument needed to be played instinctively and roughly, such as Ernest Johnson's piano in the recording of *Louisiana Bound*:

> The bass figures growl and climb, the treble notes are hammered throughout the record with alternating runs. It is not *The Forty-Fours*, but listening to the accompaniment to *Louisiana Bound* is like hearing a pianist who is exploring the piano, feeling his way to the creation of the theme. It is an impressive performance, less polished and formalized than recordings of *The Forty-Fours* and *Vicksburg Blues*, more wild and in many ways more exciting.[61]

The way Oliver perceives Johnson to "feel" his way through the recording prioritizes improvisation, and thus the instinctive aspects of performance. In other words, the pianist is playing naturally and therefore, honestly. The passage gives as much away about the author as it does of the singer. Stating that he found it "wild" and "exciting" suggests a sense of primitivism and affinity for the exotic.

This perception of the sincere approach to musicianship finds its counterpart in the analysis and judgment of singing, such as in the example of Hi-Henry Brown's "Preacher Blues": "Though the words were humorous there was little humour in Hi-Henry Brown's delivery which was deep, rough-textured and with an intonation that suggests there was some truth in the narration of the misdemeanours of the preacher."[62] This description associates the less polished qualities of Brown's voice with the singer's sincerity, invoking the repeatedly used assertion that was presented in the oral accounts of *Conversation*—the blues conveys the truth. There needed to be conviction in the unpolished delivery of the lyrics, as if to communicate innate truths that were direct and unadulterated, such as Jesse James's "Sweet Patuni": "With his guttural voice, his stomping piano breaking sometimes into boogie woogie bass figures and the rough humour of his verses with their terminal puns, Jesse James pours out a stiff draught of unadulterated, undiluted barrelhouse entertainment."[63] Oliver also repeatedly uses the terms "unbowdlerized" and "bowdlerization" to discern the level of censorship in sexual themes, and therefore make judgments on the extent to which those themes are indicative of the tradition.[64] Bessie Smith's "Empty Bed Blues," for instance, "is honest in that it does not attempt to hide its theme, the metaphors following direct statements."[65] Honesty, as the directness and frankness that early jazz critics championed in African American music, was a fundamental criterion for Oliver's tradition. What is significant, however, is that these examples demonstrate the unstable method of description that is used to define authentic blues. It is almost entirely dependent on the author's perception of sincerity as it is conveyed in the performance. Once again, one is reminded of the vitally important role of the sonic characteristics of the blues in determining written interpretations of the music.

The weakness in this method of judgment is made more evident in Oliver's criticism of singers who fail to match the standards required of the tradition. For instance, the pianist Roosevelt Sykes (singing under the pseudonym of Willie Kelly) lacked "the organic unity of the traditional theme" of *The Forty-Fours* in his recording of "Kelly's 44 Blues," and the result is a "a surprisingly poorly resolved musical composition."[66] Memphis Slim's attempt to record this traditional theme was described as "mechanical and lifeless," despite including many of the musical characteristics that shaped the tune.[67] In another example, Oliver describes Virginia Liston's delivery of "Rolls-Royce Papa" as "sung with an insipid voice and with little conviction.[68] Perhaps the most significant of these instances relates to the career of Bessie Smith:

> Rudi Blesh observes . . . that "in her later years Bessie Smith was the victim of mismanagement and, faced with diminishing returns, succumbed at times to the temptations of commercialization and pornography and even belittled herself and her race singing *coon* songs." The recordings careers of [Sara Martin and Bessie Smith] and other classic blues singers were liberally sprinkled with coon songs. Imitative of Negro song in a genre which owed more to "Nigger Minstrels" than to a part of the tradition, they were prominent not only at the conclusion but also at the commencement of their careers. The increased proportion of suggestive and pornographic material in their late sessions does lend support to the view that the record companies, confronted with the Depression, attempted to revive flagging sales with records of this character.[69]

What seems significant here is that Oliver not only shared Blesh's interpretation, he emphasizes the view to the extent that Smith "belittled herself and her race." The categorization of music that fails to respect the anticommercial nature of the tradition is now made into a racial discourse. In other words, to seek commercial reward through the music is to betray the race, and therefore the tradition. The African American blues tradition is thus seen as a form based on antimodern stance, centered on human relationships of direct and frank expression, the antithesis of the commercial and materialistic principles of Western Anglo-Saxon culture.

In *Screening* Oliver clearly shared the aversion for the influence of white mainstream popular culture and its postwar incursion into the black vernacular music that had been expressed by LeRoi Jones in *Blues People* (1963). Jones had suggested that the effects of the Depression on the recording industry forced some musicians to try and satisfy white audiences, and when that happened, "many times no more real blues ever left their lips." He went on to argue that in the postwar years continuity was traceable from the prewar blues into the newly labeled rhythm and blues category, which "though largely commercialized, was still exclusive enough to escape the bloodless commercialism of the white entertainment world." Jones termed this "the blues continuum," which was largely orientated toward fostering a sense of pride in African American cultural heritage, which would serve as a consolidator for "black pride" at a time of increased militancy and revolt at social injustice.[70] Keil also saw Jones's "continuum" in the urban blues sounds of the sixties. However, this was not a tradition in the sense that a specific and historically identifiable practice was held as the standard for contemporary interpretations. Instead, Keil's concept of black expression through the "unspeakable essence" of expressing "soul" allowed music to draw on older forms while reforming them for deployment in the present day.[71] Thus, while there was continuity, there was also change and modernization in the new age.

By contrast, Oliver's analysis of the blues tradition, while establishing continuities in thematic and melodic characteristics, functioned as a means of demarcating and creating categorical boundaries and imposing limits where Jones and Keil saw evolution. It distinguished authentic African American blues from the imitations and interpretations of the sixties and the commercial blues that were becoming ever more prominent. In the process of "screening" the blues, of filtering the authentic from the inauthentic, Oliver placed a gulf between prewar African American cultural expression and the postwar era. In privileging of the past over the present, Oliver fell into the trap of romanticizing a vibrant, human, and honest folk culture, but also into making sometimes fairly limiting assumptions about African American character and consciousness in order to defend his blues culture from the white invasions of the sixties. The tradition therefore functioned as a means of creating links to the past, and paving the way for Oliver's next book, which narrated the story of the music. The focus on the upkeep of the tradition, and on the dominance of the past over the scholarship of the blues in the late sixties, highlights Oliver's aesthetic allegiance to the standards set by the blues of the interwar years. In addition, the romantic tone of Oliver's personalized passages suggest that the blues used to be at the heart of a racial defiance of social injustice through cultural practice rather than political protest, creating the narrative of human tenacity and survival against all odds, of beauty being born of tragedy, a motif that would become central in *The Story of the Blues*. It also further removes the world of the blues from the contemporary social and cultural context of African Americans. While Jones's "blues continuum" represented a part of the formation of a strong African American cultural and historical identity being constructed around the time of the Black Arts movement and Black Power in the late sixties, as the next chapter will explore in *The Story of the Blues*, the allegiance to the glory of days gone by would inevitably result in the end of the tradition and the "death" of the blues.

5 • The Blues Narrative

A Story of Triumph over Tragedy

The Story of the Blues was Oliver's last major book of the sixties and was probably the most influential in future scholarship, as it represented one of the first formal attempts to narrate a history of the genre. At the time of the book's publication, British jazz writer Max Harrison argued that *The Story of the Blues* was "the only complete history of the music we have."[1] Although by this time there had been a number of other books on the subject, none had dedicated their efforts to trace the emergence and development of the music in any great length. For this reason the editor of *Blues Unlimited* described Oliver's monograph as "the most lavish book on the subject to date."[2] The closest to a blues history before then was undoubtedly LeRoi Jones's (Amiri Baraka) *Blues People* (1963). However, this was a history that sought to emphasize the value and vitality of black music and simultaneously, as William Harris highlighted, to critique white America and the black middle classes that had shunned folk and vernacular art forms.[3] Consequently, Jones was not as determined to maintain the categorical definitions between blues and other genres, as he was to distinguish "free" African Americans from slaves and white Americans. Many blues writers still maintain today that *The Story of the Blues* "represents the best synthesis/reportage of the 'real thing'" and that it "was the best popular introduction to the music in its day." The first major attempt at what I term the "blues narrative," *The Story of the Blues* provides a comprehensive survey of the differing range of musicians, styles, and geographical areas involved in the music's development, as well as acknowledging the various social and economic circumstances that conditioned the emergence of the blues across the African American landscape. Oliver's sensitivity to these diverse elements has been appreciated by blues musicologists such as Evans, who argues that the author "has learned that the history of blues is complex and cannot be neatly packaged or reviewed as a unilinear development and that the blues has many meanings for many different people."[4]

As has been the focus of this book, in his writing during the fifties and sixties Oliver had elected to demonstrate that the blues was a distinct musical category worthy of attention in its own right. His exploration of meaning in lyrics saw the blues as a reflection of the African American experience of the lower classes, and the identification of the blues as a tradition by "screening" the real from the inauthentic functioned to separate it from other forms of music, as well as root its origins within a distant folk culture from the past. In this context, a historical narrative would complete the process of isolating the blues as a distinct and identifiable form with its own particular story. *The Story of the Blues* is interesting precisely for this reason, as representing the blues through the historical narrative suggests that the music exists not only as a stable and definable idiom, but also as a music that had a unique history that legitimized its consideration apart from other forms. Oliver's history examines the origins and development of the blues in sixteen chapters that span a century. It begins in the music's obscure origins from the ashes of slavery and Emancipation, through to its development from folk idiom to popular culture at the turn of the twentieth century, the start of the recording industry in the twenties, the Depression, to its decline as a folk music in the postwar blues revival of the sixties. While accounting for the genesis of the music from the often tragic circumstances of the African American experience, the author was indirectly proclaiming the "death" of the blues at a time when the blues revival itself was in the process of petering out. Incidentally, Oliver's emphasis on the demise of the blues as a genre coincides with Wald's assertion that by the end of the sixties, the revivalist and romanticized interpretations of the blues had become fully established.[5]

Despite Oliver's sensitive appreciation of the complexity of blues history, however, an examination of *The Story of the Blues* reveals the manner in which his blues narrative contributed to the production of a constructed representation of the music at the end of the 1960s. When Oliver described the book as "a brief outline," he modestly underestimated both its impact on future blues historians and its power to reify an idea of the blues.[6] The blues narrative would be frequently rewritten in years to come by notable writers such as Giles Oakley, Robert Palmer, William Barlow, Francis Davis, and former Rolling Stones bassist Bill Wyman.[7] Notable historians such as Lawrence Levine and Leon Litwack have also given space to the blues in their African American histories. The romantic slant of these narratives that represents the blues as the voice of an African American consciousness, opposed to the soulless commercialism of the capitalist world has been the focus of criticism in recent revisionist scholarship. Perhaps Palmer's now iconic quotation (also used by Litwack) has come to symbolize the lure of blues history: "How much history can be transmitted by pressure on a guitar string? The thought of generations, the history of every human being who's ever felt the blues come down like showers of rain."[8] This pushes Hamilton to comment that "it is curious . . . to find an historian as sophisticated as Litwack framing the blues in this populist way as the voice of the folk, the pure and unmediated cry of the masses."[9] Revisionists have concentrated on the manner in which romanticism has obscured more factual histories, in the sense of actual events that occurred in the past. While this criticism allows for the use of more empirical data in discerning fact from fiction, it does not fully take account of the manner in which the actual process of *writing* history can contribute to misrepresentations and reifications of an imagined blues.

This chapter will examine the construction of the historical narrative in *The Story of the Blues*, as it is the process of writing a history—a "blues narrative"—characterized by the inevitable clash of historical evidence and literary artifice that destabilizes the tangible appearance of that same story. Importantly, what is omitted from the story is also telling of the manner in which the history is shaped by the author. The production of the narrative undermined the notion that a coherent, linear, and identifiable history of the blues could be known and accurately told. This will entail a discussion of the very nature of historical writing and the ambiguities that characterize the writer's negotiation of historical information in the contemporary social, cultural, and political context of the late sixties. In addition, the chapter will explore Oliver's use of a range of different images, from his own photographs, the portraits of singers, and advertisements from the Race Records era to the photographs from the Farm Security Administration of the New Deal, which help to establish the iconography of the blues while complicating the representation of blues history.

Writing History and the "Blues Narrative"

Oliver's work in *Blues Fell This Morning*, *Conversation with the Blues*, and the British jazz press of the 1950s had always been characterized by an emphasis on the past, while not being formally in the discipline of history. In collecting records from the interwar years, examining lyrics within the context of interwar African American life, collecting singers' memories of those experiences, and tracing a blues tradition, the representation of the music was dictated by an idealized version of the past with which the contemporary postwar world was repeatedly confronted. *The Story of the Blues* represents a more formal attempt to narrate a history, and as such requires analysis precisely as a historical work. However, it is not the purpose here to debate the accuracy of historical events presented in the book, as these discussions have taken place elsewhere.[10] Also, this would contradict the historical deconstructionist approach that has characterized the preceding chapters. Instead, it is the actual process of writing a blues history that is of interest, as the putting together of information gathered from records, oral history, and literature on the subject of the blues and African American culture provides a window into the process of constructing the blues.

This analysis takes as its basis a deconstructionist historical analysis as explained by Alun Munslow:

> History is first and foremost a literary enterprise. Its cognitive function derives from the complex interpretive structure of narrative defined as a set of proposals or suggestions about past events. . . .
>
> Constituting a narrative explanation requires the ordering, selection and omission of events and occurrences, and by our study of how the historian does it this ought to be possible to reveal something of his/her rationale or motive for producing this or that choice of narrative.[11]

It would be unproductive to take the linguistic discourses of deconstructionist thought to their ends. What becomes the focus of deconstructive analysis in this case is what the "literary enterprise" of the historian highlights. The emphasis is placed on the construction of the historical text, the way history is *done*, rather than the past on which the text is based. Historians are therefore regarded as much as "authors" as they are historians, acknowledging the literary activity that characterizes the process of selecting and piecing together historical elements into a written narrative. Much of the criticism on the literary practice of historical work emanates from the writings of Hayden White, who argues that all historical evidence is "value neutral" and lacking in meaning prior to its organization into a narrative form. An order is achieved through a process of "emplotment" in which the author's "literary imagination" adds "fictive elements" in order to adequately organize and give meaning to historical events.[12] For White, it is in this capacity to mold historical information that the authorial characteristics of the process emerge. A *story* is created from the information of historical events that have a beginning, a purpose, and an ending, and its protagonists must be able to attract some form of response from the reader through their struggles. All of these characteristics can be traced in Oliver's aptly titled book. Importantly, this is not to say that Oliver's historical narrative was fictional, that it was deliberately misleading, or overtly romanticized, as this was far from the case. It is to say, rather, that due to the problematic nature of adequately representing and knowing the past, the process of piecing together a historical narrative carries inevitable elements of literary craft that shape the ultimate representation of the subject at hand. These elements, however, have contributed a great deal to the present-day images and interpretations of the blues.

In the emphasis on the disconnection between signifier and signified, deconstructionist theories have tended to point to the existence of a world without meaning, and claimed that all history is therefore "invented." However, as suggested above, the implication of applying these theoretical principles would make any form of analysis redundant, and, as Georg Iggers reminds us, the production of the historical text "does not occur in a vacuum."[13] What must be remembered, therefore, is that history can never be fully divorced from the reasons motivating people to write:

> We are all imprisoned in the present as we narrate the past. This is the historian's perennial double-bind. . . .
>
> . . . the historical imagination itself exists intertextually within our own social and political environment, the past is never discovered in a world set aside from everyday life. History is designed and composed in the here and now.[14]

In other words, the construction of the narrative must also take account of the contemporary ideological, political, and social contexts that shape and motivate the production of the historical text. The context of the blues revival and the white discovery of African American music played a considerable role in Oliver's framing of the past. Herein lies the "intertextuality" of blues scholarship, with scholars examining records and memories of the past on the one hand, but on the other carrying out the research in their own contemporary social, political, and cultural context. While actual blues songs had lost their popular appeal in the charts, the number of blues enthusiasts had grown toward the end of the sixties. These were ever more hungry for information, records, and history, a hunger that can be detected in the growth in the number of articles that looked at the historical and sociological background of the music, such as Lawrence Skoog's series in *Blues Unlimited* entitled "The Negro in America: His Life and Times."[15] Following the publication of *The Story of the Blues*, Oliver kicked off the second National Blues Convention in September 1969. A reviewer argued that Oliver "really put the stamp of authority on proceedings with a relaxed, but splendidly succinct lecture."[16] While the fact that blues was no directly longer topping the music charts at this point supports Wald's view that the histories blues scholars were writing reflected "an elite, extremely minority taste," it was nonetheless within this context of a minority of connoisseurs that Oliver's history of the blues was shaped.[17]

The analysis of the literary construction of a blues history has many parallels with Scott DeVeaux's criticism of jazz historiography and official jazz histories:

> Jazz is presented as a coherent whole, and its history as a skilfully contrived and easily comprehended narrative. After an obligatory nod to African origins and ragtime antecedents, the music is shown to move through a succession of styles and periods, each with a conveniently distinctive label and time period: New Orleans jazz up through the 1920s, swing in the 1930s, bebop in the 1940s, cool jazz and hard bop in the 1950s, free jazz and fusion in the 1960s. Details of emphasis vary. But from textbook to textbook, there is substantive agreement on the defining features of each style, the pantheon of great innovators, and the canon of recorded masterpieces.[18]

For DeVeaux, the narrative reifies jazz as a stable and identifiable category, with histories presenting a continuum traceable throughout the twentieth century. He also adopts White's concept of literary emplotment, arguing that the mode in which jazz histories are told varies from the Tragic to the Romantic. In essence, the evolution and establishment of the blues narrative from Oliver's history to the writings of Oakley, Palmer, Davis, and even Bill Wyman display a remarkable similarity to DeVeaux's critique of the jazz narrative. It may well be that modern music histories, even of rock, punk, new wave, metal, or grunge, are all characterized by a process of literary construction. This is in combination with the retrospective character of writing histories that often constitutes a divorce of historians from the historical context they are narrating.[19] In the specifics, however, what differentiates jazz from blues in the historiographical sense is that jazz, or "America's classical music," retains a strong presence in the twenty-first century both musically and economically, and still retains numerous figureheads seen to be keeping the tradition alive.[20] The "blues narrative," on the other hand, has often rested on the assumption that the music has been on the verge of demise or, depending on the time in which the history was written, extinct in its "truest" and most "authentic" forms. This has meant its transition from a form of folk music to popular music and ending with a "roots" music label.[21] Indeed, in the introduction to *The Story of the Blues,* Oliver wraps his narrative in the context of a fading musical form that in its time of dying has inspired the burgeoning success of many others:

> *Roll over, Beethoven!* When the Beatles recorded the iconoclastic title it wasn't only Beethoven who had to move aside but the composer of the song, the rhythm-and-blues singer, Chuck Berry, as well. When the Rolling Stones were *Confessing the Blues* they were confessing, too, to the influence of Walter Brown and B.B. King; when the Animals acclaimed the *Big Boss Man* the real boss man was Jimmy Reed. It was Lightnin' Hopkins who was preserved when The Lovin' Spoonful put the *Blues In the Bottle*; it was a Mississippi Negro, Bukka White, on parole from Parchman Farm, who was Bob Dylan's muse for *Fixin' to Die Blues*. Using the words and music of a Memphis "gum-ball raker," Gus Cannon, the Rooftop Singers offered the invitation to *Walk Right In*. Popular music has been walking in on the blues ever since.

The boundaries are clearly drawn here: the blues and white popular music of the sixties are two different things, and the end of the story is set with the invasion of latter on the territory of the former. However, Oliver again makes clear the purpose of his narrative by drawing a line in the sand: "this is not a book about the current trends in popular music, but about the blues."[22]

Beginnings: Framing the Story

From the outset, in his acknowledgments Oliver directly sets the backdrop for the story: "my greatest debt of gratitude, of course, is to the blues singers and musicians themselves whose creative abilities, born in painful experience have immeasurably enriched our musical experience."[23] Similar sentiments would be endlessly repeated in blues narratives that followed, as exemplified by Stephen C. Tracy: "It is a story as old as the American genesis . . . and it is, to a great degree, a myth of inferiority that is forcefully dispelled musically, poetically, and spiritually by this century's humbly towering art form, the blues."[24] While this is a perfectly understandable ode to the creators of the music, it also sets the context for the blues narrative. Given the absence of concrete historical evidence on the origins of the music, Oliver elects to focus on the wider historical context of the African American experience. It is their "painful experience" of the latter part of the nineteenth and the beginning of the twentieth centuries that frames the history of the blues. The story therefore begins from the legacies of slavery. The inclusion of a full page poster from 1853 in which a slave buyer offered "$1200 to $1250 for Negroes," which is representative of the antebellum slave trade, looms large over Oliver's introduction, indicating the burden that the protagonists of Oliver's story must carry. Thus in the opening chapters the story emphasizes the quiet resistance and tenacity of African Americans who, despite the continued presence of the slave trade in the nineteenth century, the failed promises of Reconstruction and Emancipation, and the disenfranchisement of Jim Crow, retained the ability to express themselves creatively. This has its origins within the Atlantic crossings of African slaves:

> There had been sustained contact with Africa for more than two centuries, and in spite of the barbarities of the slave-ships, the inhumanity of the auction block and the brutalities of the slave-drivers that were all designed to break the spirit, the African displayed a remarkable capacity for survival under deplorable conditions.[25]

Accompanying this description is a large image of a "Guinea-man" slave ship loading plan, displaying the shocking harshness of the crossings. The effect of the image is to stress the human suffering and tragedy characterizing the beginning of the African experience. Here the British scholar seems to lean toward LeRoi Jones's analysis of the blues—born in the African slave's path to becoming African American. Jones argued that slavery dictated to a large degree the emergence of the music, and would go on to argue militantly that "the only so-called popular music in this country of any real value is of African derivation."[26] Oliver, however, is not declaring that the blues was the music of slaves, but rather is attempting to demonstrate the manner in which African Americans were able to survive despite the suppression of their African culture with the use of spirituals and work songs. The effect of this framing is to create a distinctly powerful image of beauty emerging from tragedy, of a spiritual triumph over physical and material despair, or in White's words, "the triumph of good over bad, of virtue over vice, of light over darkness."[27] Oliver uses an example from the diary of the young black freewoman Charlotte Forten from 1862, where a slave woman is quoted commenting on the spiritual "Poor Rosy," stating that "it can't be sung widout *a full heart and a troubled spirit.*" Despite focusing here on early traces of African American songs, Oliver regards the sentiment evoked by the slave woman as a link to the emergence of the blues around half a century later: "A full heart and a troubled spirit has been the inspiration and the reason for countless blues."[28] This helps to establish the "emplotment" of Oliver's narrative as a battle between the human spirit and oppression, which is depicted as being played out throughout African American history.

While Oliver is not directly linking the blues to slavery, he does attempt to trace a continuity of consciousness based on human endurance. The brutal manner of the transatlantic slave trade meant that inevitably some elements of African identity and culture were forcibly eroded in transplanted slaves, but, as in the case of those spirituals that were supposedly white in origin, their "African means of expression and [their] ability to extemporise soon moulded them as something apart from the European tradition." Equally, the call-and-response patterns of the work songs allowed them to impose their own rhythms on the toil of the field gangs.[29] This ability to adapt and reshape music to suit their demands is represented as the constant that transcends historical events:

> It may be seen that Negro traditions of music, song and dance had a long history extending far back in slavery and to an African heritage. Vestiges of Africa remained in their arts where they were permitted to do so, and in the dialect of the Georgia Sea Islands, of the Gullah Negroes and in scattered fragments throughout the South, may be heard African words and phrases. The ability of the Negro to adapt his music, to create anew, to improvise words and themes is evident in innumerable reminiscences and reports. All this has relevance to the blues and has had, in some way, an influence on the shaping of the music, its content or its function.[30]

Indeed, the imagery used in the book supports the idea of African retentions, by presenting an image of inmates at the Angola Penitentiary in Louisiana, singing a "cutting song as they wield their axes, in a manner that recalls that of African work gangs" (fig. 22). Oliver makes use of some his own photographs from his experiences in Ghana in 1964, where he spent some months as a visiting lecturer at the Faculty of Architecture at the University of Science and Technology in Kumasi, and at the University of Ghana in Legon. While there he gave a number of talks on African American vernacular music, including blues and jazz. These experiences allowed him to conduct fieldwork that would eventually be published in *Savannah Syncopators: African Retentions in the Blues* (1970), the first in a series of "Blues Paperbacks" that

Oliver edited.[31] The images show African American banjo players next to similar stringed instruments from the savannah regions of West Africa, which Oliver stated were "related to the banjo." Similarly, a photograph of an Ashanti dance to a drum orchestra appears on the same page that Oliver discusses the Saturday night "frolics" and "jigs" that characterized the plantation lives of slaves.[32] Once again, this creates a sense of continuity. While Oliver notes that African and European cultures met and formed hybridized versions in the antebellum South, there remains the suggestion that the African elements were better positioned to resist total suppression. In the battle of good over evil, then, African heritage takes on the part of the good, whereas the imperial white oppressor takes the bad. The use of African photographs demonstrates the author's emphasis on the past and more specifically with the origins of the blues from the black experience of slavery.

The manner in which free African Americans coped with the social and economic conditions of the late nineteenth century inspires similar imagery of human survival against the odds. According to the author, the combined effect of the catastrophic failure of Emancipation after the Civil War, the eventual institutionalization of the "separate but equal" laws through the Supreme Court in 1896, and the entrapment in exploitative employment practices such as sharecropping, "was to impress upon [the African American] a sense of his own identity." For Oliver, these events gave rise to Booker T. Washington's and W. E. B Dubois's two different approaches to tackling the underprivileged position of the African American, but most importantly for the story, also triggered an internal revolution within black culture that would give rise to not only blues but jazz, ragtime, gospel, and ballad folk heroes such as John Henry and Ella Speed.[33] That it was possible to forge such distinctive cultural forms amid dire social and economic circumstances impresses on the reader a sense that the African American story was an extraordinary one. Indeed, the experience of black Americans from slavery through to segregation was one of the greatest struggles in human history. But by establishing a firm link between this history and the emergence of the blues, and placing emphasis on the experience and survival of cultural practices amid tragic events, the music became well worthy of its own history.

What emerges, however, is an internalized and inward looking African American world, a recurrence of the "Negro world" Oliver describes in his writing of the fifties. The opening chapters of *The Story of the Blues* create a middle ground occupied by this African American space. Oliver states that the book is an attempt to show "the evolution of a modern folk music," which places the blues in a category between the modern world and the old. Labeling the blues in this way is demonstrative of the cultural constructs that categories such as "folk" point to, but Oliver's purpose is once again one of demarcation. In this way, the blues belongs neither to the world of the slaves, or the modern world of popular entertainment and mass culture, instead it is in-between, in a place and culture of its own. In addition to the cultural "in-betweenness" of the African American world, Oliver provides rich imagery to describe the geographical separation of the black world from the white:

> When the blues began, the countryside was quiet. Loudest of the sounds to break the stillness was the roar of the steam train as it traced its way through the lowlands, leaving a smudge of smoke against the blue sky. A brief moment of excitement as it passed, a shrill whistle, dipping and wailing like a blues and it would be gone. . . .
>
> There was little to listen to. No airplanes overhead, no automobiles lifting clouds of dust from the dirt roads, no television aerials on the cabin roofs, no tractors and mechanical cotton-pickers, no transistor radios to place on them. . . . In the early years of the blues, their counterparts were the creaking of wagon axles, the groaning of gang planks, the cries of occasional street vendors—the tamale man, the charcoal man and the blackberry woman. Or perhaps the blind guitarist on the community steps.

Perhaps there is no better example of literary craft in Oliver's history than in this passage, where the sound of a passing train in this quiet country is likened to the sound of a blues. The scenes described here are of an isolated world cut off from modernity, although the passing train that passes by acts as a reminder of the modern world's existence. From Oliver's description this is a primitive, almost Arcadian rural world where modern life and technology have yet to make their presence felt. Oliver's summary of African American life in the South of early twentieth century portrays a simple way of life:

> At the height of the cotton-picking season, there was little time for anything else but hard work during the day and the rest of aching limbs for a brief night, but during the rest of the year, when the sun went down, there was time for relaxation. At the end of the week the hands would go into town to bring produce to the market, to spend a little change, have a haircut and swap lies. Saturday night has always been the big night in southern rural communities; there were fish-fries and country suppers to the music of a string band or of a guitarist and fid-

> dler by the river's edge when the weather was warm, and wilder pursuits in the hot, ill-ventured juke joints. On the Sunday, for the godly there was church, with services lasting on and off all day, the hoarse exhortations of the preachers leading to the lining-out of old spirituals or to the joyous sounds of the gospel song which was to become the successor of the shout. But that was Sunday. Saturday night was for good times, with the liquor flowing, the shouts and laughter of dancers rising above the noise of juke band or gin-mill piano, and sometimes the staccato report of a revolver fired in jest—or in earnest.[34]

Here Oliver strengthens his interpretation of the African Americans as the "humble, obscure, unassuming men and women" that make up the story of the blues.[35] Life in the black world of the rural South in the early twentieth century appears to oscillate simply between labor and leisure, with little concern for anything outside this realm of experience.

The images that accompany theses passage both support and challenge this depiction (fig. 23). At first glance, the pictures of cotton pickers and a close-up of a cotton boll illustrate the rural character and centrality of the cotton to African American livelihoods. And this indeed was the case. Right up to the stock market crash of 1929, cotton was the focus of three out of four of all black sharecroppers, and two-thirds of tenant farmers.[36] This is contrasted by the two images of a riverboat and a freight train transporting industrial quantities loads of 500-pound cotton bales, highlighting that the production of cotton was part of a larger and modern economic system. Images of a country juke joint and of dancing present a similar paradox. While the image of the smiling dancers inspires a sense of joy and ecstasy, the sign reading "colored juke" on the building reminds of the racial segregation that characterized the South. Interestingly, the description of black life demonstrates that the isolation from the outside world is not wholly negative. In Oliver's portrayals the exceptionalism of the middle ground acquires a romantic beauty, once again recalling Big Bill Broonzy's description of the blues and the relation to its place in the rural South, narrated to his British audiences in the early fifties: "in Mississippi and Arkansas. That's where you hear the blues hollerin' across the fields at sundown."[37]

The Plot, the Protagonists, and the Setting

Having framed the context of story in the African American experience of the postbellum era, Oliver's history moves in chronological order from the turn of the twentieth century up to the 1960s. As an instance of the early state of the music, Oliver draws upon a now legendary instant in blues history"

> "One night at Tutwiler, as I nodded in the railroad station while waiting for a train that had been delayed nine hours, life suddenly took me by the shoulder and wakened me with a start." The event which, quite literally, altered the life of William Christopher Handy and also, to a considerable degree, the course of the blues, was the playing and singing of a ragged, lean Negro guitarist. "As he played, he pressed a knife on the strings of the guitar in a manner popularized by Hawaiian guitarists who used steel bars. The effect was unforgettable. His song, too, struck me instantly.
>
> Goin' where the Southern Cross the Dog.
>
> The singer repeated the line three times, accompanying himself on the guitar with the weirdest music I had ever heard." It's one of the earliest dateable references to a specific blues and is important because of the evident folk character of the singer, the location, the idiom—which W. C. Handy later used in his *Yellow Dog Blues*—and the technique of playing the guitar.[38]

So much has this encounter from 1903, narrated by the African American composer Handy in his autobiography of 1941, become a staple of blues histories that the U.S. Congress marked the centenary by naming 2003 as "The Year of the Blues." This year also saw director Martin Scorsese commission a series of blues documentaries by the likes of Mike Figgis and Clint Eastwood.[39] Hamilton's study has drawn attention to the reliance on this retrospective encounter that has been repeatedly used in blues histories as a symbol of the genesis of the genre. She argues convincingly that Handy's account matched the blues scholars' ideal of the music "as it sounded before the record companies got to it," in its original and uncorrupted state. Thus, "In their hands Handy's Delta vagrant has been transformed into the archetypal bluesman . . . the story became a foundation myth, seeming to convey something essential and incontrovertible about the origins of the blues tradition."[40] To a great extent, Hamilton's observations apply to Oliver's use of the story, as it is clear that the image painted here resonated with the author's interpretation of the blues in its pre-record industry days. This is demonstrated by his focus on the "folk character" of the situation in terms of sound (slide guitar), appearance ("ragged, lean Negro"), and place (railway platform in a small Mississippi Delta town). However, Oliver's "scholasticism" ensures that Handy's experience does not become simply a "foundation" story, and instead serves as a rare example of the condition and function of the blues at the turn of the century. Oliver was appreciative of the fact that examples of the music had been recorded as early as 1911 in the work of the folklorist Howard B. Odum, and as discussed above, was keen to place the music within the context of the development of African American vernacular music.[41] Nonetheless, Oliver's use of the Tutwiler narrative is still indicative of the attachment to a romantic image, a real historical event repackaged through Handy's memory. Oliver may not have regarded this as the beginning of the story of the blues, but it conformed to a preexisting notion of the music's function before recording—*who* played it and *where* it was played. Interestingly, it also seemed to echo the author's own experience of hearing African American music for the first time in the summer of 1942 in Britain, when the sound of black GIs singing as they worked left a lasting impression on the young Oliver.

Throughout his writing of the fifties and sixties, Oliver had rarely privileged Mississippi or the Delta as the unquestionable home of the music. During the blues revival, this idea had taken shape in the early sixties with the founders of the Origins Jazz Library (OJL) and the American collector James McKune, and it went on to seduce the growing world of blues scholars, enthusiasts, and musicians. Hamilton demonstrates that by 1965 even writers such as Charters, who had originally proposed a blues canon more appreciative of audience behavior, believed that "nowhere else in the South . . . could have bred a music so raw, so primal, for nowhere else was so cut off from the currents of modern life."[42] And in *The Story of the Blues* Oliver also began to fall for the lure of the Mississippi story:

> The sheer crudity of segregation in Mississippi, the barbarity of the measures to enforce it, the rich and yet despairing landscape with its low, red clay hills and the monotony of the flat bottomlands combine to give the state a perverse fascination. It is occasionally beautiful, but mostly it is elemental, cruel even, stifling in its feudalism. That a folk music of such stature and dignity took root and thrived in this soil continues to thrill and astonish, and for this reason perhaps, the view of the Mississippi as the birthplace of blues and the epitome of the whole music is seldom questioned. And perhaps, when all is told in the story of the blues, this may be true. But blues is not a music of a state and county lines or river boundaries, but of a people. While the blues was taking shape in Mississippi other traditions were emerging elsewhere.

Once again, Oliver's appreciation for Mississippi is more considered and appreciative of the fact that the story of the blues was not only from this part of the South. However, it also demonstrates the focus on the motif of triumph over tragedy. The Mississippi Delta has a special place not only because of the singers and the music that came from the region, but also because the harsh conditions that characterized African American life seemed more extreme. Two images accompany this description: the first shows a cotton picker alongside a white man in a suit, and the second an aerial shot of the river running through the Delta. These images are captioned as "many Mississippi blues singers . . . were underprivileged members of the community in their home districts, subject to exploitation . . . and the rigours of a hard life growing cotton in the fertile, black Delta lands." These pictures reference the subordinate social standing of the African American of the Delta to his white "boss," while showing the enormous scale and wild character of the land they work (fig. 24). What is significant here is that an almost supernatural link is established between the musicians and the Delta. The music of Delta singers such as Charley Patton, who "sang with such fierce conviction and with such growling earthiness," was the fruit of a land described as "rich and yet despairing," "elemental," and "cruel."[43]

This link is explored further in a chapter that examines the "back home" music of the thirties, when the older generations of singers who had stayed in the rural South, instead of venturing northward or westward, recorded for local talent scouts such as H. C. Speir. Undoubtedly, the intimate connections that existed between Delta singers such as Patton, Son House, Tommy Johnson, Willie Brown, and Ishmon Bracey in a relatively small space adds to the appeal of the Delta tradition narrative. It seems clear that a motivating force behind the emphasis on the Delta region was the fact that often conditions there were harshest, and therefore the blues here was at its most powerful:

> Three years earlier the terrible disaster of the Mississippi floods had occurred; the ravages of the boll weevil were still being felt; after the inundations had come an equally devastating drought, and the full effect of the Wall Street crash was beginning to hit the South. It must have seemed that there was no end to the troubles that a Mississippi field hand had to bear.

Oliver describes Son House's singing as "hypnotic," and his voice as "full" and "raw." Similarly, the singer Bukka White, who enjoyed some success and recognition during the blues revival, "had a tough life" and thus his singing held "a primitive force." The focus on the blues of this region allows Oliver to briefly highlight the presence of Robert Johnson. Here, Oliver relies on the testimony of Johnson's friend David "Honeyboy" Edwards to OJL's founder, Pete Whelan. While Oliver describes Johnson as "the most important musician" to work with the likes of House and Brown, his importance is only justified in terms of his influence on the postwar Chicago blues scene. As Wald has recently reminded blues scholars, Johnson sold very few records in the late 1930s and was practically unknown to interwar African American audiences. It is unlikely that Oliver was unaware of Johnson's poor commercial success, but his brief description indicates that the lure of this obscure singer's life and death was compelling. Oliver argues that the lyrics of songs such as "Hellhound on my Trail" and "If I Had Possession over Judgement Day" reveal "a tormented spirit" that was "undoubtedly . . . rocking to his end."[44]

It is not surprising that Oliver decided to give space to the Mississippi in his narrative. After all, many of the rediscoveries of the early sixties were from the region, and many collectors and folklorists had devoted attention to uncovering the recordings and lives of Delta musicians, peaking with the crowning of Robert Johnson as "The King of the Delta Blues Singers" by Columbia Records in 1961. The popularity of Johnson's recordings among white audiences of the sixties had made it so that his story could not be ignored. However, while Oliver gives ample space to the Mississippi bluesmen in his story, as he stated above, "other traditions were emerging elsewhere." He takes on a comprehensive survey of the various geographically based styles that characterized the origins and development of the music, espousing a view of the music's polygenetic nature. In addition to the Mississippi Delta bluesmen, also examined are the Texas styles of singers such as Blind Lemon Jefferson, the popularity of string and jug bands such as the Mississippi Sheiks and the Memphis Jug Band among black audiences, the piano blues that emanated from the sawmills and lumber camps, the piano and guitar duos such as Leroy Carr and Scrapper Blackwell, the success of the classic blueswomen such as Bessie Smith, Ida Cox, and Gertrude "Ma" Rainey, from the minstrel and traveling shows to the vaudeville era, the East Coast style of Blind Blake and Blind Willie McTell, the postwar jazz-influenced sounds of the "shouters" such as Jimmie Rushing and Jimmie Witherspoon, the music of the younger generations that amplified their juke joint sounds in cities, and the emergence of rhythm and blues in the postwar era. These are considered in unison with social changes such as World War I and the migrations from the rural South to urban areas across the country (predominantly the North), the decline of agriculture and mechanization of farming practices, the emergence of the race records industry in the 1920s, the Great Depression, the emergence of mass media in the postwar era, to the white discovery of African American music in the revival.

One of the main characteristics of Oliver's narrative is its focus on movement, and journeys that African Americans made throughout the first half of the twentieth century. The back inside cover of the book includes a large map of the East, South, and Midwest showing "migratory routes" via railroads and highways (fig. 25). Whether spurred on by the labor shortages in the factories during World War I, pushed by the intolerance of Jim Crow segregation, or urged to seek fortunes elsewhere due to the Depression, the protagonists of Oliver's story, like the millions of African Americans involved in the Great Migrations, are continually on the move. While the predominant direction of this movement in blues histories was from rural South to urban North, exemplified by Palmer's use of Muddy Waters's journey from the plantation to Chicago, Oliver's use of a map and the focus on migrations northward, westward, as well as to urban centers of the South demonstrate the author's consideration for more accurate historical realities.[45] Indeed, the Great Migrations were predominantly a rural to urban migration, rather simply from South to North. However, what makes the focus on movement significant in *The Story of the Blues* is its representation. On the one hand, numerous pictures show freight trains, railway tracks, some with people walking alongside them, roadside signposts, bird's-eye view images of cities, and urban ghetto housing, highlighting the destinations of the migrations (figs. 26–27). On the other, the factual description of the scale of African American migration (e.g., "by 1900 the colored population in [Chicago] was ten times that of fifty years before")[46] is under umbrella chapter headings such as "Travelin' Men" and "Back to Mississippi," and passages that state historical facts are blended with a sense of stoicism: "The struggle to gain work, to eat and to raise a family was sometimes too much to cope with, and many blues singers, like other jobless rootless men, took to the highways."[47] It is here possible to relate the sense of affinity with the idea of movement with what Hamilton describes as the postwar Beat-inspired "male flight from commitment." Migration and travel are not simple consequences of historical events, but made into conscious acts of empowerment.

The common thread linking the development of the music amid the movements of African Americans through various historical events is that the blues is considered "a state of mind: the blues singer didn't reason himself into a different frame of mind, he sang himself into it," and the blues is therefore "a means by which a man may give expression to his feelings."[48] Thus, the blues becomes much more than just music or entertainment; it is given symbolic significance as an attitude, a means of approaching life, and a collective consciousness required to deal with the difficulties presented by the racial segregation. This is made clear in the descriptions of the singers' styles. In a style remarkably similar to Oliver's writing during the fifties, Blind Lemon Jefferson is described as singing "with a deep pathos, a feeling that stemmed from the being of a man forever in darkness."[49] Considered in conjunction with the descriptions of singing with language such as "raw," "guttural," "instinctive," it is clear that blues has an almost spiritual force. This intangible, abstract power endows the music with the ability to create a strong connection between singer and audience, and for Oliver, the audience is never white or European, but African American. He states that Ida Cox's songs "were aimed . . . at her Southern audiences." Similarly, Big Bill Broonzy "sang for the South in Chicago," and "was neither motherless nor sisterless, but he sang for those who were."[50] Effectively, the lyrics of songs therefore carry the duty of communicating this "state of mind" and solidifying the collective consciousness: "the blues records conveyed the feelings and experiences of ordinary men . . . and the content of blues lyrics spoke for the black masses."[51]

Oliver had been defining the blues as "a state of mind" for almost two decades, but in the context of the blues narrative, the underlying motif of the blues as a psychological standpoint serves to unify and link together diverse historical events and music in various regions of the South by creating a sense of continuity. From the early records of black songs in Charlotte Forten's diary to the Depression of the thirties, the collective consciousness fostered by the practice and performance of music permits the transcendence of tragedy:

> In the post-Depression years, Negroes seemed to need to be given the assurance that their economic and social stresses were shared and understood, and if no-one else could give it without appearing condescending, the blues singer could. The blues in this period was sometimes less rich musically than it had been hitherto, but the content of the verses, which mattered greatly to those who bought the discs, was of more immediate social relevance than at any other previous time.

Here the blues is seen as a unifying medium, bringing together the experiences of millions of African Americans across the country and providing reassurance. It is for this reason that Oliver regarded black life of the interwar years as "mirrored" in lyrics.[52] Whether through the experience of debt peonage and sharecropping, the consequences of natural disasters such as the Great Mississippi Flood of 1927, the economic effects of the Depression, the displacement of the Great Migration, or life in urban ghettoes, Oliver believed that "blues singers . . . offered an indication of the hopes and fears of black people, sometimes their anger and sometimes their apathy."[53] Importantly, what is created here is something that the outside world cannot destroy or appropriate, thus remaining distinctly African American. As Oliver bases much of his scholarship on the lyrics of recordings, and as exemplified in the identification of the blues tradition in *Screening the Blues*, he endows blues musicians and audiences with the ability to utilize the recording industry as a means of creating and harboring a collective "folk" African American consciousness, and therefore establishing a continuity with the past, the survival through slavery and Emancipation. Importantly, however, Oliver was not trying to claim that blues reflected the experience of all African Americans:

> Blues singers sang for the "Race" audience exclusively in the 'twenties and 'thirties and not even the Negro political organisations chose to listen. In the 'thirties the Negro was a forgotten man, and he required of the blues singer and his records the confirmation that he was not alone.[54]

As highlighted in all of his previous publications, the music did not resonate with black civil rights organizations such as the NAACP or CORE that sought social change, and thus in terms of protest, the music was predominantly "accommodative."[55] Therefore, the world of the blues was not only one that had been "forgotten," but one that seemingly accepted the world as it was and perhaps "forgot" about the outside world. This strengthens the idea of a separate black world far removed from contemporary life and social struggles.

Fundamental to this separate world is an intimate connection between the blues and the spaces it occupies. In Oliver's narrative the story of the blues becomes not just a story about "a people," but importantly about specific places. In a double-page map of the East, Midwest, and South of the United States on the inside cover of the book, Oliver pinpointed his "blues centres and recording locations" (fig. 28). With the telling of the story a clearer picture of these "blues centres" emerges. The aforementioned descriptions of southern fields, where sounds of modern life are absent, and memories of lonely figures playing blues to themselves on train platforms of sleepy Delta towns combine to root the earlier forms of the blues in a rural and premodern South. As the story progresses with the Great Migration of agricultural hands to the industries of urban areas, and the development of African American music in the ghettoes, places such as Chicago's South Side also become "blues centres":

> There was little chance for the majority of blues singers to escape the lives they described; by 1925 literally half the Negro families in the North were living on relief, but still the cities attracted Negroes from the South although the disillusioned trickled back. Ghettoes burst at the seams, "hot-bed" apartments operated on a shift basis. . . . Under such conditions crime was rife, prostitution was a commonplace, the courts filled on Friday nights and weekends with delinquents pulled almost at random off the streets. . . .
>
> Everyday conditions in the ghetto, which constantly recur in the blues, were shared by countless singers. But even the more extreme and dramatic circumstances were to be found in the lives of some of them.[56]

Therefore, as the "back home" blues was at its most powerful in areas where conditions were harshest, so did the urban side of the music flourish in parts of St. Louis, Chicago and Detroit where African Americans were the most socially and economically deprived, but importantly, where the old "folk-ways" could be maintained.[57] The ghetto described above, as well as recalling Oliver's earliest descriptions of urban life (chapter 1), is akin to the "barbarity" imagined in the Delta. While violence, crime, and poor living conditions were consequences of the mass concentration of African Americans into urban ghettoes, the growth of these black areas also fostered what Oliver terms "urban folk communities," that is, the transplanted culture of ordinary African Americans from the South. From these were drawn the "star" singers of the thirties, among them Big Bill Broonzy, Tampa Red, Bumble Bee Slim, Lonnie Johnson, and Walter Davis, whom record companies relied on for record sales at the expense of the "effete and stage-directed 'classic singers' of minor calibre whose work ended with the Depression."[58] Oliver commented that the lives of African Americans, whether in the South or the city ghettoes, were often too real and harsh to be subjected to romanticism. While the author avoids romanticizing, he emphasizes the narrative of beauty born from tragedy. He describes singers who had been stabbed, shot, blinded, served in prison for homicide, and bore the scars of shackles, but "however complex the circumstances or repressing the conditions of living, so many had the creative ability and the artistic stature to develop a folk music of such richness from such experience."[59]

The Imagery of the Story

As in *Conversation with the Blues*, the range of photographs and the additional posters, advertisements, and illustrations used in *The Story of Blues* function to fix Oliver's blues centers in distinct geographical realities. Descriptions of agricultural life in the South are accompanied by images of cotton fields, sharecropper homes, railroad workers, ditch-diggers, muleskinners, country juke joints, and singers playing on their front porches or for dances. Conversely, as African American life became more urbanized in Oliver's narrative, pictures begin to show the deprived housing of the black ghettoes, the smokestacks of city industries, an image of a young black man being treated at the emergency ward of a Chicago hospital, as well as blues musicians playing inside the city nightclubs (figs. 29–30). In this manner, Oliver helps to establish some of photographic iconography of the blues. What distinguishes the use of images from *Conversation*, however, is that Oliver uses a wide range of sources. As well as reusing photographs from his 1960 field trip, Oliver borrows images from a number of other folklorists and blues scholars such as Frederic Ramsey, Harry Oster, Jacques Demetre, George Adins, Mike Leadbitter, Mack McCormick, Val Wilmer, Pete Welding, and William Russell. In addition, Oliver made use of material from governmental organizations such as the United States Information Service (USIS) and the Farm Security Administration (FSA), including photography from the thirties and forties obtained through the Library of Congress.

One of the most significant aspects of the images used in the book is that the range of sources and types of image used appears as a pastiche that complicates and destabilizes the narrative. The majority of the photographs are not dated, with the effect of blurring the historical specificity of the story. Thus, images from a range of historical periods spanning almost a century, from the immediate postbellum period, the thirties, to the author's own photographs from 1960 are shown alongside one another (figs. 31–33). The effect is somewhat paradoxical. On the one hand, the pictures are real and specific enough to link the written narrative with specific geographical spaces, such as the landscapes of the South. On the other hand, the scant dating of the images and lack of specific explanation color the visual element of the book with a sense of timelessness. The absence of details about the photographs often means that the only element indicating a historical difference between the images is the quality of the photograph itself. The effect is to blur the various historical events of the African American past into a more simple whole. Despite the fact the images portray very different circumstances and provide visual references to events that are either very distant from one another temporally or not directly related, their presentation in *The Story of the Blues* helps them to blend into a unified narrative: the African American experience that produced the blues.

The images therefore reinforce the narrative by strengthening the triumph-over-tragedy motif. This is made much clearer in pictures that attempt to highlight the subordinate and disenfranchised social standing of African Americans and the physical reality that have given birth to the blues. The photographs Oliver selected from the Library of Congress collection of interwar photography in particular attempt to show the more vividly disturbing scenarios that are ambiguously grouped together: the squalid living conditions of ordinary black laborers and families; a picture of hundreds standing in line in relief camps following the 1927 Mississippi flood; families watching their buildings burning down; inmates kept in cramped quarters under armed guard; a man grieving at the grave of a loved one (figs. 34–36). What is presented, therefore, is a much more explicitly graphic representation not only of the history of the blues, but the places in which this history occurred. Many of the images taken from the FSA photographers, USIS, and the Library of Congress most probably had very little to do with blues when they were taken. But presented alongside the written narrative they become representative of the story. For instance, an image of a sharecropper and his family give an indication of the living conditions of agricultural laborers. However, it is not clear if the sharecropper was a blues singer or a musician at all. But in the context of the story, the family stood almost in a horizontal line and, facing the camera, become representative of the blues life. Similarly the picture of African Americans inside a liquor store has no direct relevance to the music, but the solemn expressions on their faces comes to symbolize the sentiment of "a full heart and a troubled spirit" (fig. 37). Max Harrison described the images in the book as "acutely depressing," and for this reason he believed the story of the blues was a testament to the "tenacity of the human spirit."[60] The pictures Oliver selected therefore functioned to intensify the tragic element of the narrative, thus also heightening the achievement of creating music such as the blues out of the experience.

While a considerable proportion of the pictures support Oliver's description of African American life in the first half of the twentieth century, many other images contradict the seemingly separate and isolated "Negro world." The advertisements for blues records from the race records industry, press releases, record covers, and the professional portraits of musicians often smartly dressed in suits and smiling for the camera indicate a society in which music functioned not so differently from the present day, supporting Wald's view of the blues as the pop music of its time (figs. 38–39). These images complicate the story of the "humble and unassuming men and women" who had "limited aspirations." Many of the styled portraits indicate that a professional look was important to the success in an industry that sold millions of records and advertised and marketed profusely across the African American market. Considered alongside images of a more "folk" in nature, country dances, men singing the blues on the porches of their shacks, of decaying juke joints and railroads, the incongruences make it evident that the story of blues is made of a multitude of histories, multiple stories that in their similarities are unified into a single narrative.

The Death of the Blues?

As the story progresses from the Depression through World War II and the postwar era, the narrative describes the musicians and styles that became prominent in the late thirties and forties in other parts of the country, moving away from the predominant "South to North" motif. While the chapter entitled "Travelin' Men" considers the music and movements of musicians of the East Coast and Piedmont style, such as Blind Blake, Blind Willie McTell, Sonny Terry, Blind Boy Fuller, Brownie McGhee, Josh White, and Sleepy John Estes, the following chapter examines the music that developed in the westward part of the country, from Texas and Kansas to California in the late thirties and early forties. Among other musical developments, this period saw the emergence of hybridized forms of electrified music with the likes of T-Bone Walker, the fusion of Kansas City jazz bands, group ensembles, and blues "shouting." Concurrently, the early forties were also characterized by the increase in the influence of radio and the boom in the jukebox industry. Since the 1920s, music had been sent to millions of homes across America, with radio beginning to replace the more expensive phonograph as the primary source of music in the home.[61] As discussed in chapter 4, in terms of the relationship between the blues and the recording industry, while Oliver identified positive effects from technological developments, such as in the potential for audiences to hear more than was possible from their immediate experience, and the mixture of musical styles that radio permitted, on the whole mass media diffusion through radio and jukeboxes "was damaging to music making."[62] The author's language thus begins to take on a more pessimistic tone than in *Screening the Blues*. While phonographs could substitute live performance, jukeboxes, which became highly influential and ever-present between 1940 and 1960, could offer more choice than the repertoire of a single musician.[63] Similarly, while radio could open up markets for certain musicians, it also made the "exploitation" of the market through the commodification of blues records more straightforward.[64]

Simultaneously, Oliver believed that in this period some singers had begun to "move further away from blues and into commercial popular music with blues colouration" and learned to blend different sounds into popular styles, such as Ray Charles, whose music is described as a "studied exploitation of blues idioms."[65] However, the predominant migration northward to Chicago and Detroit during the late forties and fifties was accompanied by a great concentration of a newer generation of blues singers, seen as continuing the "back home" blues tradition in its most authentic forms. Musicians such as Elmore James, Muddy Waters, Little Walter, and Howlin' Wolf began to be heard over the airwaves with the growth of black radio stations during the late 1940s, and they could been seen performing regularly in a small nucleus of Chicago venues such as Sylvio's, Smitty's Corner, and the Big Squeeze Club. That the tradition was alive in the mid-fifties was evident, as lesser-known blues singers such as Jimmy Davis and Little David could be heard on Maxwell Street, depicted as the "training ground." Playing on streets for change or for pure enjoyment presents the link back to the southern tradition of music making, as represented by the espoused depiction of the singer on the train platform in Tutwiler. It also transposed the iconographic landscapes of the South to the contemporary streets of the northern cities. But importantly, it was also signaling the beginning of the end in the story of the blues:

> Through the heavy amplification, the smoke, the urban haze, could be discerned still a line of descent which was sired in the music of Charley Patton, Son House and Robert Johnson. It was a thrilling, dramatic culmination of a remarkable tradition exemplified in numerous lesser bands led by Snooky Prior or J. B. Hutto, Walter Horton or J. B. Lenoir all over the South and West Sides. But it was not to last much longer.[66]

From the very beginning of Oliver's narrative, the story is set to end with the postwar discovery of the blues. The sense of decline had been building in Oliver's writing prior to *The Story of the Blues*, as there was always an underlying premonition that the music's days were numbered, whether that was manifested in the concentration on the blues from the interwar years in *Blues Fell This Morning*, the memories and images in *Conversation*, or the focus on the tradition in *Screening the Blues.* However, in *The Story of the Blues* it is made clear in several instances that while the blues developed and evolved through the African American experience of the late nineteenth and first half of the twentieth centuries, the demise of the music would come with the onset of the sixties: the huge influence of black music on white groups in this decade is framed as an invasion of popular music ("walking right in on the blues"); at the time of writing it was "still possible, but only just, to hear the history of the blues from the mouths of many of them who shaped it"; the blues on record reflected the life of African Americans during the twenties and thirties, and began to lose relevance to the changing nature of black society in the postwar era; little more than memories remained of the classic blues singers; and the story is told in progressive stages (i.e., "down in Memphis, the last act in the city's important part in the story of the blues was being played out"),with each part inching closer to the end.[67] Overall the "death of the blues" results as a combination of three primary occurrences: the industrialization and commercialization of music; changes in African American culture and society; and the white discovery of black music.

The first of these concentrates on the Adornian interpretation of music as a commercialized industry. The folkloric view of the blues as a music born in an oral tradition and morally opposed to any aspects of profit making, success, or fame is dependent on an adverse view of the recording industry. Oliver became more and more aware of the double-edged nature of the recording process, as a tool for preserving folk culture and allowing the mass dissemination of African American culture, but also standardizing the genre and diluting the nature of the music through the influence of commercialism. Additionally, Oliver had appreciated the fact that what was available on record was only an approximation of the culture to which the music pointed. Thus, the race records market between 1920 and the early 1940s was not a simple and definable thing, but was complex, diverse, and "illusive." Power often rested within the record companies, and blues musicians were sometimes equipped with the necessary skills of playing the market to their advantage, while others succumbed to commercial demands of control and censorship.[68] But ultimately the recording industry, the growth of radio and jukeboxes replacing the traditional role of live musicians, changed the function of music making from predominantly active participation to passive consumption. Once the blues became more popular on record and on the airwaves, the traditional function of singer and audience, releasing tensions and collectively facing their troubles through the cathartic performance of the music, described in the first half the book and in *Blues Fell This Morning*, was waning. The author could therefore conclude that for over a decade there had been very few blues songs that were "lyrically significant," as the blues lost the power for social commentary it possessed prior to World War II.[69]

While the music industry represented an external development that exerted its influence upon the blues, there was an "internal" shift among African American culture that favored its decline. This change was twofold. First, the postwar period saw the burgeoning of younger generations of African American musicians and performers that gave rise to rhythm and blues, which also meant the transformation of the "race" label. For Oliver, these new performers varied in their allegiance to the blues tradition. While the likes of Jimmy Reed maintained "roots [that] were still deep in the blues" and held an appeal to younger generations, others such as Chuck Berry and Bo Diddley "played on the current fads, fears and fantasies of the young Negroes."[70] B. B. King is described as "impassioned, if somewhat uninvolved," and Buddy Guy's popularity is given to his showmanship on stage rather than to his skill as a blues musician.[71] As in *Screening the Blues*, this form of subjective categorization rests upon deeply personal interpretations of authenticity, with certain lyrics and sounds being identified as traditional, and other mannerisms as the flight from the tradition. Inherent in this portrayal of the new rhythm-and-blues musicians was the belief that younger audiences identified with a more confident and assertive stage presence that the seemingly accommodationist blues of the interwar years could provide, and thus turned to soul culture as the sixties wore on:

> That the Soul trend—the blend of gospel techniques of exaggerated mannerisms and screaming, passionate entreaties with blues instrumental techniques and commercial "pop" words—has been immensely popular with young Negroes and whites alike is undeniable. It has meant vastly increased sales for the record companies and, combined with the sleek and successful Detroit Tamla-Motown "sound," has dominated the record catalogues which are directed at a Negro market, and so in turn, the juke-box and disc-jockey promotional devices. This has been damaging to the blues as a form in its own right and blues singers who have been unwilling or unable to adapt their music demands of "soul" have found themselves without engagements. The more geared to the record and radio industries music has become, the greater has been the pressure on blues singers to accede to popular taste. As Buddy Guy explained to Peter Guralnick, "you got to keep up with the latest songs. You got to have it down, man, what James Brown or Wilson Pickett may put out. You forget your own. . . . Unless you make a hit."

> Soul, it seems, has replaced the blues as the music that speaks for the younger generation of Negroes, while it draws from the blues as part of its expression.[72]

While this represents a change in the music of the period, it also points to the second aspect of the internal shift. Guy's reference to James Brown was probably a response to the singer's 1968 hit "Say it Loud, I'm Black and I'm Proud," which came to be the musical expression of black militancy. It was one of the most prominent songs in a body of music from the mid-sixties onward, including figures such as Marvin Gaye, Curtis Mayfield, and Berry Gordy, that became representative of an African American culture that both "celebrated blackness and challenged white dominance in equal measure." As Stephen Tuck argues, in this scenario music was not simply an abstraction of the racial struggle, it was the actual "battleground."[73] As much of Oliver's writing had indicated, none more so than *Conversation with the Blues*, the blues represented a realm of experience that was not akin to that of the generations involved in the civil rights or Black Power movements. Oliver's focus on the past was therefore confirming what many African American writers of the Black Arts movement thought, that the "blues was how we felt yesterday."[74] In *The Story of the Blues*, the blues had been described as the music of "humble, obscure, unassuming men and women," seemingly accommodative, while simultaneously fostering a sense of group solidarity. He stated, "The blues singer has yet to declare 'I'm black and I'm beautiful and I'm Afro-American,'" thus leading to a decline in relevance of the blues to a generation that required loud political voices. Oliver hoped that in a post-civil rights world "black Americans may be able to look back with pride upon the creation of one of the richest and most rewarding of popular arts and perhaps the last great folk music that the western world may produce." If the political objectives of the more assertive postwar African Americans had colored the interpretation of the blues as a negative symbol of the past, in his closing remarks the author remarked that the achievement of these political objectives would hopefully open the doors to a renewed appreciation for the music as a form of African American cultural heritage. Gussow's essay argues that while for many black cultural critics and writers of the late sixties the blues *was* significant, for younger African American audiences the blues was not particularly popular or interesting.[75] Nonetheless, what is significant here is that in the description of the blues' decline, Oliver strengthens the racial categorization of the music by hoping for a future reconciliation of African Americans with their past. This is reinforced by separating African American discourses of history from the white discovery of the blues.

That this discovery represented a threat to the authenticity of the blues was nothing new. However, in *The Story of the Blues* it is made clearer by the fact that little more than a few paragraphs are dedicated to the blues revival in the sense of the music played by white rhythm-and-blues bands of the sixties. Instead, the revival that Oliver discusses is the research and fieldwork of American and European folklorists, musicians, and enthusiasts of the post-war era that led to a growth in knowledge about the blues, but also to the rediscovery of a number of elderly and forgotten bluesmen. In this way, the author focuses more on the fact that the veterans of the music, and those who have supplied more information than anyone else, were dying out. This establishes the sense of nostalgia that accompanies the narrative, visually reinforced by images that appear like distant memories of the past, when the blues was part of a living folk culture. From the very beginning of the book, the white discovery of the blues is framed in terms of an invasion and appropriation, a process of popular music "walking in on the blues" that will bring about its decline. While Oliver described the popularity of the blues among European audiences as a "phenomenon that deserves more attention," he also attempted a brief analysis:

> In the [European] clubs, many of the young dancers hardly knew who they were dancing to; they like the music, it was great for the twist or the frug, and a whole generation seemed to find an affinity with the men who made the blues. A generation in revolt found that the music of a segregated minority was the symbol of a gulf between themselves and the values and attitudes of their parents.[76]

He therefore suggests that the popularity of the music was perhaps more indicative of a social and generational crisis within European society than it was about a genuine interest in the culture of African Americans. Accompanying this cultural disconnection between black music and white audiences is the fact that the blues played by European musicians was markedly different from the real thing: "White singers could play the blues too well and, up to a point, could sing them, but they hadn't got the magical quality of 'soul'" (the only exception seems to have been English harmonicist Cyril Davies).[77] While skillful, white imitators could only approximate as they lacked something that was intangible, something that came from deep within the experience of the African American. From this viewpoint, Oliver's historical narrative framed in terms of a triumph over tragedy serves as a legitimizing factor, giving the blues a firm link within the experiences of segregation and disenfranchisement in the United States. In the fifties, Oliver criticized Lonnie

Donegan and Ken Colyer for attempting to sing black music while they themselves were not of the same folk heritage. In the late sixties, Oliver's language adapts to the new developments within African American culture to adopt the term "soul," distinctive for its relation to African American cultural expression and identity. Importantly, lacking this fundamental characteristic meant that the "black youth [had] turned away" from the blues.

The "death" of the blues highlights some of the major contradictions in *The Story of the Blues*. The very genesis of the music explained through the coming together of the work songs, field hollers, and spirituals of the nineteenth century, combined with the Anglo-European influence of instrumentation and melody, allows for a certain amount of hybridity. The blues was born of the African American experience, but also as a product of many cultural and musical interchanges that resulted amid the events of the late nineteenth and early twentieth centuries. Inherent in Oliver's description of the blues before World War II was a sense that the African American progenitors of the music retained a certain autonomy over their own music and their own culture. However, in the postwar era, when the culture is more exposed to growing forms of mass media and thus open to "invasion" of the white world, the cross-cultural possibility for a multiracial hybrid of the blues is deplored, seen as a form of cultural colonialism, a barbaric violation of something pure and meaningful. Therefore, while Jones and Keil saw the evolution of older forms in the soul of the sixties, Oliver and many of the readers who valued his book saw the last days of the genre. In the analysis of the blues' decline in the sixties a clearer picture emerges of the representation of the blues as an organic whole, made of sound and a cultural and often racial consciousness that has a beginning, a story, and an end.

The construction and piecing together of the "blues narrative" demonstrates the manner in which the music was imagined by the leading writer on the subject at the end of the sixties. After having established that the blues constituted a tradition, Oliver attempted to fix categorical boundaries by narrating the music's history, legitimizing its existence as a distinct musical form, with a story and history of its own. While this history is highly informative in that Oliver appreciates the complex historical nuances of the African American experience, the framing of the narrative through the "triumph over tragedy" motif maintains the portrayal of African Americans largely as accommodative, and as the predecessors of those who made up the civil rights groups of the fifties and sixties. The narrative thus locks the protagonists of the story firmly within the past, as the people that make up the story in Oliver's book seem closer to the disappointments of Emancipation, the endurance of Jim Crow segregation, and the experiences of the Depression years than the young activist African Americans of the postwar years. The pastiche of imagery present in large quantities throughout the book also adds geographical specificity by attempting to reveal the places in which the story evolved. While many of the pictures are starkly real in their presentation of the physical realities of African American life, as in *Conversation with the Blues*, they are also distinctly elusive in the way they appear timeless, in the mixture of their sources and styles, thus complicating the fluidity of Oliver's narrative of the blues as folk music. Nonetheless, the images in Oliver's book help to establish some of the visual iconography that was associated with the music by blues scholars during the revival: the rural landscapes of the South and the Mississippi Delta, the urban ghettoes of the North, the railways that transported millions out of the South, the economic poverty and despair on the faces of African Americans. In conjunction with the author's increased emphasis on more "revivalist" aspects of the music, such as the role of the Mississippi Delta, Robert Johnson, and Handy's encounter with the music for the first time, *The Story of the Blues* reveals the blending of fact and imagination in the formation of the "blues narrative," and how the interpretation of the music always rested on the aesthetic criteria imposed by the scholar's idealized view of the music. In this way, *The Story of the Blues* functioned not only as a means of legitimizing the blues through the telling of its history, but also as a means of reifying the imagined world of the blues, of trying to fix categorical meanings and aesthetic criteria by narrating *the* story, which brought together the experiences of blues singers in a generalized experience that made up the blues life. The book would therefore both inform readers on the experiences of many African Americans in the late nineteenth and early twentieth centuries and conform to visions of a folk world constructed in opposition to the commercialism, cultural capitalism, and musical miscegenation of the fifties and sixties. These visions simplified the many different tales and events that made up the history of the blues into a single and more compelling *story*.

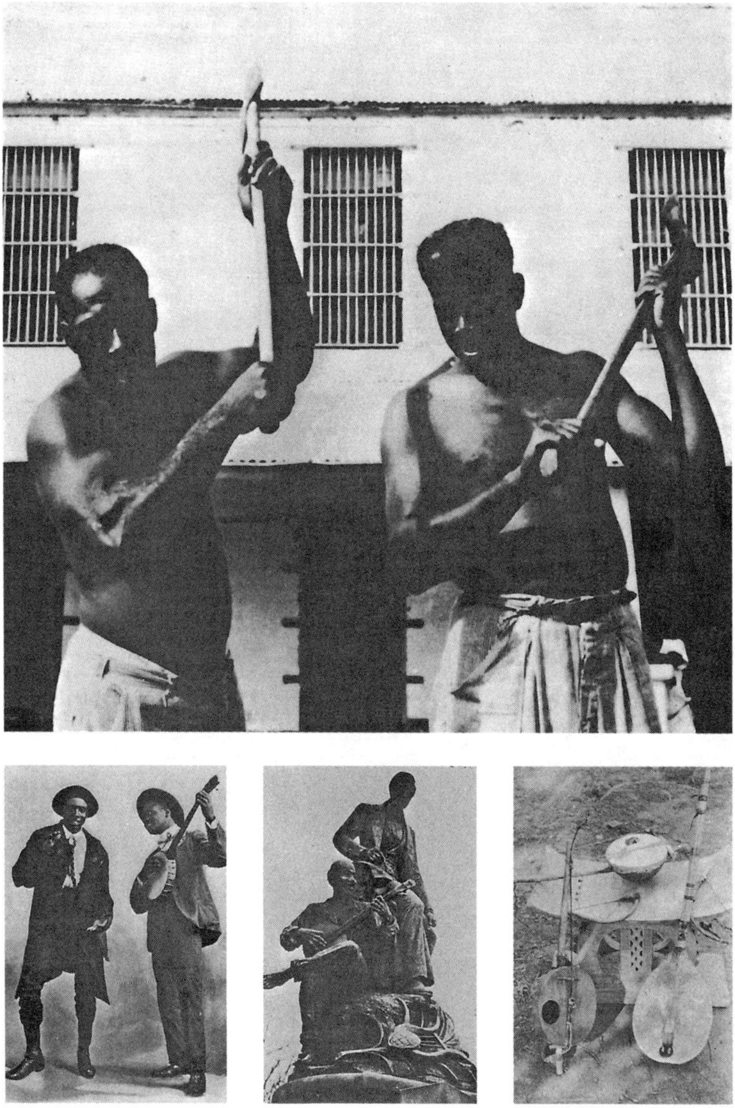

Figure 22. Oliver's caption reads, "Convicts in Angola Penitentiary, Louisiana, sing a 'cutting song' as they wield their axes, in a manner which recalls that of African work gangs. *Bottom left*: banjo player and dancer about 1890. *Center*: Negro songs were sentimentalised in the 'Plantation Melodies' of Stephen Foster, and here a banjo-playing slave sits at Foster's feet on the Pittsburgh Memorial. *Right*: Hausa and Fulani stringed instruments from the savannah regions of West Africa are related to the banjo." It is interesting that the raised arms of the convicts almost remind of the postures of the dancer and banjo player. (Top image from Harry Oster, bottom center from United States Information Service, remaining images from Paul Oliver.)

Figure 23. Images of the cotton bolls, pickers, railroad cars, and riverboats transporting large loads of 500-pound cotton bales. (Top left and bottom right Paul Oliver; top right and bottom left USIS.)

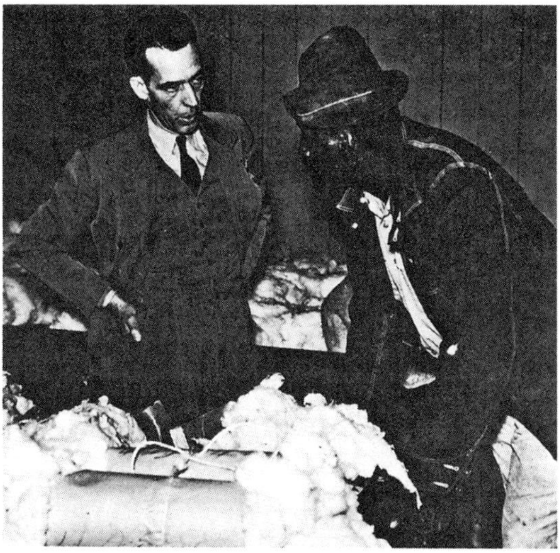

Figure 24. Images of the fertile but hostile Delta region of northern Mississippi, accompanied by picture of a cotton-picker and the white landowner referred to as "The Man." Also included is the advertisement for Crying Sam Collins's Jail House Blues." (Top right from FSA; bottom from USIS; top left from Nick Perls, Yazoo Records.)

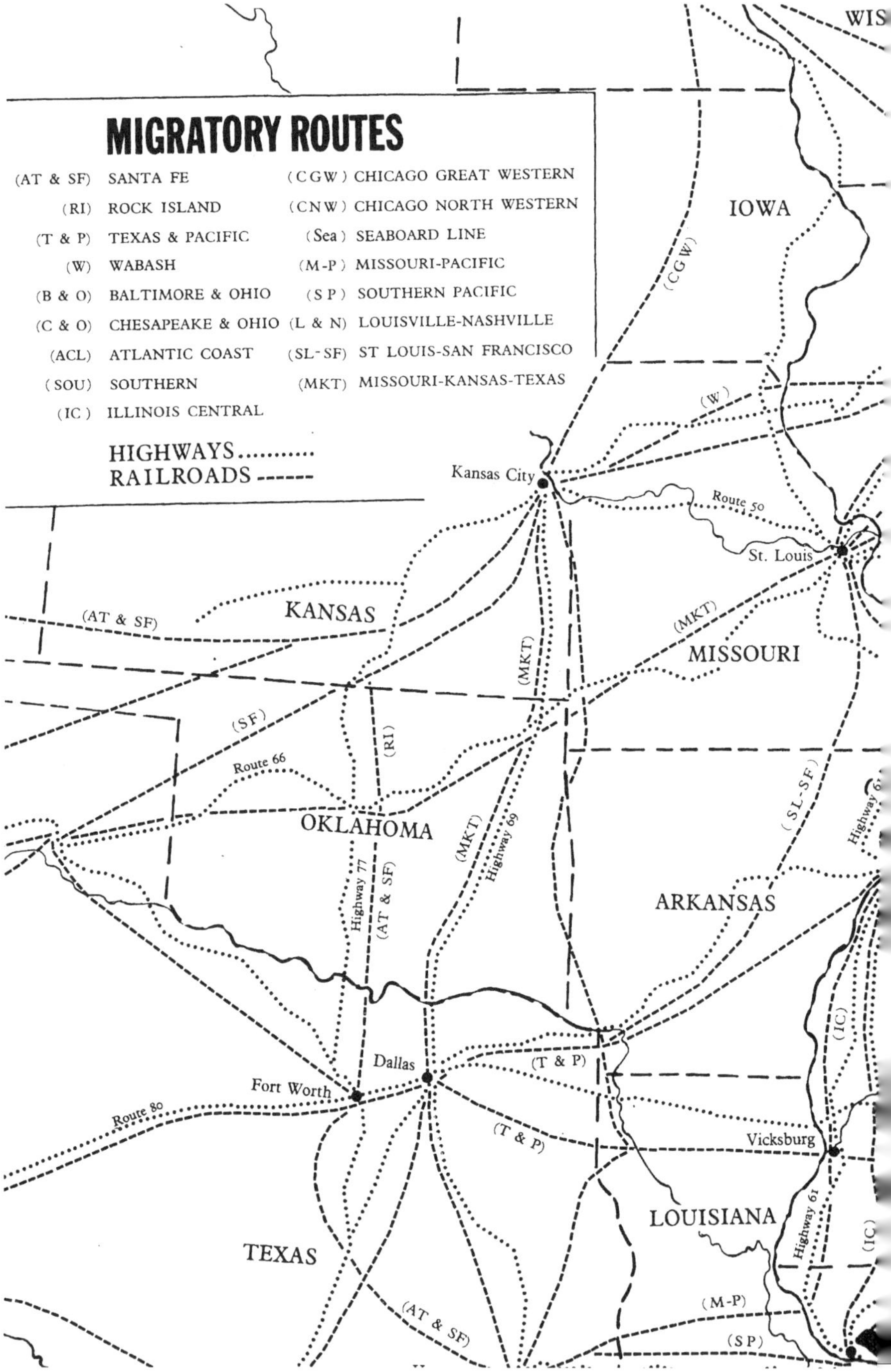

Figure 25. Migratory Routes on back inside cover of the book

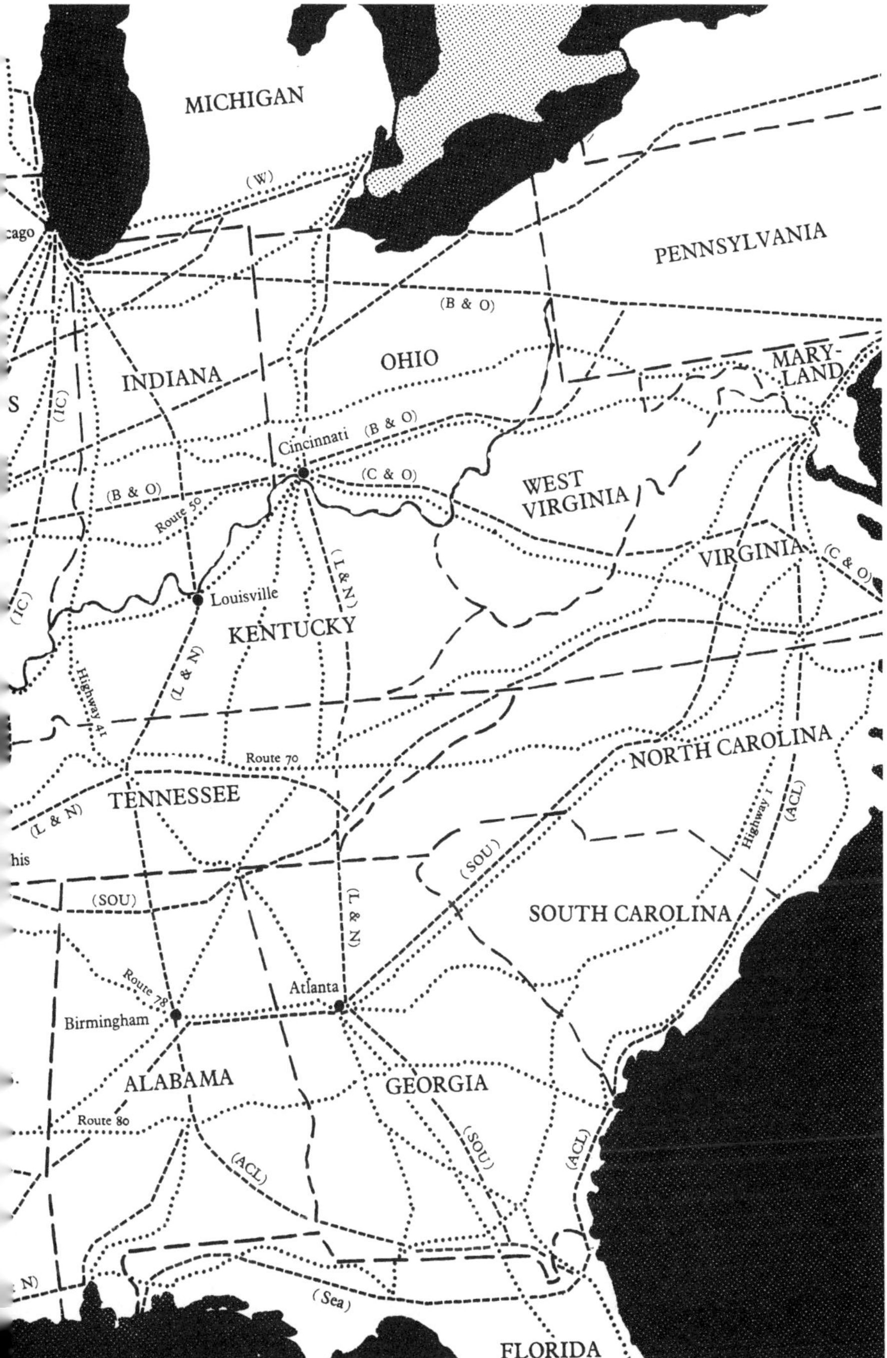
MICHIGAN
(W)
PENNSYLVANIA
(B & O)
OHIO
MARY-
LAND
INDIANA
(IC)
Cincinnati
(B & O)
(C & O)
(B & O)
Route 50
WEST
VIRGINIA
(L & N)
VIRGINIA
(C & O)
Louisville
KENTUCKY
(IC)
Highway 41
(L & N)
Route 70
NORTH CAROLINA
TENNESSEE
(L & N)
Highway 1
(ACL)
(SOU)
(SOU)
(L & N)
SOUTH CAROLINA
Route 78
Atlanta
Birmingham
ALABAMA
GEORGIA
Route 80
(ACL)
(SOU)
(ACL)
(Sea)
FLORIDA

Figure 26. Urban housing in the black ghettoes (FSA)

Figure 27. Images of "movement." (Top FSA; bottom USIS.)

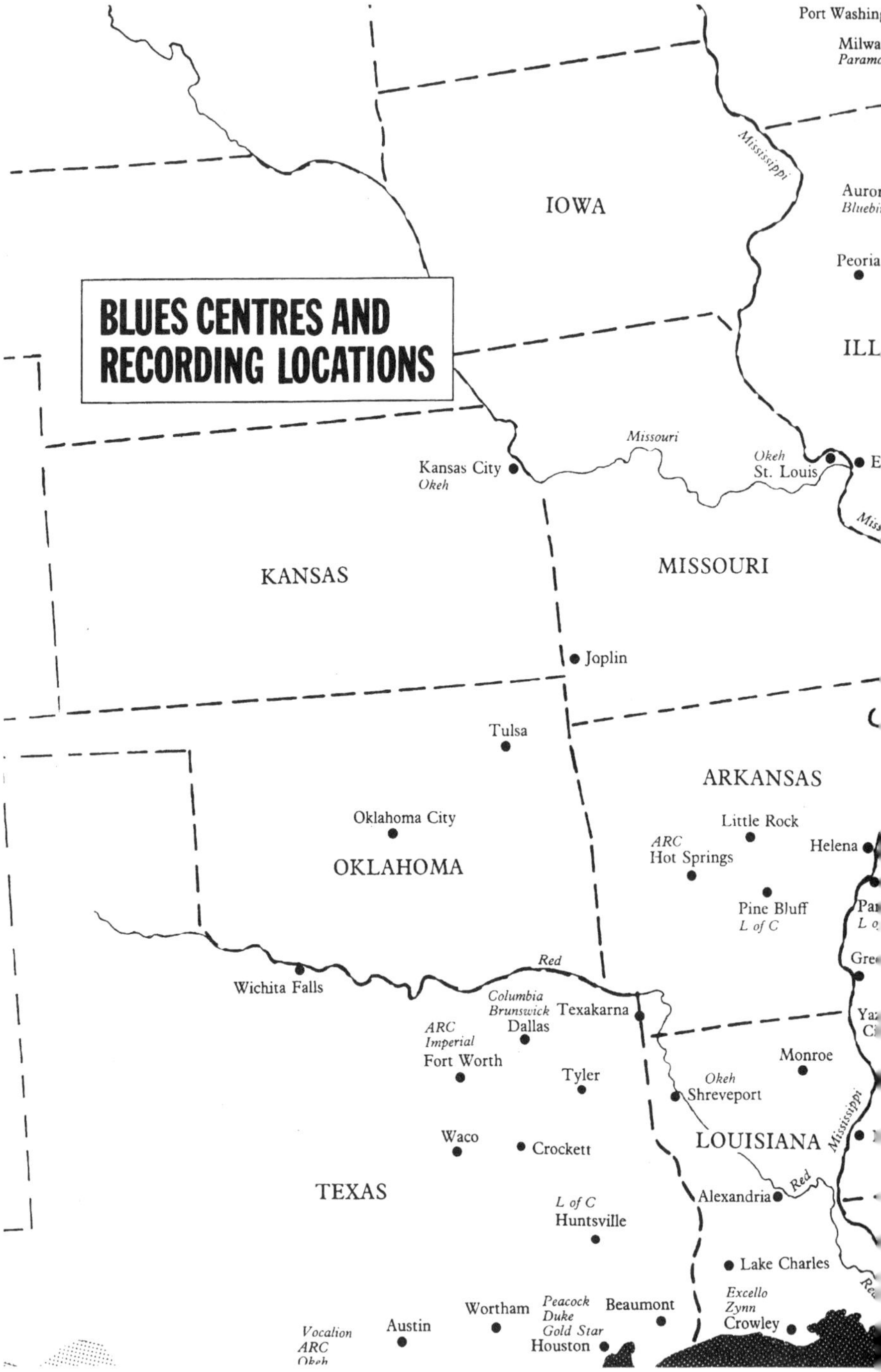

Figure 28. Blues Centres and Recording Locations on front inside cover

Detroit
J & B
Fortune
Modern
Cleveland
PENNSYLVANIA
Philadelphia
Gotham
Pittsburgh
Gary
OHIO
Baltimore
MARY-
LAND
Kokomo
Wabash
Columbus
Washington
Vocalion
Indianapolis
Ohio
King
De Luxe
Cincinnati
Richmond
Champion
Gennett
WEST
VIRGINIA
VIRGINIA
INDIANA
Lynchburg
Richmond
L of C
Louisville
Okeh
Victor
Ohio
Durham
KENTUCKY
Winston-Salem
Raleigh
L of C
Knoxville
NORTH CAROLINA
Charlotte
Bluebird
Nashville
Bullet
Excello
Spartanburg
TENNESSEE
Greenville
Chattanooga
SOUTH CAROLINA
Rome
Columbia
Okeh
ARC
Atlanta
Columbia
Vocalion
Charleston
Gennett
Birmingham
Macon
Statesboro
Savannah
Columbus
ALABAMA
GEORGIA
Selma
Montgomery
Federal
Waycross
Mobile
Tallahassee
Pensacola
Columbia
Victor
De Luxe
Biloxi
FLORIDA
Tampa

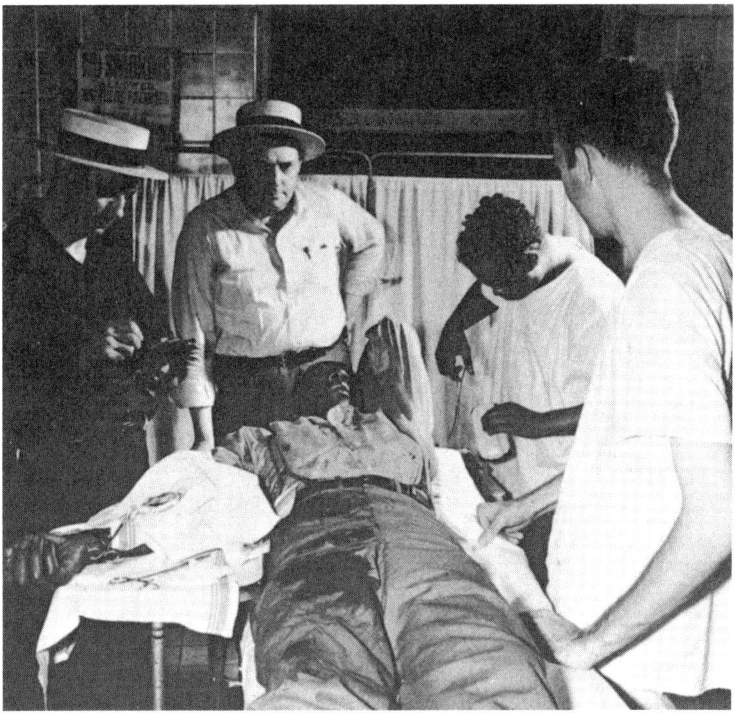

Figure 29. A man being treated in an emergency ward (FSA)

Figure 30. Downtown Atlanta (USIS)

Figure 31. Richmond, Virginia, in April 1865 (USIS)

Figure 32. The image is captioned by Oliver as "the slaves freed at the end of the Civil War looked uncertainly to the future." (New York Public Library.)

Figure 33. The picture is of workers in the fifties lining the rail tracks in Alabama under the watchful eye of the section boss in the background (Frederic Ramsey).

Figure 34. Picture of the Red Cross-maintained relief camps following the 1927 Mississippi flood (Library of Congress)

Figure 35. Families look on as a building is burning (FSA).

Figure 36. A man grieving at a grave site (FSA). Both figures 35 and 36 are captioned by Oliver as follows: "The blues mirrored Negro life in the 'twenties and 'thirties."

Figure 37. A black liquor store (FSA)

Figure 38. "Professional" portraits of (from left to right) Big Bill Broonzy, Georgia Tom, and Roosevelt Sykes. (Left and right Paul Oliver; center Philips Phonographische Industries)

Figure 39. Race records advertising (Nick Perls, Yazoo Records).

Afterword

Paul Oliver has had an enormous impact on blues scholarship in the last sixty years, and while this study has focused on his writing during the 1950s and 1960s, he has continued to work and publish on the subject of African American music throughout his life. Indeed, the year after *The Story of the Blues* was published, Oliver edited a series of "Blues Paperbacks" that included books by a number of now established blues scholars. The series began with Oliver's *Savannah Syncopators: African Retentions in Blues*, a work that John Baily praised for its innovative ethnomusicological approaches, which widened the narrow scope of existing research on the subject of African retentions.[1] It also represented the first of many attempts to establish links between the music of West Africa and the blues, including Sam Charters's *The Roots of the Blues: An African Search* (1981) and even Martin Scorsese's documentary starring musician Corey Harris, *Feel Like Going Home* (2003). While Oliver's book highlighted the interest in the origins of the blues at the end of the sixties, it is worth noting that in later years, as in *Songsters and Saints: Vocal Traditions on Race Records* (1984), he acknowledged that his focus on the blues, as well as the writing of other blues scholars from the revival, had resulted in the marginalization of a range of musical styles that were enjoyed and performed by African Americans in the early part of the twentieth century. He therefore examines the music of southern dances, the medicine shows, and the spirituals and gospel songs of the church congregations, and attempts to go some way to deconstructing the iconic figure of the "bluesman" by making the case that many "songsters and musicianers" had much more stylistically varied repertoires.[2] Despite Oliver's acknowledgment of the biases that had pervaded blues scholarship, including his own, the republication of *Blues Fell This Morning* (1990), *Conversation with the Blues* (1997), and *The Story of the Blues* (1997) indicates that the conceptualizations of the blues constructed during the revival were still prevalent and prominent more three decades later. The development and evolution of blues scholarship in the years after the revival are still deserving of further scholarly attention. Nonetheless, the focus of this study on Oliver's scholarship during the postwar revival was intended to contribute to the understanding the "invention" of the blues. By examining the work of the leading authority on the subject of the blues, I have aimed to locate Oliver in his rightful place—at the center of blues historiography—and in the process attempt to transcend discourses dominated by ideas of cultural ownership, whether based on notions of race or cultural nationalism, by highlighting the transatlantic nature of blues scholarship during the revival.

Paul Oliver and the "Invention' of the Blues

The lack of consideration for Oliver's scholarship in revisionist studies is surprising when one considers the ideological characteristics he shared with people like Alan Lomax, Samuel Charters, Frederic Ramsey, and even Hamilton's "blues mafia." All displayed a sense of distrust toward the music industry, harbored a nostalgic attachment to an imagined and idealized past, and exhibited a general discomfort with modernity. What differentiates Oliver is the wealth of his material available for scrutiny, and it is in his processes of interpreting and representing the music that it is possible to identify the manner in which the blues was invented. However, in Oliver's case, it is perhaps more accurate to say the blues was "reconstructed" rather than "invented." The author's conception of the blues was created in the small details rather than blatant fabrications or flights of fancy. It was built with the subtle uncertainties that lie between fact and fiction, between empirical evidence and nostalgia. In the fifties, when the blues was the interest of a small number of jazz enthusiasts who only heard the origins of jazz in the blues, the author examined the lyrics of records collected in Britain in the attempt to separate the genre from jazz. Stymied by a dearth of available documentation on the music, Oliver supplemented the information that lyrics provided with the imagery and descriptions drawn from African American literature. His representations of the blues in *Music Mirror* and *Jazz Journal* became intertwined with the memories of Richard Wright and Ralph Ellison, leading to the construction of ideas about the musical atavism of black Americans. This was also represented in a series of illustrations in which Oliver depicts his downtrodden subjects as emanating from another time. Throughout his articles, and more especially in *Blues Fell This*

Morning, Oliver used the candid and "direct" nature of lyrics to build images of an African American world that was devoid of the pretension of either modern or white middle-class culture. His semifictionalized passages, describing a particular situation pertaining to a song, continue to illustrate the manner in which the author imagined the world in which the blues had emerged.

The "imagined' confronted the "real" during his 1960 field trip to the United States. While Oliver declared that the land he visited and people he met had confirmed many of the hunches in *Blues Fell This Morning*, in *Conversation with the Blues* the reader is presented with a paradoxical world that combines memory and nostalgia with history and reality. In the oral responses of singers, memories of the past that included life experiences of toil, poverty, and deprivation are at once selected and prioritized, indicating that the world Oliver was searching for was that of the interwar era, rather than 1960. The photographs in *Conversation* strengthen the book's nostalgic attachment to the past by calling to mind the sociodocumentary-style black-and-white photography of the thirties. Importantly, they also begin to aestheticize distinct geographic locations, such as the cotton fields, sharecropper homes, levees, railroad lines, and urban ghettoes as being emblematic of blues culture, thus reifying the folkloric interpretation of the blues with specific "blues places." In his final two publications of the sixties, the author clarified that the blues was a music that belonged to an African American culture that was in the process of disappearing. By tracing a "tradition," Oliver at once categorized certain aesthetic qualities that separated the music from other genres and determined that authentic blues belonged to the past. In *The Story of the Blues*, the process of constructing a blues narrative along the lines of a triumph over tragedy, a human story of survival against the odds, contributed to its categorization as a unique musical genre, identifiable not only in its sonic and aesthetic characteristics but in its relationship to development of an African American society and culture that predated the civil rights era.

Oliver's scholarship in the fifties and sixties reveals the process by which events from the past are reconstructed into "histories." The retrospective character of blues writing, which entailed historical analysis of the meaning of lyrics, the exploration of memories in oral histories, the search for the reality of the black experience through historically significant places, and the formalization of a narrative that gave the blues a "story," contributed to the intermixture of historical fact and imagination that produced *a* blues. The sources Oliver used were similar to archaeological finds, fragments that pointed to a past culture, and what was missing was imagined to "reconstruct" Oliver's conception of the blues. Appreciating Oliver's role as an "author-historian" has made it possible to uncover the "reconstruction" of the blues through its representation in a number of texts: articles, illustrations, photographs, oral histories, and historical narratives. This reconstruction was determined by the social, cultural, and ideological context of his experiences in the postwar era. Having developed his early ideas about the blues while working within the British art school environment, and being influenced by traditionalist jazz writing and the work of folklorists, he espoused and evidenced the prevalent folkloric ideology that characterized the blues revival of the fifties and sixties. The blues is persistently championed as an expression of African American folk culture, and thus framed as antithetical to the entertainment business and music industry. Separating Oliver from many other blues writers in this regard was his considered appreciation of the blues' dual presence within the commercial music industry, and within the "folk" culture of African American society. Despite his acknowledgment of the biases that occur from the analysis of commercial records, Oliver's scholarship represented the efforts of blues scholars to continually define as "antimodern" a music that was inherently "modern": the music proliferated when record companies realized the economic opportunity of capitalizing on the African American appetite for music, and musicians developed individualized forms of expression and performance that operated within a range of shared musical styles. As Paul Gilroy argues in his chapter on black music and authenticity in *The Black Atlantic*, critics became ever more obsessed with origins and past meanings when they became ever more ungraspable.[3] Therefore, Oliver's scholarship indicates that ideas about the blues were "re-constructed" by re-creating an identifiable and suitable past that would be the antithesis of the commercial music industry, of entertainment, and of mainstream Western culture. At its heart, this past was distinctly racialized.

Race and Blues Scholarship

As I have argued throughout, Oliver's research was centered on the relationship between the blues and African American life. From his articles in the British jazz press to his major publications of the sixties, the story and meaning of the blues are intrinsically linked to the experiences of ordinary African Americans, particularly in the first half of the twentieth century: the music developed and "moved" along with the ebbs and flows of agricultural life of the South, the experiences of sharecropping and debt peonage, the Mississippi floods, Jim Crow segregation, the Depression of the thirties, and the migrations out of the South. There are two fundamental aspects to Oliver's conceptualizations of African American culture in his writing. First, the British author clearly evidences a fascination for working-class black culture, particularly in the fifties, when his descriptions of black life and of blues singers take on shades of romanticism, exoticism, and, at times, remnants of primitivism or 1920s "negrophilia." It is here that it becomes more complicated to place Oliver within the broader context of white European enthusiasm for black culture in the postwar era. According to Ulrich Adelt, "attempts by young white audiences to reject white middle-class culture, racism, colonialism, and fascism sometimes took form in a nostalgic re-creation of a safe blackness that predated the civil rights movement."[4] This identification of young white musicians with an idealized blackness that seemed to shun conventions, such as commercial success and pretension, can be identified in the fascination with gritty realism of the blues. In the BBC4's documentary *Blues Britannia*, the English musician John Mayall describes the British fascination with the blues in the sixties: "The main charm about the blues is that it has such an authenticity about it, the fact that when you listen to it, you hear the stories and you can visualize that these are real stories."[5] While musicians would feel some form of kinship with blues singers through the act of replicating the music, in Oliver's scholarship this is not possible. The author did not believe that whites could adequately reproduce the music they revered, and in this conviction effectively segregated the music based on the racial and cultural aspects of African American culture. He summarized this in *The Story of the Blues* by stating that whites did not have the quality of "soul," the innate and unspeakable characteristic that separates the imitation from the real. The memories of singers in *Conversation with the Blues* testify to their lived experience that is depicted as a fundamental aspect of the music. The language that is used to reinforce this motif oscillates between racial and class-based distinctions. When the blues is under attack from within the African American domain, from music that is considered more commercial, or not of the tradition, Oliver relies on descriptions that frame the blues' working-class and folk character, as the music of the "ordinary Negro," in order to establish its place within the totality of black culture. On the other hand, as the world of mainstream and white popular music begin to appropriate the blues in the postwar era, Oliver's language shifts toward more racialized tones, sometimes relying on stereotypical assumptions of innate and atavistic musicality, and in others justifying the black experience of segregation and discrimination as the factor determining cultural differences with the white world. Essentially, Oliver's language in explaining African American life, while evidencing a more moralistic tone in *Blues Fell This Morning* (particularly in the explanation that segregation and racism were the causes of major incomprehensions of black culture), is never too involved politically to challenge the condition of blacks in America, or to support civil rights. Instead, it tends to focus on what Adelt terms a "safe blackness" that was idealized by European blues aficionados. They envisioned a culture that was distant from the mainstream, more obscure from the perspective of white observers, but therefore also more easily available for misinterpretation.

Importantly, the process of describing the intricate relationship between the blues and the African American experience of the pre-civil rights generation highlights the second aspect of Oliver's ideas on race. By drawing a line between blues culture and postwar African American social and political activism, he tended to focus on a more accommodationist and sometimes fatalist black consciousness. And reading Oliver's descriptions of black life in the South, one can understand why some African American critics of the late sixties saw in the blues an expression that was akin to a "black slave lament" that had little relevance to Black Power or any sense of social and political empowerment. Paradoxically, however, Oliver's writing also preceded the thoughts of many African American writers of the Black Arts movement who saw a vibrant form of expression and an active cultural consciousness in the blues of the interwar years. While many black theorists and writers would challenge the notion that any white or European observers could fully understand and represent this distinctly African American music, and take exception to the fact the blues was a means of safely displacing repressed white fantasies, their objectives in arguing that the blues was socially and culturally significant for the African American were the same as Oliver's. Thus, Oliver does not display an affinity for "safe blackness" to displace his own desires, as much as take an interest in the vitality, beauty, and social significance of a "folk" culture.

The Transatlantic

If Oliver shares so many ideological characteristics with figures such as Alan Lomax, Samuel Charters, Frederic Ramsey, and a large proportion of writers of the Black Arts movement, then the question arises: what is the significance of transatlantic blues scholarship? As this study has argued from the very beginning, blues historiography has been plagued with notions of cultural nationalism and perhaps more understandably (given the social and racial cauldron that is American society) ethnocentrism, leading to clichéd questions such as, can white people sing the blues? And can white people understand the blues? It is hoped that this study has gone some way to demonstrating that, contrary to popular belief, blues scholarship did not emerge and develop along nationally divided lines. While most writing on the blues was carried out by whites—and this has had a determining impact on the interpretation of the blues—Oliver's scholarship demonstrates (along with the emerging scholarship on the transatlantic diffusion of African American culture) that ideas and conceptualizations were actively constructed in a transnational context.[6] There was widespread cooperation among folklorists and collectors during the fifties and sixties, and the major differences characterizing their work were on the basis of diverging aesthetic categorizations of authenticity. In addition, Oliver's use of commercial recordings prior to his first visit to the United States was not an indicator of the special predicament of non-American blues appreciation. After all, despite the increased opportunities of actually visiting the South and seeking out musicians, American blues researchers also were forced to rely on recordings. Separation into national (i.e., British or American) or racial categories (black versus white) has been imposed on the historiographical examination of blues scholarship by writers keen to defend American music from foreign invaders, or ensure African American music is not diluted by white cultural colonialism. More importantly, these debates do little to aid our understanding of the means by which music described as blues came to play such an important role in the development of Western popular music in the twentieth century. Perhaps the grasping of racial and nationalistic categories supports the articulations of writers such as Eric Hobsbawm and Paul Gilroy who in different terms suggest that the search for the past in terms of origins, significance, and traditions is symptomatic of a contemporary sense of cultural crisis.

It may never be fully possible to explain the British or European fascination for the blues, although it must be always be remembered that interest in the music is at some level always dictated by the aural experience of sound, and that no scholar would have ever written about the blues, put very simply, if they did not like it. Despite the fact considerable scholarship concentrates on the meaning of lyrics and the social function of the blues within African American communities, as Albert Murray argued, "the chances are that most of their [(scholars')] goose pimples and all of their finger snapping and foot tapping are produced by the sound far more than by the meanings of the words."[7] It is therefore important to recognize that white interest in the blues during the revival was initially spurred by this sensory experience, and all subsequent interpretations of race and politics were developed at a secondary stage. Nonetheless, Oliver's blues scholarship demonstrates that "invention," or the romantic interpretation of early twentieth-century African American culture as antimodern, unpretentious, and uncomplicated by the whims of the Western world, was inherently part of the process of blues writing during the revival. In other words, the "revival" of the blues constituted the "invention" of the blues. Misrepresentations of the blues—in the exaggeration of folkloric myths, or the privileging of certain blues forms over others that were closer to an imagined "tradition"—occurred even in the most carefully considered studies. Indeed, while some readers may regard this study as a criticism of Oliver's scholarship, I argue clearly that his work remains among the most important and influential in the field. However, an alternative reading of his writing on the blues gives us a window from which to understand the nature of the blues revival, and gain insights into the processes of "discovery" and "rediscovery." In this light it is possible to consider blues scholarship of the 1950s and 1960s as an example of the way in which representations of the past, like the popular representations of Native Americans or the Tudors, can be exaggerated, manipulated, or "invented" by the processes of looking backward and *doing* history.

Notes

Introduction

1. Quoted in *The Paul Oliver 70th Birthday Tribute*, www.bluesworld.com/PAULOLIVER.HTML, retrieved 22 August 2009; although the term was coined in a pejorative sense, this will be discussed in chapter 2.

2. Elijah Wald, *Escaping the Delta: Robert Johnson and the Invention of the Blues* (New York: Amistad, 2004); Marybeth Hamilton, *In Search of the Blues: Black Voices, White Visions* (London: Jonathan Cape, 2007).

3. George Lipsitz, *Time Passages: Collective Memory and American Popular Culture* (Minneapolis: University of Minnesota Press, 1990 [*sic*] 1994), p. 18.

4. Robert Palmer, *Deep Blues: A Musical and Cultural History, from the Mississippi Delta to Chicago's South Side to the World* (Harmondsworth: Penguin, 1981), p. 17.

5. Leon F. Litwack, *Trouble in Mind: Black Southerners in the Age of Jim Crow* (New York: Alfred A. Knopf, 1999), p. 452.

6. *The Mississippi Blues Trail*, http://msbluestrail.org/.

7. "poorest" and "blackest" in William Barlow, *Looking Up at Down: The Emergence of Blues Culture* (Philadelphia: Temple University Press, 1989), pp. 26–27.

8. Ted Gioia, *Delta Blues: The Life and Times of the Mississippi Masters* (London: Norton, 2008), p. 2.

9. Hamilton, *In Search of the Blues*, p. 9.

10. Seasick Steve's appearance on British TV in October 2009, retrieved from http://news.bbc.co.uk/1/hi/entertainment/8310377.stm on 5 April 2011 at 12:30 p.m.

11. Jeff Todd Titon, "Reconstructing the Blues: Reflections on the 1960s Blues Revival," in N. V. Rosenberg, ed., *Transforming Tradition: Folk Music Revivals Examined* (Urbana: University of Illinois Press, 1993), pp. 222–23.

12. Scott DeVeaux, "Constructing the Jazz Tradition: Jazz Historiography," *Black American Literature Forum*, vol. 25, no. 3, Fall 1991, pp. 525–60; Richard A. Peterson, *Creating Country Music: Fabricating Authenticity* (Chicago: University of Chicago Press, 1999); Karl Hagstrom Miller, *Segregating Sound: Inventing Folk and Pop Music in the Age of Jim Crow* (Durham: Duke University Press, 2010).

13. Wald, *Escaping the Delta*, p. xxii.

14. Hamilton, *In Search of the Blues*, p. 3.

15. Wald, *Escaping the Delta*, p. xxiii.

16. Hamilton, *In Search of the Blues*, p. 18.

17. Charles Keil, *Urban Blues* (Chicago: University of Chicago Press, 1966), pp. 34–35; Keil explains "moldy figs" as a term that was used by more modern jazz musicians and critics to describe those who defined jazz strictly as a music from New Orleans and the prewar era.

18. Albert Murray, *Stomping the Blues* (London: Quartet Books, 1975), pp. 203, 208.

19. Miller, *Segregating Sound*, pp. 6–10.

20. Titon, "Reconstructing the Blues," p. 223.

21. David Evans, *Big Road Blues: Tradition and Creativity in the Folk Blues* (Berkeley: University of California Press, 1982), p. 309.

22. Robin D. G. Kelley, "Notes on 'Deconstructing the Folk,'" *American Historical Review*, vol. 97, no. 5, December 1992, pp. 1400–1408.

23. Benjamin Filene, *Romancing the Folk: Public Memory and American Roots Music* (Chapel Hill: University of North Carolina Press, 2000), p. 77.

24. David G. Nicholls, *Conjuring the Folk: Forms of Modernity in African America* (Ann Arbor: University of Michigan Press, 2000), p. 5.

25. Hamilton, *In Search of the Blues*, p. 24; Hamilton uses the scholarship of Howard Odum (such as Howard B. Odum and Guy Johnson's *Negro Workaday Songs* [Chapel Hill: University of North Carolina Press, 1926]) in the first quarter of the twentieth century as a more reliable historical source than Handy's recollections in the autobiography, *Father of the Blues*, which was published in 1941.

26. Wald, *Escaping the Delta*, p. xv.

27. Hamilton, *In Search of the Blues*, pp. 9–10, 193.

28. Filene, *Romancing the Folk*, p. 5.

29. Ibid., p. 131.

30. Roberta Freund Schwartz, *How Britain Got the Blues: The Transmission and Reception of American Style Blues in the United Kingdom* (Aldershot: Ashgate, 2007); Ulrich Adelt, *Blues Music in the Sixties: A Story in Black and White* (New Brunswick: Rutgers University Press, 2010): in chapter 4 Adelt considers the conceptualization of race in Horst Lippmann and Fritz Rau's American Folk and Blues Festivals in Europe throughout the sixties and seventies; and edited collections such as Neil A. Wynn, ed., *Cross the Water Blues: African American Music in Europe* (Jackson: University Press of Mississippi, 2007) and Neil Wynn and Jill Terry, eds., *Transatlantic Roots Music: Folk, Blues, and National Identities* (Jackson: University Press of Mississippi, 2012).

31. Michael Bane, *White Boy Singin' the Blues: The Black Roots of White Rock* (Harmondsworth: Penguin, 1982), p. 156.

32. Wald, *Escaping the Delta*, pp. 245, 221.

33. "heads beaten" in Jon Michael Spencer, "Blues and Evil: Theomusicology and Afrocentricity," in Robert Sacre, ed., *Saints and Sinners: Religion, Blues and (D)evil in African-American Music and Literature* (Liège: Société Liégeoise de Musicologie, 1996), p. 47; "what it means to be black" in Jon Michael Spencer, *Blues and Evil* (Knoxville: University of Tennessee Press, 1993), p. xxv.

34. This is dealt with at length in Adam Gussow, "'If Bessie Smith Had Killed Some White People': Racial Legacies, the Blues Revival, and the Black Arts Movement," in Lisa Gail Collins and Margo Natalie Crawford, eds., *New Thoughts on the Black Arts Movement* (New Brunswick: Rutgers University Press, 2006), pp. 227–52.

35. James H. Cone, *The Spirituals and the Blues* (New York: Seabury, 1972); Murray, *Stomping the Blues*, p. 50; Samuel A. Floyd Jr., *The Power of Black Music: Interpreting Its History from Africa to the United States* (Oxford: Oxford University Press, 1995), p. 78.

36. *Blues Britannia: Can Blue Men Sing the Whites?* BBC4, 11:00 p.m., 9 December 2011, Chris Rodley (2009).

37. Peter Hall, *Cities in Civilization* (London: Weidenfeld & Nicolson, 1998), p. 601.

38. David Horn, "Introduction," *Popular Music*, vol. 26, no. 1, 2006, pp. 1–4, 6.

39. John Szwed, *The Man Who Recorded the World: A Biography of Alan Lomax* (London: William Heinemann, 2010), p. 3.

40. *Paul Oliver 70th Birthday Tribute.*

41. Roberta Freund Schwartz, "Preaching the Gospel of the Blues: Blues Evangelists in Britain," in Wynn, *Cross the Water Blues*, pp. 145–66; Wald, *Escaping the Delta*, p. 249; Hamilton, *In Search of the Blues*, p. 8; Palmer, *Deep Blues*, p. xvii.

42. Alun Munslow, *Deconstructing History* (London: Routledge, 1997), p. 102.

43. David Evans, ed., *Ramblin' on My Mind: New Perspectives on the Blues* (Urbana: University of Illinois Press, 2008); Peter Muir, *Long Lost Blues: Popular Music in America, 1850–1920* (Urbana: University of Illinois Press, 2009).

44. Hamilton, *In Search of the Blues*, p. 1.

45. Hayden White, "Historical Text as Literary Artifact," in *Tropics of Discourse: Essays in Cultural Criticism* (London: John Hopkins University Press, 1978).

46. Richard Middleton, *Studying Popular Music* (Milton Keynes: Open University Press, 1990), p. 14.

47. Lipsitz, *Time Passages*, p. 5.

48. Paul Gilroy, *The Black Atlantic: Modernity and Double Consciousness* (London: Verso, 1993), pp. 73–74.

49. Simon Frith and Howard Horne, *Art into Pop* (New York: Methuen, 1987), p. 74.

50. Gussow, "If Bessie Smith Had Killed," pp. 231–32: Gussow was referring to Frantz Fanon's *Toward the African Revolution* (1967) and Ron Karenga's article "Black Art: A Rhythmic Reality of Revolution," *Negro Digest*, vol. 17, no. 3, January 1968.

51. Houston A. Baker Jr., *Blues, Ideology and Afro-American Literature: A Vernacular Theory* (Chicago: University of Chicago Press, 1984), p. 3; *Black Wax: Gil Scott-Heron*, Robert Mugge (1982), Sky Arts 1, 10:00 p.m., 9 July 2012.

52. Wald, *Escaping the Delta*, p. 249; Oliver has continued to publish on the subject throughout his career.

53. Adelt, *Blues Music in the Sixties*, p. 114.

54. Alessandro Portelli, "What Makes Oral History Different," in Robert Perks and Alistair Thompson, eds., *The Oral History Reader* (London: Routledge, 1998), p. 67.

55. Paul Oliver, *Conversation with the Blues* (Cambridge University Press, 1965 [*sic*] 1997), p. xiv.

Chapter 1

1. Paul Oliver, *Blues off the Record: Thirty Years of Blues Commentary* (Tunbridge Wells: Batton Press, 1984), pp. 2–3.

2. W. C. Handy, *Father of the Blues: An Autobiography* (New York: Macmillan, 1941).

3. Wynn, *Cross the Water Blues*, p. 12.

4. "part-time degree" in John Baily, "Paul Oliver's Contribution to Ethnomusicology," *Popular Music*, vol. 26, no. 1, 2006, p. 16.

5. Oliver, *Blues off the Record*, p. 58.

6. Andrew Kellett, "Born in Chicago: The Impact of the Paul Butterfield Blues Band on the British Blues 'Network,' 1964–1970," in Wynn and Terry, *Transatlantic Roots Music*, p. 182.

7. "A Conversation with Paul Oliver," Bob Garratt, 2 June 2004, Harrow County Staff website, http://www.jeffreymaynard.com/Harrow_County/POliver.htm, retrieved 1 June 2012, 4:32 p.m.

8. These *Blues Paperbacks* were published by Studio Vista between 1970 and 1971.

9. Horn, "Introduction," p. 1.

10. "a break" in Oliver, *Blues off the Record*, p. 5; for a more detailed bibliography of Oliver's work see Robert Ford, "Paul Oliver: A Selective Bibliography," *Popular Music*, vol. 26, no. 1, 2006, pp. 157–86.

11. Frith and Horne, *Art into Pop*, p. 75.

12. Ibid., p. 71.

13. Ibid., p. 78.

14. Simon Frith, *Performing Rites: Evaluating Popular Music* (New York: Oxford University Press, 1996 [*sic*] 2002), pp. 88, 94.

15. *Blues Britannia: Can Blue Men Sing the Whites?* BBC4, 11:00 p.m, 9 December 2011, Chris Rodley (2009), "crying out" and "gutless" are the words of Chris Barber.

16. Catherine Parsonage, "Fascination and Fear: Responses to Early Jazz in Britain," in Wynn, *Cross the Water Blues*, pp. 97–98.

17. E. Simms Campbell, "Blues," in Frederic Ramsey and Charles Edwards Smith, eds., *Jazzmen* (London: Harcourt Brace Jovanovich, 1939), p. 110.

18. Rudi Blesh, *Shining Trumpets: A History of Jazz* (London: Cassell, 1949), p. 101; Mezz Mezzrow with Bernard Wolfe, *Really the Blues* (London: Corgi, 1946 [*sic*] 1961), p. 23.

19. Mike Dewe, *The Skiffle Craze* (Aberystwyth: Planet, 1998), p. 3.

20. Albert McCarthy, ed., *The PL Yearbook of Jazz* (London: Hutchison, 1946), p. vii.

21. Iain Lang, *Jazz in Perspective: The Background of the Blues* (London: Hutchison, 1947), pp. 104, 122.

22. Schwartz, *How Britain Got the Blues*, pp. 20–21.

23. Lang, *Jazz in Perspective*, p. 102.

24. Max Jones, "On Blues," in McCarthy, *PL Yearbook of Jazz*, p. 73: Jones explicitly stated that the blues "relate much of the Negro's social experiences in the Southern states," p. 86; "peak period," p. 104.

25. Francis Newton, *The Jazz Scene* (Harmondsworth: Penguin, 1958 [*sic*] 1961), pp. 3, 8; Newton could be seen as voicing concerns about mass popular culture similar to those expressed by the cultural theorist Richard Hoggart in *The Uses of Literacy* (London: Chatto and Windus, 1957).

26. Georgina Boyes, *The Imagined Village: Culture, Ideology, and the English Folk Revival* (Manchester: Manchester University Press, 1993), p. 198.

27. Michael Brocken, *The British Folk Revival, 1944–2002* (Aldershot: Ashgate, 2003), p. 20.

28. Szwed, *Man Who Recorded the World*, pp. 254–59.

29. "archaic" is taken from Rex Harris's description of blues in his booklet *Jazz* (London: Penguin, 1952).

30. Interview by the author, appendix 1.1, p. 293.

31. Schwartz, "Preaching the Gospel," p. 145.

32. Schwartz, *How Britain Got the Blues*, pp. 25–26.

33. Max Jones and Rex Harris, "Collector's Corner," *Melody Maker*, 1 December 1946, p. 4; 26 January 1946, p. 4; 27 April 1946, p. 4.

34. Derrick Stewart-Baxter, "Preachin' the Blues," *Jazz Journal*, vol. 5, no. 1, January 1952, pp. 6–7.

35. Paul Oliver, "Screening the Blues," *Jazz Monthly*, vol. 5, no. 12, February 1960, pp. 26–27.

36. Jeff Smith, "Folk Music Branches Out," *Melody Maker*, 21 November 21 1959, p. 13; Schwartz, *How Britain Got the Blues*, p. 86.

37. Audit Bureau of Circulations, 1949–1961 (London: England, 1961).

38. Oliver, *Blues off the Record*, p. 4.

39. Dewe, *The Skiffle Craze*, p. 53; interview by the author, 17 November 2009, appendix 1.1, p. 293.

40. Schwartz, *How Britain Got the Blues*, p. 33.

41. Oliver, "Talking Blues," in *Blues off the Record*, p. 208, quoted in Schwartz, *How Britain Got the Blues*, p. 27.

42. Interestingly, objectivity is a characteristic that Oliver has often been praised for (see Evans, *Paul Oliver 70th Birthday Tribute*).

43. Oliver, *Blues off the Record*, p. 2.

44. Hamilton, *In Search of the Blues*, p. 3.

45. Ralph Ellison, "Remembering Jimmy," *Jazz Journal*, vol. 11, no. 11, November 1958, pp. 10–11 and "The Charlie Christian Story," *Jazz Journal*, vol. 12, no. 5, May 1959, pp. 7–8.

46. Interview by the author, 26 November 2009, appendix 1.2, p. 304; Jacques Demetre and Marcel Chauvard, "Land of Blues," *Jazz Journal*, vol. 13, nos. 3, 5, 7–10, 1960.

47. The term "Negro" was used at Oliver's time of writing as the term "African American" is used in the present day, and in revised editions of his works it was substituted for the term "black." The use of the term "Negro" here is only to represent Oliver's work accurately and consistently, and in order to avoid confusion.

48. Oliver, "Match Box Blues: Blind Lemon Jefferson," *Jazz Review*, July 1959, in *Blues off the Record*, p. 69; Oliver, "Give Me That Old Time Religion," *Jazz Journal*, February 1952, in *Blues off the Record*, pp. 14–15; Oliver, "Match Box Blues," p. 69.

49. Oliver, "Peetie Wheatstraw: Devil's Son-In-Law," *Jazz Monthly*, May 1959, in *Blues off the Record*, p 193.

50. Wright, "Foreword," to *Blues Fell This Morning: The Meaning of the Blues*, by Paul Oliver (London: Cassell, 1960), p. 11; the personal notebooks were made available to the author by Paul Oliver.

51. Yearly visits to Paris, interview by the author, 1 June 2010, appendix 1.4, p. 329.

52. Richard Wright, *Native Son* (Harmondsworth: Penguin, 1940), p. 15; meeting Hughes and Mezzrow, and influence of Parisian experiences in Oliver, *Blues off the Record*, p. 10.

53. Paul Oliver, "Devil's Son-in-Law," *Music Mirror*, vol. 2, no. 2, March 1956, p. 8.

54. John Lowe, "Palette of Fire: The Aesthetics of Propaganda in *Black Boy* and *In the Castle of My Skin*," *Mississippi Quarterly*, vol. 61, no. 4, Fall 2008, p. 565.

55. Ralph Ellison, *Invisible Man* (Harmondsworth: Penguin, 1952), p. 141.

56. Raymond M. Olderman, "Ralph Ellison's Blues and 'Invisible Man,'" *Wisconsin Studies in Contemporary Literature*, vol. 6, no. 2, Summer 1966, p. 11.

57. Oliver, "Give Me That Old Time Religion," p. 15; Oliver, "Strut Yo' Stuff," *Music Mirror*, vol. 2, no. 3, March 1955, p. 4; Oliver, "Muddy Waters: Hoochie Coochie Man," *Jazz Monthly*, January 1959, in *Blues off the Record*, p. 259.

58. Quote from Jones, "On Blues," p. 79.

59. Oliver, "Sources of Afro-American Folk Song 1: Down the Line," *Music Mirror*, vol. 1, no. 1, May 1954, p. 42; Oliver, "In the Sticks," *Music Mirror*, vol. 2, no. 4, April 1955, p. 4. The references here are to the female singers such as "Ma" Rainey who, although more involved with the world of entertainment, are praised by Oliver for retaining the quality of singing the "music of their people".

60. Oliver, "Got the Blues," *Music Mirror*, vol. 2, no. 5, May 1955, p. 8.

61. Cone, *The Spirituals and the Blues*, p. 125.

62. "Negrophilia" is a term that emanates from the French fascination with figures such as Josephine Baker who represented the craze for African American music in Paris during the 1920s. Iris Schmeisser, "'Un Saxophone en Mouvement'? Josephine Baker and the Primitivist Reception of Jazz in Paris in the 1920s," in Wynn, *Cross the Water Blues*, p. 111.

63. Robin Kelley, "'We Are Not What We Seem': Rethinking Black Working-Class Opposition in the Jim Crow South," *Journal of American History*, vol. 80, no. 1, June 1993, pp. 75–112.

64. Oliver, "Sources of Afro-American Folk Song 1," p. 42; Oliver, "Strut Yo' Stuff," p. 4; Oliver, "Match Box Blues," p. 66.

65. Middleton, *Studying Popular Music*, p. 128.

66. Paul Oliver, *Bessie Smith* (London: Cassell, 1958), p. 6.

67. Oliver, "Devil's Son-in-Law," p. 9.

68. Oliver, "Rock Island Line," *Music Mirror*, vol. 4, no. 1, January 1957, pp. 6–8.

69. Oliver, "Got the Blues," p. 8.

70. Rod Gruver, "A Closer Look at the Blues," *Blues World*, vol. 4, no. 26, January 1970, pp. 4–10; Oliver, "Got the Blues," p. 10.

71. Oliver, "Chocolate to the Bone," *Music Mirror*, vol. 1, no. 7, November 1954, p. 41.

72. Richard Wright, *Black Boy: A Record of Childhood and Youth* (London: Longman, 1945), pp. 136–37.

73. Richard Wright, *12 Million Black Voices* (New York: Basic Books, 2008 [*sic*] 1941).

74. Interview by the author, 26 November 2009, appendix 1.2, p. 304; Big Bill Broonzy and Yannick Bruynoghe, *Big Bill Blues* (London: Cassell, 1955); Rex Harris, "Jazz: New Music with Ancient Roots," *Radio Times*, July 27, 1956.

75. Robert L. Herbert, *From Millet to Leger: Essays in Social Art History* (London: Yale University Press, 2002), pp. 32–33, "primeval innocence," p. 61.

76. Steven Feld, "Communication, Music, and Speech about Music," in Charles Keil and Steven Feld, eds., *Music Grooves* (Chicago; University of Chicago Press, 1994), p. 84.

77. Paul Oliver, "Another Man Done Gone," *Music Mirror*, vol. 1, no. 4, August 1954, p. 27.

78. Oliver, "The Folk Blues of Sonny Terry," *Music Mirror*, vol. 2, no. 10, October 1955, p. 6; Oliver, "Introduction to Odetta: An Important New Folk and Blues Singer," *Jazz Music Mirror*, vol. 5, no. 7, April 1958, p. 6.

79. Nathan I. Huggins, *Harlem Renaissance* (London: Oxford University Press, 1971), p. 64.

80. David Levering Lewis, *When Harlem Was In Vogue* (Oxford: Oxford University Press, 1979), p. 173.

81. Anita Patterson, "Jazz, Realism and the Modernist Lyric: The Poetry of Langston Hughes," *Modern Language Quarterly*, vol. 61, no. 4, December 2000, p. 667.

82. Middleton, *Studying Popular Music*, p. 127; Oliver, "The Folk Blues of Sonny Terry," p. 6; Oliver, "Forgotten Men," *Music Mirror*, June 1956, 3/5, p. 9; Oliver, "Brownie McGhee and Sonny Terry," *Music Mirror*, June 1958, 5/11, p. 17.

83. Schwartz, *How Britain Got the Blues*, pp. 8–9.

84. List of musicians who came to Britain from Dewe, *The Skiffle Craze*, p. 37; Anticipation for Josh White's tour in *Melody Maker*, vol. 27, no. 906, 27 January 1951, p. 3; Albert McCarthy, "Lonnie Johnson," *Jazz Journal*, vol. 5, no. 6, June 1952, pp. 1–2; Derrick Stewart-Baxter, "A Date with the Blues," *Melody Maker*, vol. 27, no. 939, 15 September 1951, p. 9.

85. Titon, "Reconstructing the Blues, p. 223.

86. Elijah Wald, *Josh White: Society Blues* (Amherst: University of Massachusetts Press, 2000), p. 220; Max Jones, "Josh White Pleases the Mums and Dads," *Melody Maker*, vol. 27, no. 908, 10 February 1951, pp. 6, 9; pressure on White to play solo in *Melody Maker*, vol. 27, no. 912, 10 March 1951, p. 6.

87. Dora Lowenstein and Philip Dodd, eds., *According to the Rolling Stones* (London: Phoenix, 2003), p. 38.

88. Michael Gray, *The Bob Dylan Encyclopaedia* (London: Continuum, 2006), p. 365.

89. Tony Standish, "Muddy Waters in London—Part II," *Jazz Journal*, vol. 12, no. 2, February 1959, pp. 3–6.

90. Oliver, "How Long Blues," *Music Mirror*, vol. 3, no. 6, July 1956, pp. 4–6; Oliver, "Blue-Eyed Blues: The Impact of Blues on European Popular Culture," in C. W. E. Bigsby, ed., *Approaches to Popular Culture* (Bowling Green: Bowling Green University Popular Press, 1976), p. 230.

91. Les Pythian in Stewart-Baxter, "Preachin' the Blues," pp. 6–7; Hugues Panassie, "A Date with the Blues," *Melody Maker*, vol. 27, no. 939, September 1951, p. 9.

92. "it's fortunate" in Arthur Jackson, "Review of Big Bill Bronzy in Cambridge," *Jazz Journal*, vol. 5, no. 12, December 1952, p. 3; "his hollering" in Oliver, "Blue-Eyed Blues," p. 231.

93. Interview by the author, 11 March 2010, appendix 1.3, p. 317.

94. "held audiences" in Oliver, "Blue-Eyed Blues," p. 231; Alexis Korner, "Big Bill Broonzy: Some Personal Memories," *Jazz Journal*, vol. 11, no. 3, March 1958, p. 1; Harry Shapiro, *Alexis Korner: The Biography* (London: Bloomsbury, 1996), p. 61; Big Bill cooking at the Olivers, interview by the author, 11 March 2010, appendix 1.3, p. 317.

95. Roger House, *Blue Smoke: The Recorded Journey of Big Bill Broonzy* (Baton Rouge: Louisiana State University Press, 2010), p. 145.

96. Wald, *Josh White*, p. 221; Bob Riesman, *I Feel So Good: The Life and Times of Big Bill Broonzy* (Chicago: University of Chicago Press, 2011), pp. 164–65.

97. Interview by the author, 17 June 2011, appendix 1.9, p. 395.

98. Broonzy as a blues historian, Riesman, *I Feel So Good*, p. 164; Broonzy mentioning Waters, interview by the author, appendix 1.3, p. 317; Oliver, "Blues Backstage," *Music Mirror*, vol. 4, no. 4, May 1957, p. 23; Oliver, "Forgotten Men," p. 9.

99. Interview by the author, 17 November 2009, appendix 1.1, p. 293.

100. Interview by the author, 11 March 2010, appendix 1.3, p. 317.

101. Oliver, "Special Agents: How the Blues Got on Record," *Jazz Review*, February 1959, in *Blues off the Record*, p. 48; "golden rule," Oliver, "Big Bill Broonzy on Vogue," *Music Mirror*, vol. 3, no. 7, August 1956, p. 4.

102. Riesman, *I Feel So Good*, p. 165.

103. "fascination," Oliver, "Problems of Collecting Race Records," p. 14; Oliver, "We're Gonna Rock This Joint: Jimmy Rushing's Early Years," *Jazz Monthly*, December 1957, in *Blues off the Record*, p. 146.

104. Tona Hangen, "Man of the Hour: Walter A. Maier and Religion by Radio on the Lutheran Hour," in M. Hilmes and J. Loviglio, eds., *Radio Reader: Essays in the Cultural History of Radio* (London: Routledge, 2002), pp. 113–34.

105. Oliver, "Forgotten Men," p. 8.

106. For more detail about Robert Johnson's lack of commercial success see Wald, *Escaping the Delta*.

107. Brian Ward, *Just My Soul Responding: Rhythm and Blues, Black Consciousness and Race Relations* (Berkeley: University of California Press, 1998), p. 1.

108. Dewe, *The Skiffle Craze*, pp. 58–59.

109. Derrick Stewart-Baxter, "Blues in the Country," *Jazz Journal*, vol. 12, no. 4, April 1959, p. 3.

110. Interview by the author, 17 June 2011, appendix 1.9, pp. 395–96.

111. Dewe, *The Skiffle Craze*, pp. 1, 22; McGuiness, interview by the author, 17 June 2011, appendix 1.9, p 395.

112. "imitation," Oliver, "Blues Backstage," p. 23; Oliver, "Hometown Skiffle," *Music Mirror*, vol. 3, no. 11, February 1956, p. 9.

113. Oliver, "Blue-Eyed Blues," p. 231.

114. The term "blues evangelists" is taken from Schwartz's article subtitle in "Preaching the Gospel"; Schwartz, *How Britain Got the Blues*, p. 40.

115. Oliver, "Introduction to Odetta," p. 6.

116. Max Jones, "Blues from the Gutter," *Melody Maker*, December 19, 1959, p. 25.

117. W. E. B. DuBois, *The Souls of Black Folk* (London: Penguin, 1903), p. 206; Alain Locke, *The Negro and His Music* (Port Washington: Kennikat Press, 1936).

118. Oliver, "Problems of Collecting Race Records," *Music Mirror*, vol. 2, no. 9, September 1955, p. 13.

119. Oliver, "Match Box Blues," p. 69.

120. Oliver, "Devil's Son-in-Law," p. 9.

121. B. A. Botkin, in the *New York Times Book Review*, quoted on reverse of *The Meaning of the Blues*.

122. These ideas are explored at length in Wald and Hamilton.

Chapter 2

1. Paul Oliver in "A Conversation with Paul Oliver," Bob Garratt, 2 June 2004, Harrow County Staff, http://www.jeffreymaynard.com/Harrow_County/POliver.htm, retrieved 16 June 2012, 4:32 p.m.; interview by the author, 18 November 2009, appendix 1.10, p. 411.

2. The Groundhogs, *Blues Obituary*, Arkama LP5271 (1969).

3. Quoted in *Paul Oliver 70th Birthday Tribute.*

4. Val Wilmer quoted in Schwartz, *How Britain Got the Blues*, p. 115.

5. Oliver, *Blues Fell This Morning*, p. xviii.

6. Ibid., p. xvii.

7. Wright, "Foreword," pp. x–xi.

8. Gunnar Myrdal, *An American Dilemma: The Negro Problem and Modern Democracy* (London: Harper and Row, 1944 [*sic*] 1962), p. xlviii.

9. Samuel B. Charters, *The Country Blues* (New York: Da Capo, 1975 [*sic*] 1959), p. x.

10. Wright, "Foreword," p. vii.

11. Oliver, *Blues Fell This Morning*, p. 5.

12. Spencer, "Blues and Evil," p. 38; Spencer, *Blues and Evil*, p. xx.

13. Ward, *Just My Soul Responding*, p. 4.

14. See, for instance, Riesman, *I Feel So Good.*

15. Charters, *The Country Blues*, p. 19.

16. Richard Middleton, *Pop Music and the Blues: A Study of the Relationship and Its Significance* (London: Gollancz, 1972), p. 27.

17. Barlow, *Looking Up at Down*, pp. 4, 327.

18. LeRoi Jones, *Blues People: The Negro Experience in White America and the Music That Developed from It* (New York: Morrow, 1963), pp. 86, 93.

19. See Gussow, "If Bessie Smith Had Killed."

20. Stanley Edgar Hyman, "The Folk Tradition" (1958), in Alan Dundes, ed., *Mother Wit from the Laughing Barrel: Readings in the Interpretation of Afro-American Folklore* (New York: Garland, 1981 [*sic*] 1973), pp. 45–56.

21. Ralph Ellison, *Shadow and Act* (New York: Signet, 1966), p. 242.

22. Derrick Stewart-Baxter, "Blues Fell This Morning," *Jazz Journal*, vol. 13, no. 4, April 1960, pp. 18–19; G. E. Lambert, "Blues Fell This Morning," *Jazz Monthly*, vol. 6, no. 12, February 1961, pp. 28–29.

23. Shapiro, *Alexis Korner*, p. 91; Bob Dawbarn, "This Could Have Been the Book on the Blues," *Melody Maker*, 2 April 1960, p. 8; Philip Larkin, "A Racial Art: *Blues Fell This Morning* by Paul Oliver," *Observer*, 27 March 1960, in Richard Palmer and John White, eds., *Larkin's Jazz: Essays and Reviews 1940–1984* (London: Continuum, 1999 [*sic*] 2001), pp. 43–44; Charles Fox, "Book and Disc Review: Blues Fell This Morning, Paul Oliver," *Gramophone*, August 1960, p. 91, http://www.gramophone.net/Issue/Page/August%201960/91/853199/, retrieved 20 June 2012 at 5:15 p.m.

24. Paul Oliver, "Apropos 'Blues Fell This Morning,'" *Jazz Monthly*, vol. 7, no. 1, March 1961, pp. 12, 20; *Blues Fell This Morning: Rare Recordings of Southern Blues Singers*, Philips BBL 7369 (1960).

25. Oliver, *Blues Fell This Morning*, p. 12.

26. Paul Garon, *Blues and the Poetic Spirit* (London: Eddison Press, 1975), pp. 8, 39; Angela Y. Davis, *Blues Legacies and Black Feminism: Gertrude "Ma" Rainey, Bessie Smith and Billie Holiday* (New York: Vintage, 1998), p. xv; see, for instance, Guido Van Rijn, *Roosevelt's Blues: African-American Blues and Gospel Songs on FDR* (Jackson: University Press of Mississippi, 1997) and *The Truman and Eisenhower Blues: African-American Blues and Gospel Songs, 1945–1960* (New York: Continuum, 2006).

27. Simon Frith, "Jazz and Suburbia," in Simon Frith, ed., *Music for Pleasure: Essays in the Sociology of Pop* (New York: Routledge, 1988), p. 112.

28. Oliver, *Blues Fell This Morning*, p. 2.

29. Friedrich Nietzsche, *The Use and Abuse of History* (1874), quoted in James Longenbach, *Modernist Poetics of History: Pound, Eliot, and the Sense of the Past* (Princeton: Princeton University Press, 1987), p. 6.

30. Paul Oliver, "Preface to the Revised Edition," *Blues Fell This Morning: Meaning in the Blues* (New York: Cambridge University Press, 1994), p. xxiv.

31. Oliver, *Blues Fell This Morning*, p. 9.

32. This will be discussed in more detail in chapters 4 and 5.

33. Wald, *Escaping the Delta*, p. 36.

34. Lowenstein and Dodd, *According to the Rolling Stones*, pp. 6/, 8–9.

35. Oliver, *Blues Fell This Morning* (1994), p. 281.

36. Alexis Korner, "The Evolution of Muddy Waters," *Recorded Folk Music*, vol. 2, September–October 1959, pp. 5–8.

37. Keith Richards, *Life* (New York: Little, Brown, 2010), p. 82.

38. Paul Oliver, "Blue-Eyed Blues: The Impact of Blues on European Popular Culture," in C. W. E. Bigsby, ed., *Approaches to Popular Culture* (Bowling Green: Bowling Green University Popular Press, 1977), p. 239.

39. Ibid., p. 5.

40. Oliver, *Blues Fell This Morning*, p. 8.

41. Ibid., pp. 11–12.

42. Ibid., pp. 15–16: lyrics from Ramblin' Thomas, "Poor Boy," 1929.

43. Ibid., p. 40: lyrics from Peetie Wheatstraw, "Working on the Project," 1937.

44. Ibid., p. 260: lyrics from St. Louis Jimmy, "Bad Condition," 1944.

45. Ibid., James "Boodle-It" Wiggins, p. 207, Mississippi floods, pp. 234–38.

46. Jones, "On Blues," p. 90; Lang, *Jazz in Perspective*, p. 122; Harris, *Jazz*; Newton, *The Jazz Scene*, p. 150.

47. Oliver, *Blues Fell This Morning*, pp. 111, 116.

48. Ibid., p. 117.

49. Ibid., p. 110.

50. Ibid., p. 298.

51. Ibid., p. 75.

52. Ibid., p. 32: lyrics from Blind Blake, "Detroit Bound Blues," 1928.

53. Ibid., pp. 42–43: lyrics from Roosevelt Sykes, "Southern Blues," 1948.

54. Stephen Tuck, *We Ain't What We Ought to Be: The Black Freedom Struggle from Emancipation to Obama* (Cambridge: Harvard University Press, 2010), pp. 145–46; see also Joe William Trotter Jr., *The African American Experience* (Boston: Houghton Mifflin, 2001), pp. 373–401.

55. Oliver, *Blues Fell This Morning*, p. 170: lyrics from Peetie Wheatstraw, "Beer Tavern," 1939.

56. Ibid., pp. 58–59: lyrics from Peetie Wheatstraw, "Road Tramp Blues," 1938.

57. Harvard Sitkoff, *A New Deal for Blacks: The Emergence of Civil Rights as a National Issue. The Depression Decade*, 30th anniversary ed. (New York: Oxford University Press, 2009), pp. 26–27.

58. Oliver, *Blues Fell This Morning*, pp. 36–37: lyrics from Walter Davis, " My Friends Don't Know Me," 1945.

59. Ibid., "Negro's despairing fatalism," p. 246; "seldom seek," p. 267; "Fatalistically," p. 274.

60. Ibid., p. 59.

61. Ibid., p. 12.
62. Ibid., p. 281.
63. Ibid., p. 61.
64. Larkin, "A Racial Art," p. 44.
65. Oliver, *Blues Fell This Morning*, p. 89.
66. Ibid., p. 133.
67. Ibid., "gambling," p. 151, "health," p. 268.
68. Graham Smith, *When Jim Crow Met John Bull: Black American Soldiers in World War II* (London: I.B. Taurus, 1987), p. 217.
69. "Black and White Minstrel Creator Dies," www.guardian.co.uk, 29 August 2002, http://www.guardian.co.uk/media/2002/aug/29/broadcasting2, retrieved 23 July 2012 at 4:28 p.m.; Michael Keith, *Race, Riots and Policing: Lore and Disorder in a Multi-racist Society* (London: University College London Press, 1993), pp. 44–45.
70. Schwartz, *How Britain Got the Blues*, p. 266.
71. Oliver, *Blues Fell This Morning*, p. 101: lyrics from Leroy's Buddy, "Triflin' Woman Blues," 1939.
72. Ibid., p. 89.
73. Ibid., p. 86.
74. Ibid., p. 245.
75. Ibid., p. 216.
76. Ibid., p. 97: lyrics from Lonnie Johnson, "I Ain't Gonna Be Your Fool," 1938.
77. Ibid., p. 99: lyrics from Lightnin' Hopkins, "Automobile," 1946.
78. Melville Herskovitz, *The American Negro* (New York: Knopf, 1928).
79. Oliver, *Blues Fell This Morning*, p. 230.
80. *Blues Fell This Morning: Rare Recordings of Southern Blues Singers* (1960).
81. Oliver, *Blues Fell This Morning*, pp. 292–93.
82. Theodore Rosengarten, *All God's Dangers: The Life of Nate Shaw* (University of Chicago Press, 2000); Kelley, "We Are Not What We Seem."
83. House, *Blue Smoke*, p. 114.
84. Daphne Duval Harrison, *Black Pearls: Blues Queens of the 1920s* (New Brunswick: Rutgers University Press, 1988), pp. 7–8.
85. Cone, *The Spirituals and the Blues*, p. 124; Barlow, *Looking Up at Down*, p. 29; Cone and Barlow are just two examples of writers sharing the vision of the blues' function as a form of release.
86. Oliver, "Preface to the Revised Edition," p. xiv.
87. W. G. Roy, *Reds, Whites, and Blues: Social Movements, Folk Music, and Race in the United States* (Princeton: Princeton University Press, 2010), p. 192.
88. Middleton, *Studying Popular Music*, pp. 36, 378.
89. Oliver, *Blues Fell This Morning*, p. 10.
90. *Blues Fell This Morning: Rare Recordings of Southern Blues Singers* (1960).
91. Oliver, *Blues Fell This Morning*, p. 277.
92. Ibid., p. 265.
93. Middleton, *Studying Popular Music*, p. 127—"sense of mission."
94. John Dougan, "Objects of Desire: Canon Formation and Blues Record Collecting," *Journal of PopularMusic Studies* , vol. 18, April 2006, p. 55.
95. Newton, *The Jazz Scene*, p. 8.
96. Quoted in Keil, *Urban Blues*, p. 49.

97. Roland Barthes, "Musica Practica" (1970), in *Image, Music, Text*, trans. Stephen Heath (New York: Oxford University Press, 1977 [*sic*] 1984), pp. 149–50.
98. Theodor W. Adorno, "On the Fetish-Character in Music and the Regression of Listening," in Andrew Amato and Eike Gebhardt, eds., *The Essential Frankfurt School Reader* (Oxford: Blackwell, 1978), p. 271.
99. Hamilton, *In Search of the Blues*, p. 10.
100. Oliver, *Blues Fell This Morning*, p. 2.
101. Brocken, *The British Folk Revival*, p. 23.
102. Stephen C. Tracy, ed., *Write Me a Few of Your Lines: A Blues Reader* (Amherst: University of Massachusetts Press, 1999), p. xiii.
103. Seth Moglen, *Mourning Modernity: Literary Modernism and the Injuries of American Capitalism* (Stanford: Stanford University Press, 2007), p. 5.
104. "natural and uninhibited," Oliver, *Blues Fell This Morning*, p. 102; Moglen, *Mourning Modernity*, p. 35.
105. Longenbach, *Modernist Poetics of History*, p. 11.
106. Tracy, *Write Me*, p. xiii.
107. Wald, *Escaping the Delta*, p. 3.
108. Hamilton describes the world of a group of American blues enthusiasts and collectors in the fifties, spearheaded by the enigmatic James McKune, which eventually started the Origins Jazz Library label and canonized what they believed to be the "real" blues over commercial offshoots. Hamilton, *In Search of the Blues*, chapter 6.
109. Roy, *Red, White and Blues*, p. 64.
110. Munslow, *Deconstructing History*, p. 162.

Chapter 3

1. The quotation in the title of this chapter is taken from the blues musician Will Shade in Oliver, *Conversation with the Blues*, p. xiii.
2. Paul Oliver, "Crossroads Blues," *Jazz Beat*, vol. 1, no. 6, February 1965, pp. 20–21: the quotation is taken from the subtitle of Oliver's article.
3. David M. Breeden, review, "*Conversation with the Blues* by Paul Oliver," *Music Educators Journal*, vol. 53, no. 6, February 1967, pp. 97–98.
4. Quoted in Schwartz, *How Britain Got the Blues*, p. 177; Val Wilmer described *Conversation with the Blues* as the "Hear Me Talkin' to Ya" of the blues, *Jazz Beat*, vol. 2 no. 7, 1965; Nat Shapiro and Nat Hentoff, *Hear Me Talkin' to Ya: The Story of Jazz as Told by the Men Who Made It* (New York: Dover Publications, 1966), p. xii.
5. Mervyn Cooke, review, "*Conversation with the Blues* by Paul Oliver," *Music and Letters*, vol. 79, no. 4, November 1998, pp. 638–39.
6. Schwartz, *How Britain Got the Blues*, p. 177.
7. Barry Lee Pearson, *"Sounds Good to Me": The Bluesman's Story* (Philadelphia: University of Pennsylvania Press, 1984).
8. Alan Lomax's trips to the South were the subject of his book, *The Land Where the Blues Began* (New York: Pantheon Books, 1993); Lomax and Collins's trip in 1959 from Shirley Collins, *America over the Water* (London: SAF Publishing, 2005); Frederic Ramsey Jr., *Been Here and Gone* (New Brunswick: Rutgers University Press, 1960).

9. Demetre and Chauvard, "Land of Blues"; Oliver, *Conversation with the Blues*, p. xiii; Stewart-Baxter, "Blues in the Country," p. 4.

10. "Obtaining grant," Oliver, *Conversation with the Blues*, p. ix; "use of USIS at American Embassy," interview by the author, 1 June 2010, appendix 1.4, p. 329.

11. Schwartz, *How Britain Got the Blues*, p. 117; Penny Marie Von Eschen, *Satchmo Blows Up the World: Jazz Ambassadors Play the Cold War* (Cambridge: Harvard University Press, 2004), pp. 20–21.

12. Oliver, *Conversation with the Blues*, p. ix.

13. Interview by the author, July 2011, appendix 1.8, p. 383.

14. Albert McCarthy, "Blues Recording Fund," *Jazz Monthly*, vol. 6, no. 1, March 1960, p. 3.

15. John Street, "Shock Waves: The Authoritative Response to Popular Music," in Dominic Strinati and Stephen Wagg, eds., *Come On Down? Popular Media Culture in Post-war Britain* (London: Routledge, 1992), p. 306.

16. Derrick Stewart-Baxter, "Curtis Jones," *Jazz Journal*, vol. 13, no. 3, March 1960, p. 3.

17. Oliver, "Crossroads Blues," p. 21.

18. Oliver, *Conversation with the Blues*, p. xiv, 12; Paul Oliver, "Blues '65," *Jazz*, vol. 4, no. 7, July 1965, pp. 26–29.

19. Oliver, *Conversation with the Blues*, p. 10.

20. Ibid., p. 12.

21. Ibid., p. xiv; "desire to visit Texas," interview by the author, 20 June 2010, appendix 1.5, p. 349.

22. Oliver, *Conversation with the Blues*, p. 4.

23. Ibid., pp. xv, 3.

24. Paul Thompson, "The Voice of the Past: Oral History" in Perks and Thompson, *The Oral History Reader* , p. 26.

25. Oliver, *Conversation with the Blues*, p. 12.

26. Rebecca Sharpless, "The History of Oral History," in Thomas L. Charlton, Lois E. Myers, Rebecca Sharpless, and Leslie Roy Ballard, eds., *The History of Oral History: Foundations and Methodology* (Lanham: Rowman and Littlefield, 2007), pp. 9–32.

27. Alan Tratchenberg, *Reading American Photographs: Images as History—Matthew Brady to Walker Evans* (New York: Hill and Wang, 1989), pp. 245–46.

28. John F. Szwed, "Review of *Conversation with the Blues* by Paul Oliver," *Western Folklore*, vol. 25, no. 3, July 1966, pp. 202–3; in his review Breeden argued that the images "prove that poverty breeds a need for creative outlet, and that it is in such conditions that blues music frequently, if not always, comes to play an essential role in people's lives" (pp. 97–98)..

29. Schwartz, *How Britain Got the Blues*, p. 175.

30. Hamilton, *In Search of the Blues*, pp. 184–85.

31. Schwartz, *How Britain Got the Blues*, p. 145.

32. Ibid., pp. 182–83; Rolling Stones, "Little Red Rooster," mentioned in BBC4 documentary *Blues Britannia: Can Blue Men Sing the Whites?* Chris Rodley (2009), BBC4, 11:00 pm, 9 December 2011.

33. Paul Oliver, "Blues Festival '65," *Jazz Monthly*, vol. 11, no. 10, December 1965, pp. 18–20; Schwartz, *How Britain Got the Blues*, pp. 182–85.

34. Alan Lomax interviewing the New Orleans clarinet player Louis deLisle Nelson in Alan Lomax, *Mister Jelly Roll: The Fortunes of Jelly Roll Morton—New Orleans Creole and "Inventor of Jazz"* (London: Pan Books, 1959 [*sic*] 1952), p. 88.

35. Ibid., pp. 218–19.

36. Hamilton, *In Search of the Blues*, pp. 140–42.

37. Shapiro and Hentoff, *Hear Me Talkin' to Ya*, p. x.

38. Szwed, *Man Who Recorded the World*, p. 185.

39. The 1947 interviews are available on the Cultural Equity Research Center website, http://research.culturalequity.org/get-audio-detailed-recording.do?recordingId=11941, retrieved 27 June 2011 at 3:45 p.m.

40. Thompson, "Voice of the Past," p. 28.

41. Szwed, *Man Who Recorded the World*, p. 244.

42. Oliver, *Conversation with the Blues*, pp. 1–3.

43. Ibid., p. 7.

44. Ibid., p. 10.

45. Frith, "Playing with Real Feeling: Making Sense of Jazz in Britain," *New Formations*, No. 4, Spring 1, 1998, pp. 7-24; p. 22.

46. Oliver, *Conversation with the Blues*, p. xv.

47. Ronald J. Grele, "Movement without Aim: Methodological and Theoretical Problems in Oral History," in Perks and Thompson, *The Oral History Reader* , pp. 38–52; Portelli, "What Makes Oral History Different," pp. 63–74.

48. Oliver, *Conversation with the Blues*, p. 11.

49. Ibid., p. 11.

50. Collins, *America over the Water*, p. 114.

51. Interviews by the author, 20 June 2010, "Harlem" in appendix 1.5, p. 349; "Oliver's wife," July 2011, appendix 1.8, p. 383; Oliver comments on this visit to a barrelhouse, without mentioning that his wife spent time with Mrs. Walton, in *Conversation with the Blues*, p. xiii.

52. Oliver, *Blues off the Record*, p. 11.

53. Other blues researchers on Oliver's trip in Paul Oliver, *The Story of the Blues* (Harmondsworth: Penguin, 1972), p. 164; Chris Strachwitz's recordings in Lee Hildebrand, "Chris Strachwitz: The Life of a Sound Catcher," *Living Blues*, issue 211, vol. 42, no. 1, February 2011, pp. 28–33.

54. Pearson, *Sounds Good to Me*, p. 30.

55. Ibid., p. 39.

56. Colin Harper, *Dazzling Stranger: Bert Jansch and the British Folk and Blues Revival* (London: Bloomsbury, 2000), p. 17.

57. Jeff Todd Titon, "The Life Story," *Journal of American Folklore*, vol. 93 no. 369, July–September 1980, pp. 276–92.

58. Portelli, "What Makes Oral History Different," p. 65.

59. Jeffrey Hadler, "Remus Orthography: The History of the Representation of the African-American Voice," *Journal of Folklore Research*, vol. 35 no. 2, May–August 1998, pp. 100–101.

60. Oliver, *Conversation with the Blues*, p. xi.

61. Interview by the author, 1 June 2010, appendix 1.4, p. 329.

62. Oliver, *Conversation with the Blues*, pp. 19, 21–22.

63. Ibid., pp. 46, 22, 125–26.

64. Interview by the author, July 2011, appendix 1.8, p. 383; Oliver states that McCormick and Strachwitz had discovered the singer a few days earlier.

65. Oliver, *Conversation with the Blues*, pp. 23, 53, 36.

66. Ibid., pp. 40, 26, 39.

67. Trotter, *The African American Experience*, p. 435; the percentage of African Americans living in cities increased from less than 50 percent in 1940 to over 80 percent in 1970, p. 519.

68. Lil' Son Jackson, ibid., p. 31.

69. Track 4 by Lil' Son Jackson, "The Onliest Way," on the *Conversation with the Blues* record, contains a sentence that has been removed from the transcription quoted here.

70. Oliver, *Conversation with the Blues*, p. 31.

71. Michael Frisch, "Oral History and *Hard Times*: A Review Essay," in Perks and Thompson, *The Oral History Reader*, p. 33.

72. Oliver, *Conversation with the Blues*, p. 11.

73. Portelli, "What Makes Oral History Different," p. 67.

74. Frisch, "Oral History and *Hard Times*," p. 36.

75. Szwed, *Man Who Recorded the World*, p. 250.

76. Oliver, *Conversation with the Blues*, p. xiv.

77. Lomax was critical of Ben Botkin's *A Treasury of Southern Folklore* (1949); quoted in Szwed, *Man Who Recorded the World*, p. 250.

78. Oliver, *Conversation with the Blues*, p. 1.

79. Roy, *Reds, Whites, and Blues*, p. 192; protest in the blues has also been the subject of widespread historical debate. Many have criticized Oliver's thesis in *Blues Fell This Morning* that denied the existence of any significant form of social protest. See, for instance, Spencer, *Blues and Evil*, or Bruce Conforth, *African American Folksong and American Cultural Politics* (Lanham: Rowman and Littlefield, 2013).

80. "Alice Moore," interview by the author, 1 June 2010, appendix 1.4, p. 329; "Marion Oldham," in Oliver, *Conversation with the Blues*, p. 1.

81. Adam Fairclough, *Better Day Coming: Blacks and Equality, 1890–2000* (London: Penguin, 2002), pp. 241–43.

82. "Wife hiding in car," Michael Roach interview with Paul Oliver, http://www.euroblues.org/members/podcast, retrieved 1 July 2011 at 1:50 p.m., and Paul Oliver and Michael Roach on Paul Jones, BBC Radio 2, 7:00 p.m., 30 May 2011; interviews by the author, 1 June 2010, "run out of town in Texas" appendix 1.4, p. 330, "escorted from Mississippi" and "Alex Moore," 20 June 2010, appendix 1.5, p. 349.

83. Interview by the author, 1 March 2011, appendix 1.7, p. 373.

84. Collins, *America over the Water*, p. 114.

85. Oliver, *Conversation with the Blues*, pp. 35, 50.

86. Lil' Son Jackson, in ibid., p. 31.

87. "Oliver editing out," interview by the author, 1 March 2011, appendix 1.7, p. 373.

88. Oliver, *Blues off the Record*, p. 11.

89. Oliver, *Conversation with the Blues*, p. 9.

90. Schwartz, *How Britain Got the Blues*, pp. 116–17.

91. Notable examples are Whistlin' Alex Moore's photograph for *Alex Moore Piano Blues*, Arhoolie LP1008, Lil' Son Jackson's *Blues Come to Texas*, Arhoolie LP1004, and Mance Lipscomb's *Texas Songster*, Arhoolie 306.

92. An example of the lack of consideration for photography is *In Search of the Blues*,

where Hamilton concentrates on the author's suggestion that the poverty-ridden, rural black South retains human qualities that the modern world has lost, pp. 157–60.

93. Breeden, review of *Conversation with the Blues*, p. 98.

94. Interview by the author, July 2011, appendix 1.8, p. 383.

95. Tratchenberg, *Reading American Photographs*, p. 288.

96. Lawrence Levine, "The Historian and the Icon: Photography and the History of the American People in the 1930s," in Carl Fleishhauer and Beverly W. Brannan, eds., *Documentary America, 1935–1943* (Berkeley: University of California Press, 1988), p. 17.

97. Susan Sontag, *On Photography* (London: Penguin, 1977), p. 4.

98. Ibid., p. 6.

99. Wright, *12 Million Black Voices*, p. 110.

100. Nicholas Natanson, *The Black Image in the New Deal: The Politics of FSA Photography* (Knoxville: University of Tennessee Press, 1992), p. 251.

101. Interview by the author, July 2011, appendix 1.8, p. 383—Oliver was referring in particular to a photo of Mance Lipscomb that will be discussed later in the chapter (figure 10).

102. Tratchenberg, *Reading American Photographs*, p. 19.

103. Roland Barthes, "The Photographic Message," in *Image, Music, Text*, pp. 17–18.

104. Derrick Price, "Surveyors and Surveyed: Photography out and about," in Liz Wells, ed., *Photography: A Critical Introduction*, 4th ed. (London: Routledge, 2009), p. 107.

105. Natanson, *Black Image*, p. 89.

106. Oliver, *Conversation with the Blues*, pp. xvi, 5.

107. William Stott, *Documentary Expression and Thirties America* (New York: Oxford University Press, 1973), p. 20.

108. Lili Corbus Bezner, *Photography and Politics in America: From the New Deal into the Cold War* (Baltimore: John Hopkins University Press, 1999), pp. 5, 10; John Roberts, *The Art of Interruption: Realism, Photography and the Everyday* (New York: St. Martin's Press, 1998), p. 81.

109. Joseph Millichap, "James Agee, Walker Evans, and the Dialectic of Documentary: Representation in *Let Us Now Praise Famous Men*," *Southern Quarterly*, vol. 48, no. 1, Fall 2010, p. 88.

110. Stott, *Documentary Expression and Thirties America*, pp. 58–59.

111. The image used was an AP photograph, Wright, *12 Million Black Voices*, p. 45.

112. Stott, *Documentary Expression and Thirties America*, pp. 8 and 18–20.

113. Palmer, *Deep Blues*, p. 6.

114. Oliver, *Blues off the Record*, p. 11.

115. Interview by the author, 1 June 2010, appendix 1.4, p. 329.

116. Wright, *12 Million Black Voices*, pp. 114–15—Russell Lee's photographs were entitled *Empty Lot and Houses, Chicago, IL* and *Negro Housing, Chicago, IL*.

117. US Bureau of the Census, 1940, 1950, and 1970 in T. C. Holt and E. B. Brown, *Major Problems in African-American History: From Freedom to "Freedom Now," 1865–1990s* (Boston: Houghton Mifflin, 2000); Trotter, *The African American Experience*, p. 551.

118. Tuck, *We Ain't*, pp. 340–41.

119. These portraits include J. B. Lenoir, Otis Spann, Whistlin' Alex Moore, Black Ace, Ernest Roy, and a famous group image of Roosevelt Sykes, Little Walter, Sunnyland Slim, Armund Jump Jackson, and Little Brother Montgomery.

120. Photo of Arvella Gray in figure 7; image of Butch Cage and Willie Thomas in *Conversation*, p. viii.

121. Lee's photograph was used as the front cover for the 2008 edition of Richard Wright's *12 Million Black Voices*; the camera IS positioned to capture a corridor running through the church with two people in the background, while the young girl in the foreground looks across the camera.

122. Oliver, *Conversation with the Blues*, p. 4.

123. Ibid., Beale Street image, p. 97; Hastings Street, p. 143.

124. Stott, *Documentary Expression and Thirties America*, pp. 218–20.

125. Oliver, *Conversation with the Blues*, pp. 90–91.

126. Ibid., pp. 29, 43–44.

127. Bezner, *Photography and Politics in America*, p. 204—Bezner highlights how images such as Palfi's *Somewhere in the South* were aimed at challenging Jim Crow segregation.

128. Tratchenberg, *Reading American Photographs*, p. 258.

129. Oliver, *Conversation with the Blues*, p. xiii.

130. Prior to the publication of *Conversation with the Blues* Oliver commented that British groups playing African American–derived rhythm and blues often made him "shudder." Paul Oliver, "Review of R&B," *Jazz Monthly*, vol. 10, no. 7, November 1964, p. 24.

Chapter 4

1. Schwartz, *How Britain Got the Blues*, pp. 185–86; "discovery fatigue" quoted by Simon Napier in Schwartz, p. 190.

2. "re-discoveries" in Adelt, *Blues Music in the Sixties*, p. 43.

3. Paul Oliver, "Slidin' Delta—Fred McDowell," *Jazz Beat*, vol. 2, no. 9, August 1965, pp. 12–13, 23.

4. Oliver, "Blues '65," p. 26.

5. For instance see *Blues Unlimited*, no. 26, October 1965.

6. Schwartz, *How Britain Got the Blues*, pp. 199–200.

7. Paul Oliver, "Blues in the Bran-Tub," *Jazz Beat*, vol. 2, no. 4, April 1965, pp. 12–13.

8. Schwartz, *How Britain Got the Blues*, p. 202; Advertisement for First National Blues Convention, Conway Hall, Red Lion Square London, 7–8 September 1968. in *Blues Unlimited*, no. 54, June 1968, p. 19; "Review of National Blues Convention," *Blues Unlimited*, no. 57, November 1968, p. 16.

9. Adelt, *Blues Music in the Sixties*, p. 2.

10. Oliver, "Crossroads Blues," p. 21; Bob Dawbarn, "Are British Acts Just Imitating the Negro Sound?" *Melody Maker*, 26 June 1965, p. 8.

11. Oliver's talk at the EFDSS in Schwartz, *How Britain Got the Blues*, p. 189; Blind Gary Davis at EFDSS in Paul Oliver, "Blind Gary Davis," *Jazz Beat*, vol. 2, no. 8, July 1965, pp. 12–13; Harry Belafonte in Paul Oliver, "Sellers Market," *Jazz Beat*, vol. 2, no. 5, May 1965, pp. 12–13.

12. Adelt, *Blues Music in the Sixties*, pp. 79, 97.

13. Derek Jewell, advertisement for *Screening the Blues*, *Blues Unlimited*, no. 57, November 1968, p. 27.

14. Paul Oliver, *Screening the Blues: Aspects of the Blues Tradition* (London: Cassell, 1968), p. 13.

15. Keil, *Urban Blues*, pp. 34, 38.

16. Oliver, *Screening the Blues*, p. 38.

17. Ibid., p. 75, 85: Oliver demonstrates how many blues singers grew up directly involved with the church, and many often included religious material in their repertoires.

18. Ibid., p. 126.

19. Hamilton, *In Search of the Blues.*

20. Charters, *The Country Blues*, and Keil, *Urban Blues.*

21. Eric Hobsbawm and Terence Ranger, eds., *The Invention of Tradition* (Cambridge: Cambridge University Press, 1983), pp. 1, 4.

22. Oliver, *Screening the Blues*, p. 9.

23. DeVeaux, "Constructing the Jazz Tradition," p. 530.

24. Oliver, *Screening the Blues*, p. 13.

25. DeVeaux, "Constructing the Jazz Tradition," p. 527.

26. Oliver, *Screening the Blues*, p. 18.

27. Ibid., p. 90.

28. Ibid., p. 18.

29. Ibid., p. 41.

30. Ibid., p. 1; quote from Henry Edward Kreihbel, *Afro-American Folksongs: A Study in Racial and National Music* (New York: G. Shirmer, 1914), p. 2, quoted in *Screening the Blues*, p. 1.

31. Oliver, *Screening the Blues*, p. 2.

32. Ibid., p. 252.

33. Ibid., p. 10.

34. Ibid., p. 128.

35. Ibid., pp. 138, 144.

36. Ibid., p. 251.

37. Ibid., p. 2.

38. Ibid., p. 216.

39. Ibid., p. 214.

40. Ibid., p. 149.

41. Hamilton, *In Search of the Blues*, p. 193.

42. Oliver, *Screening the Blues*, p. 12.

43. Ibid., p. 149.

44. Ibid., p. 259.

45. Ibid., p. 257.

46. Ibid., pp. 260–61; Abraham Kardiner and Lionel Ovesey, *The Mark of Oppression: Explorations in the Personality of the American Negro* (Cleveland: World Publishing Co., 1962), pp. 340–41.

47. Oliver, *Screening the Blues*, p. 44.

48. Ibid., p. 53.

49. Ibid., p. 258.

50. Ibid., p. 255.

51. Ibid.

52. Spencer, "Blues and Evil," p. 39.

53. Oliver, *Screening the Blues*, p. 254.

54. Filene, *Romancing the Folk*, p. 24.
55. Wald, *Josh White*, p. 99.
56. Oliver, *Screening the Blues*, p. 260.
57. Ibid., p. 257.
58. Ibid., p. 163.
59. Ibid., p. 90.
60. Oliver, *Conversation with the Blues*, p. xiii.
61. Oliver, *Screening the Blues*, p. 101.
62. Ibid., p. 50.
63. Ibid., p. 225.
64. Ibid., pp. 230, 239.
65. Ibid., p. 180.
66. Ibid., p. 111.
67. Ibid., p. 113.
68. Ibid., p. 215.
69. Ibid., p. 180.
70. Jones (Amiri Baraka), *Blues People*, p. 167, 169.
71. Keil, *Urban Blues*, p. 185.

Chapter 5

1. Max Harrison, "The Blues: Review of *The Story of the Blues* by Paul Oliver," *Musical Times*, vol. 111, no. 1523, January 1970, pp. 48–49.

2. Simon Napier, "Review of 'The Story of the Blues,'" *Blues Unlimited*, no. 65, September 1969, p. 20.

3. William Harris, "Manuals for Black Militants," *Antioch Review*, vol. 27 no. 3, Autumn 1967, pp. 408–16.

4. "represents," Amy Van Singel; "best popular introduction," Jeff Titon; "has learned," David Evans, quoted in *Paul Oliver 70th Birthday Tribute*.

5. Wald, *Escaping the Delta*, p. 249.

6. Oliver, *Conversation with the Blues*, p. 7.

7. See Giles Oakley, *The Devil's Music: A History of the Blues* (New York: Da Capo, 1976); Palmer, *Deep Blues*; Barlow, *Looking Up at Down*; Francis Davis, *The History of the Blues: The Roots, the Music, the People* (New York: Da Capo, 2003); Bill Wyman and Richard Havers, *Bill Wyman's Blues Odyssey* (New York: DK Publishing, 2001).

8. Palmer, *Deep Blues*; used by Litwack, *Trouble in Mind*, p. xvii.

9. Hamilton, *In Search of the Blues*, p. 8.

10. See for instance Wald's discussion on Robert Johnson's minor role in the history of African American music, which contradicts revivalist interpretations of the singer, in *Escaping the Delta*; also see Hamilton's discussion on the inaccurate use of W. C. Handy's first encounter with the blues as a point of origin in blues histories in *In Search of the Blues*, pp. 22–23.

11. Munslow, *Deconstructing History*, p. 118.

12. White, "Historical Text as Literary Artefact," pp. 84, 99.

13. Georg G. Iggers, *Historiography in the Twentieth Century: From Scientific Objectivity to the Postmodern Challenge* (Middletown: Wesleyan University Press, 1997), pp. 11, 145.

14. Munslow, *Deconstructing History*, pp. 129, 148.

15. Lawrence Skoog, "The Negro in America: His Life and Times," *Blues Unlimited*, no. 63, June 1969, pp. 4–7.

16. "Review of "The 2nd National Blues Convention, 1969, Conway Hall, 21st/22nd September," *Blues Unlimited*, no. 67, November 1969, p. 16.

17. Wald, *Escaping the Delta*, p. 188.

18. DeVeaux, "Constructing the Jazz Tradition," p. 525.

19. "retrospective" nature of writing histories highlighted by Wald, *Escaping the Delta*, p. xv.

20. DeVeaux argues that Wynton Marsalis has been depicted as having "rescued jazz from extinction," and also that "jazz has, in many ways, never been better supported or appreciated," in "Constructing the Jazz Tradition," p. 527.

21. Filene, *Romancing the Folk*, p. 123; Filene argues that places such as Chicago and the Chess Records label became pilgrimage sites for European blues enthusiasts in search of the music's roots.

22. Oliver, *Story of the Blues*, p. 6.

23. Ibid., p. 4.

24. Tracy, *Write Me*, p. xi.

25. Oliver, *Story of the Blues*, p. 9.

26. Jones, *Blues People*, p. 28.

27. Hayden White, *Metahistory: The Historical Imagination in Nineteenth-Century Europe* (Baltimore: John Hopkins Press, 1973), p. 9.

28. Oliver, *Story of the Blues*, p. 8.

29. Ibid., pp. 10–11.

30. Ibid., p. 13.

31. Paul Oliver, "Savannah Syncopators: African Retentions in the Blues," in Paul Oliver, Tony Russell, Robert M. W. Dixon, John Godrich, and Howard Rye, *Yonder Come the Blues* (New York: Cambridge University Press, 2001), p. 15.

32. Oliver, *Story of the Blues*, pp. 12–13.

33. Ibid., p. 15.

34. Ibid., p. 21.

35. Ibid., p. 6.

36. Gunnar Myrdal, *Black and African-American Studies: American Dilemma, the Negro Problem and Modern Democracy* (Transaction, 1995), p. 223.

37. Riesman, *I Feel So Good*, p. 165.

38. Oliver, *Story of the Blues*, p. 26.

39. http://www.yearoftheblues.org/about.asp, retrieved 19 April 2012 at 2:09 p.m.; Scorsese films in Dave Allen, "Feelin' Bad This Morning: Why the *British* Blues?" *Popular Music*, vol. 26, no. 1, 2007, pp. 141–56.

40. Hamilton, *In Search of the Blues*, p. 21.

41. Interestingly, Odum is the subject of Hamilton's second chapter. She argues that his account of African American music at the turn of the century has been largely overlooked by blues scholars, although Oliver was appreciative of his writings in works such as Odum and Johnson, *Negro Workaday Songs*.

42. Hamilton, *In Search of the Blues*, pp. 186–87.

43. Oliver, *Story of the Blues*, "dark intensity' p. 31; quote and photo caption, p. 34.

44. Ibid., pp. 118–20.

45. Palmer, *Deep Blues*, p. 6.

46. Oliver, *Story of the Blues*, p. 74.
47. Ibid., p. 106.
48. Ibid., pp. 30, 46.
49. Ibid., p. 37.
50. Ibid., "Ida Cox," p. 61; "Broonzy," pp. 101–2.
51. Ibid., p. 99.
52. Ibid., p. 103–4.
53. Ibid., p. 106.
54. Ibid.
55. Oliver stated that in the blues "Negro self-assertiveness found expression instead in sexual themes," ibid., p. 104.
56. Ibid., pp. 105–6.
57. Ibid., p. 42.
58. Ibid., p. 107.
59. Ibid., p. 106.
60. Harrison, review of *The Story of the Blues*, pp. 48–49.
61. Susan J. Douglas, *Listening In: Radio and the American Imagination* (Minneapolis: University of Minnesota Press, 1999), p. 84.
62. Oliver, *Story of the Blues*, p. 139.
63. Tyler Cowen, *In Praise of Commercial Culture* (Cambridge: Harvard University Press, 2000), p. 164.
64. Oliver, *Story of the Blues*, p. 140.
65. Ibid., p. 145.
66. Ibid., pp. 154–56.
67. Ibid., "walking in' and "still possible," p. 6; memories, p. 72; "down in Memphis," p. 134.
68. Ibid., p. 99.
69. Ibid., p. 168.
70. Ibid., pp. 158–59.
71. Ibid., pp. 160–61.
72. Ibid., p. 161.
73. Brown's song got to number ten in the R&B singles chart following its release in September 1968. *The 500 Greatest Songs of All Time*, http://www.rollingstone.com/music/lists/the-500-greatest-songs-of-all-time-20110407/james-brown-say-it-loud-im-black-and-im-proud-19691231, retrieved 30 April 2012 at 10:51 a.m.; Tuck, *We Ain't*, pp. 340–41.
74. The quote is from black DJ Reggie Lavong speaking to Michael Haralambos at New York's WWRL in 1968, in Gussow, "If Bessie Smith Had Killed," p. 232.
75. Ibid., p. 237.
76. "soul," in Oliver, *Story of the Blues*, p. 167; Cyril Davies, in Oliver, *Blues off the Record*, p. 58.
77. Ibid., p. 168.

Afterword

1. John Baily, "Paul Oliver's Contribution to Ethnomusicology," *Popular Music*, vol. 26, no. 1, 2007, p. 21.

2. Paul Oliver, *Songsters and Saints: Vocal Traditions on Race Records* (Cambridge: Cambridge University Press, 1984).

3. Gilroy, *The Black Atlantic*, pp. 73–80.

4. Adelt, *Blues Music in the Sixties*, p. 2.

5. John Mayall, *Blues Britannia: Can Blue Men Sing the Whites?* Chris Rodley (2009), BBC4, 11:00 p.m., 9 December 2011.

6. See, for instance, Heike Raphael Fernandez, ed., *Blackening Europe: The African American Presence* (New York: Routledge, 2003); Wynn, *Cross the Water Blues*; Wynn and Terry, *Transatlantic Roots Music.*

7. Murray, *Stomping the Blues*, p. 76.

Bibliography

Primary Sources

Paul Oliver's personal notebooks using during his research and record collecting of the 1950s were consulted at Paul Oliver's house. Visits took place several times between October 2009 and August 2012.

Interviews were conducted by the author with Paul Oliver, Tom McGuiness and Bob Groom between October 2009 and August 2012. The transcripts are presented in the Appendix. In addition, the following interviews with Paul Oliver were used:

Garratt, Bob. 'A Conversation with Paul Oliver,' 2/6/2004, From Harrow County School Website http://www.jeffreymaynard.com/Harrow_County/POliver.htm Retrieved 16/06/2012 16:32

Horn, David, 'An Interview with Paul Oliver,' *Popular Music,* 2007, 26/1, pp. 5–13

Jones, Paul. 'Paul Oliver and Michael Roach Interview,' *The Paul Jones Show*, BBC Radio 2, 7pm 30/5/2011

Books & Book Chapters:

Oliver, Paul. *Bessie Smith* (London: Cassell, 1958)

Oliver, Paul. *Blues Fell This Morning: the Meaning of the Blues* (London: Cassell, 1960)

Oliver, Paul. *Conversation with the Blues* (Cambridge University Press, 1997 [sic]1965)

Oliver, Paul. *Screening the Blues: Aspects of the Blues Tradition* (London: Cassell, 1968)

Oliver, Paul. *The Story of the Blues* (London: Penguin, 1972[sic]1969)

Oliver, Paul. *Savannah Syncopators: African Retentions in the Blues* (London: Studio Vista, 1970—reprinted in *Yonder Come the Blues: the Evolution of a Genre* (Cambridge University Press, 2001))

Oliver, Paul. 'Blue-Eyed Blues: The Impact of Blues on European Popular Culture' in Bigsby, C. W. E. (ed), *Approaches to Popular Culture* (Bowling Green: Bowling Green University Press, 1976), pp. 227–239

Oliver, Paul. *Blues Off The Record: Thirty Years of Blues Commentary* (Tunbridge Wells: Batton Press, 1984)

Oliver, Paul. *Songsters and Saints: Vocal Traditions on Race Records* (Cambridge University Press, 1984)

Oliver, Paul. *Blues Fell This Morning: Meaning in the Blues* (Cambridge University Press, 1994)

Journal and magazine articles:

Many of the journal articles used were taken from *Blues Off The Record* (above) and therefore do not appear in the list below, but are specified throughout the text along with the details of their original publication.

Oliver, Paul. 'Sources of Afro-American Folk Song. 1: Down the Line,' *Music Mirror*, May 1954, 1/1, pp. 41–3
Oliver, Paul. 'Another Man Done Gone,' *Music Mirror*, August 1954, 1/ 4, pp. 26–8
Oliver, Paul. 'Chocolate to the Bone,' *Music Mirror*, November 1954, 1/7, pp. 38–41
Oliver, Paul. 'Strut Yo' Stuff,' *Music Mirror*, March 1955, 2/3, pp.4–7
Oliver, Paul. 'In The Sticks,' *Music Mirror*, April 1955, 2/4, pp. 4–6
Oliver, Paul. 'Got the Blues', *Music Mirror*, May 1955, 2/5, pp. 8–10
Oliver, Paul. 'Problems of Collecting Race Records', *Music Mirror*, September 1955, 2/9, pp. 13–14
Oliver, Paul. 'The Folk Blues of Sonny Terry', *Music Mirror*, October 1955, 2/10, pp. 6–7
Oliver, Paul. 'Hometown Skiffle,' *Music Mirror*, February 1956, 3/11, pp. 8–10
Oliver, Paul. 'Devil's Son-In-Law,' *Music Mirror*, March 1956, 3/2, pp. 8–9
Oliver, Paul. 'Forgotten Men,' *Music Mirror*, June 1956, 3/5, pp. 8–9
Oliver, Paul. 'How Long Blues,' *Music Mirror*, July 1956, 3/6, pp.4–6
Oliver, Paul. 'Big Bill Broonzy on Vogue,' *Music Mirror*, August 1956, 3/7, pp.4–6
Oliver, Paul. 'Rock Island Line,' *Music Mirror*, January 1957, 4/1, pp. 6–8
Oliver, Paul. 'Blues Backstage,' *Music Mirror*, May 1957, 4/4, pp. 22–3
Oliver, Paul. 'Introduction to Odetta: An important new folk and blues singer,' *Jazz Music Mirror*, April 1958, 5/7, pp. 6–7
Oliver, Paul. 'Brownie McGhee and Sonny Terry,' *Music Mirror*, June 1958, 5/11, pp. 6–7, 17
Oliver, Paul. 'Screening the Blues,' *Jazz Monthly*, February 1960, 5/12, pp.26–7
Oliver, Paul. 'Apropos 'Blues Fell This Morning,'' *Jazz Monthly*, March 1961, 7/1, pp. 12/20
Oliver, Paul. 'Review of R&B,' *Jazz Monthly*, November 1964, 10/7, p. 24
Oliver, Paul. 'Crossroads Blues,' *Jazz Beat*, February 1965, 1/6, pp. 20–1
Oliver, Paul. 'Blues in the Bran-Tub,' *Jazz Beat*, April 1965, 2/4, pp. 12–3
Oliver, Paul. 'Sellers Market,' *Jazz Beat*, May 1965, 2/5, pp. 12–3
Oliver, Paul. 'Blind Gary Davis,' *Jazz Beat*, July 1965, 2/8, pp. 12–3
Oliver, Paul. 'Blues '65,' *Jazz*, July 1965, 4/7, pp. 26–9
Oliver, Paul. 'Slidin' Delta—Fred McDowell,' *Jazz Beat*, August 1965, 2/9, pp. 12–3, 23
Oliver, Paul. 'Blues Festival '65,' *Jazz Monthly*, December 1965, 11/10, pp. 18–20

Secondary Sources:

Adelt, Ulrich. *Blues Music in the Sixties: A Story in Black and White* (New Brunswick: Rutgers University Press, 2010)
Adorno, Theodor W. 'On the Fetish-Character in Music and the Regression of Listening' in Andrew Amato & Eike Gebhardt, *The Essential Frankfurt School Reader* (Oxford: Blackwell, 1978), pp. 270–299

Advertisement for 1st National Blues Convention, Conway Hall, Red Lion Square London, 7–8 September 1968, *Blues Unlimited*, June 1968, No. 54, p. 19

Allen, Dave. 'Feelin' Bad this Morning: Why the *British* Blues?' *Popular Music*, 2007, Vol. 26 No. 1, pp. 141–56

Audit Bureau of Circulations Ltd, 1949–1961 (London: England, 1961)

Baily, John. 'Paul Oliver's Contribution to Ethnomusicology,' *Popular Music*, 2007, Volume 26/1, pp. 15–22

Baker, Houston A. Jr., *Blues, Ideology and Afro-American Literature: a Vernacular Theory* (Chicago: University of Chicago Press, 1984)

Bane, Michael. *White Boy Singin' the Blues: the Black Roots of White Rock* (Harmondsworth: Penguin, 1982)

Barlow, William. *Looking Up at Down: the Emergence of Blues Culture* (Philadelphia: Temple University Press, 1989)

Barthes, Roland. *Image, Music, Text: Essays Selected and Translated by Stephen Heath* (Oxford University Press, 1984 [sic]1977)

Bezner, Lili Corbus. *Photography and Politics in America: from the New Deal into the Cold War* (Baltimore & London: John Hopkins University Press, 1999)

Blesh, Rudi. *Shining Trumpets: A History of Jazz* (London: Cassell, 1949)

Boyes, Georgina. *The Imagined Village: Culture, Ideology, and the English Folk Revival* (Manchester University Press, 1993)

Breeden, David. M. 'Review of '*Conversation with the Blues*' by Paul Oliver' in *Music Educators Journal*, Vol. 53, No. 6 (Feb. 1967), pp. 97–98

Brocken, Michael. *The British Folk Revival*, 1944–2002 (Aldershot: Ashgate, 2003)

Broonzy, Big Bill and Bruynoghe, Yannick. *Big Bill Blues* (London: Cassell, 1955)

Charters, Samuel B. *The Country Blues*, (New York: Da Capo, 1975 [sic]1959)

Collins, Shirley. *America Over the Water* (London: SAF Publishing, 2005)

Cooke, Mervyn. 'Review—'*Conversation with the Blues*' by Paul Oliver,' *Music & Letters*, Vol. 79 No. 4, (Nov. 1998), pp. 638–639

Cone, James H. *The Spirituals and The Blues* (New York: Seabury, 1972)

Cowen, Tyler. *In Praise of Commercial Culture* (Harvard University Press, 2000)

Davis, Angela Y. *Blues Legacies and Black Feminism: Gertrude 'Ma' Rainey, Bessie Smith and Billie Holiday* (New York: Vintage, 1998)

Davis, Francis. *The History of the Blues: the Roots, the Music, the People* (Da Capo, 2003)

Dawbarn, Bob. 'This could have been THE book on the Blues,' *Melody Maker*, April 2 1960, p. 8

Dawbarn, Bob. 'Are British Acts just imitating the Negro Sound?' *Melody Maker*, June 26 1965, p. 8

Demetre, Jacques and Chauvard, Marcel. 'Land of Blues,' *Jazz Journal*, 1960, Vol. 13 Issues 3, 5, 7–10

Dewe, Mike. *The Skiffle Craze* (Aberystwyth: Planet, 1998)

DeVeaux, Scott. 'Constructing the Jazz Tradition: Jazz Historiography,' *Black American Literature Forum*, Fall 1991, Vol. 25 Issue 3, pp. 525–60

Dougan, John. 'Objects of Desire: Canon Formation and Blues Record Collecting,' *Journal of Popular Music Studies,* April 2006, Vol. 18, pp. 40–65

Douglas, Susan J. *Listening In: Radio and the American Imagination* (University of Minnesota Press; London, 1999)

DuBois, W. E. B. *The Souls of Black Folk* (Oxford University Press, 2008 [sic]1903)

Ellison, Ralph. *Invisible Man* (Harmondsworth: Penguin 1952)

Ellison, Ralph. *Shadow and Act* (New York: Signet; 1966)
Ellison, Ralph. 'Remembering Jimmy,' *Jazz Journal*, November 1958, 11/11, pp.10–11
Ellison, Ralph. 'The Charlie Christian Story,' *Jazz Journal*, May 1959, 12/5, pp. 7–8
Evans, David. *Big Road Blues: Tradition and Creativity in the Folk Blues* (California: Da Capo, 1982)
Evans, David. (ed), *Ramblin' On My Mind: New Perspectives on the Blues* (Chicago: University of Illinois Press, 2008)
Fairclough, Adam. *Better Day Coming: Blacks and Equality, 1890–2000* (London: Penguin, 2002)
Feld, Steven. 'Communication, Music, and Speech about Music,' in Charles Keil & Steven Feld (eds), *Music Grooves* (Chicago; University of Chicago Press, 1994), pp. 77–95
Ferris, William. *Give My Poor Heart Ease: Voices of the Mississippi Blues* (University of North Carolina, 2009)
Filene, Benjamin. *Romancing the Folk: Public Memory and American Roots Music* (Chapel Hill: University of North Carolina Press, 2000)
Floyd, Samuel A. Jr. *The Power of Black Music: Interpreting its History from Africa to the United States* (Oxford: Oxford University Press, 1995)
Ford, Robert. 'Paul Oliver: A Selective Bibliography,' *Popular Music*, 2006, Vol. 26 Issue 1, pp. 157–86
Frisch, Michael. 'Oral History and *Hard Times*: A review essay,' in Perks, A. & Thompson, A. (eds), *The Oral History Reader* (London: Routledge, 1998), pp. 29–37
Frith, Simon. *Music For Pleasure: Essays in the Sociology of Pop* (New York: Routledge, 1988)
Frith, Simon. *Performing Rites: Evaluating Popular Music* (Oxford University Press, 2002 [sic]1996)
Frith, Simon. 'Playing with Real Feeling: Making Sense of Jazz in Britain,' *New Formations*, No. 4, Spring 1, 1988, pp. 7-24; p. 22
Frith, Simon & Horne, Howard. *Art Into Pop* (London & New York: Methuen, 1987)
Garon, Paul. *Blues and The Poetic Spirit* (London: Eddison Press Ltd, 1975)
Gilroy, Paul. *The Black Atlantic: Modernity and Double Consciousness* (London: Verso, 1993)
Gioia, Ted. *Delta Blues: the Life and Times of the Mississippi Masters* (London: W.W. Norton, 2008)
Gray, Michael. *The Bob Dylan Encyclopedia* (London: Continuum, 2006)
Grele, Ronald J. 'Movement Without Aim: Methodological and Theoretical Problems in Oral History' in R. Perks & A. Thompson (eds), *The Oral History Reader* (London: Routledge, 1998), pp. 38–52
Gruver, Rod. 'A Closer Look at the Blues,' *Blues World* (January 1970), No. 26/4, pp. 4–10
Gussow, Adam. '"If Bessie Smith Had Killed Some White People," Racial Legacies, the Blues Revival, and the Black Arts Movement,' in Lisa Gail Collins and Margo Natalie Crawford (eds), *New Thoughts on the Black Arts Movement* (New Brunswick; Rutgers University Press, 2006), pp.227–52
Hadler, Jeffrey. 'Remus Orthography: the History of the Representation of the African-American Voice,' *Journal of Folklore Research*, Vol. 35 No. 2, (May-Aug, 1998), pp. 99–126

Hagstrom Miller, Karl. *Segregating Sound: Inventing Folk and Pop Music in the Age of Jim Crow* (Durham and London; Duke University Press, 2010)

Hall, Peter. *Cities in Civilization* (London: Weidenfeld & Nicolson, 1998)

Harris, William. 'Manuals for Black Militants,' *The Antioch Review*, Vol. 27 No. 3 (Autumn, 1967), p. 408–16

Hamilton, Marybeth. *In Search of the Blues: black voices, white visions* (London: Jonathan Cape, 2007)

Hangen, Tona. 'Man of the Hour: Walter A. Maier and Religion by Radio on the Lutheran Hour' in Hilmes, M. & Loviglio, J. (eds), *Radio Reader: Essays in the Cultural History of Radio* (London: Routledge, 2002), pp.113–134

Harper, Colin. *Dazzling Stranger: Bert Jansch and the British Folk and Blues Revival* (London: Bloomsbury, 2000)

Harris, Rex. *Jazz* (London: Penguin, 1952)

Harris, Rex. Jazz: New Music with Ancient Roots,' *Radio Times*, July 27, 1956

Harris, William. 'Manuals for Black Militants,' *The Antioch Review*, Vol. 27 No. 3 (Autumn, 1967), pp. 408–16

Harrison, Daphne Duval. *Black Pearls: Blues Queens of the 1920s* (New Brunswick: Rutgers University Press, 1988)

Harrison, Max. 'The Blues: review of *The Story of the Blues* by Paul Oliver,' *The Musical Times*, Vol. 111, No. 1523, (Jan. 1970), pp. 48–9

Herbert, Robert L. *From Millet to Leger: Essays in Social Art History* (London: Yale University Press, 2002)

Herskovitz, Melville. *The American Negro* (New York: Knopf, 1928)

Hildebrand, Lee. 'Chris Strachwitz: The Life of a Sound Catcher,' *Living Blues,* February 2011, Issue #211, 42/1, pp.28–33

Hobsbawm, Eric & Ranger, Terence (eds). *The Invention of Tradition* (Cambridge: Cambridge University Press, 1983)

Hoggart, Richard. *The Uses of Literacy* (London: Chatto and Windus, 1957)

Holt, Thomas C. & Brown, Elsa B. *Major Problems in African American-History: from Freedom to 'Freedom Now,' 1865–1990s* (Houghton Mifflin, 2000)

Horn, David. 'Introduction,' *Popular Music*, 2006, Vol. 26 Issue 1, pp. 1–4

House, Roger. *Blue Smoke: The Recorded Journey of Big Bill Broonzy* (Louisiana State University Press, 2010)

Huggins, Nathan I. *Harlem Renaissance* (London: OUP, 1971)

Hyman, Stanley Edgar. 'The Folk Tradition' (1958), in Alan Dundes (ed) *Mother Wit from the Laughing Barrel: readings in the Interpretation of Afro-American Folklore* (New York & London: Garland, 1981[sic]1973)

Iggers, George G. *Historiography in the Twentieth Century: from Scientific Objectivity to the Postmodern Challenge* (Middletown: Wesleyan University Press, 1997)

Jackson, Arthur. 'Review of Big Bill Bronzy in Cambridge,' *Jazz Journal*, December 1952, 5/12, p. 3

Jewell, Derek. Advertisement for *Screening the Blues, Blues Unlimited,* November 1968, No. 57, p. 27

Jones. LeRoi (Amiri Baraka). *Blues People: The Negro Experience in White America and the Music that developed from it* (New York: Morrow, 1963)

Jones, Max. 'On Blues,' in Albert J. McCarthy (ed), *The PL Yearbook of Jazz* (London: Nicholson & Watson, 1946), pp. 71–107

Jones, Max and Harris, Rex. 'Collector's Corner,' *Melody Maker*, January 12 1946, p.4; January 26 1946, p.4; April 4 1946, p.4

Jones, Max. 'Josh White Pleases the Mums and Dads', *Melody Maker*, 27/908, February 10 1951, pp. 6/9

Jones, Max. 'Blues from the Gutter,' *Melody Maker*, December 19 1959, p. 25

Kardiner, Abraham and Ovesey, Lionel. *The Mark of Oppression: Explorations in the Personality of the American Negro* (World Publishing Co., 1962)

Keil, Charles. *Urban Blues* (Chicago: University of Chicago Press, 1966)

Keith, Michael. *Race, Riots and Policing: Lore and Disorder in a Multi-racist Society* (London: UCL Press, 1993)

Kellett, Andrew. 'Born in Chicago: the Impact of the Paul Butterfield Blues Band on the British Blues "Network," 1964–1970,' in Neil Wynn and Jill Terry (eds), *Transatlantic Roots Music: Folk, Blues, and National Identities* (Jackson: University Press of Mississippi, 2012), pp. 179–204

Kelley, Robin D. G. 'Notes on "Deconstructing the Folk"' in *American Historical Review*, December 1992, pp. 1400–1408

Kelley, Robin D. G. '"We Are Not What We Seem": Rethinking Black Working-class Opposition in the Jim Crow South' in *The Journal of American History*, June 1993, Vol. 80 Issue 1, pp. 75–112

Kolchin, Peter. *American Slavery, 1619–1877* (London: Penguin, 1993)

Korner, Alexis. 'Big Bill Broonzy: some personal memories,' *Jazz Journal*, March 1958, 11/3, p. 1

Korner, Alexis. 'The Evolution of Muddy Waters,' *Recorded Folk Music,* Sep-Oct 1959, Vol. 2, pp. 5–8

Lambert, G. E. 'Blues Fell This Morning,' *Jazz Monthly*, February 1961, 6/12, pp. 28–9

Lang, Iain. *Jazz in Perspective: the background of the Blues* (London: Hutchinson & Co., 1947)

Larkin, Philip. 'A Racial Art: *Blues Fell This Morning* by Paul Oliver,' *Observer*, 27 March 1960, in Richard Palmer and John White (eds), *Larkin's Jazz: Essays and Reviews 1940-1984*. (London: Continuum, 1999[sic]2001), pp. 43–4

Levine, Lawrence. *Black Culture and Black Consciousness: Afro-American Folk Thought from Slavery to Freedom* (Oxford University Press, 1978)

Levine, Lawrence. 'The Historian and the Icon: Photography and the History of the American People in the 1930s,' in Carl Fleishhauer and Beverly W. Brannan (eds), *Documentary America, 1935–1943* (Berkeley, London & L.A.: University of California Press, 1988), pp. 15–42

Lewis, David Levering. *When Harlem Was In Vogue* (Oxford: OUP, 1979)

Lipsitz, George. *Time Passages: Collective Memory and American Popular Culture.* (London & Minneapolis: University of Minnesota Press, 1994 [sic]1990)

Litwack, Leon F. *Trouble In Mind: Black Southerners in the Age of Jim Crow* (New York: Alfred A. Knopf, 1999)

Locke, Alain. *The Negro & His Music* (Port Washington: Kennikat Press, 1936)

Lomax, Alan. *Mister Jelly Roll: The Fortunes of Jelly Roll Morton—New Orleans Creole and 'Inventor of Jazz'* (London: Pan Books Ltd, 1959[sic1952])

Lomax, Alan. *The Land Where the Blues Began* (Patheon Books, 1993)

Longenbach, James. *Modernist Poetics of History: Pound, Eliot, and the Sense of the Past* (Princeton: Princeton University Press, 1987)

Lowe, John. 'Palette of Fire: the Aesthetics of Propaganda in *Black Boy* and *In the Castle of My Skin*' in *Mississippi Quarterly*, Fall 2008, Vol. 61, Issue 4, p. 565

Lowenstein, Dora and Dodd, Philip (eds). *According to the Rolling Stones* (Phoenix: London, 2003)

McCarthy, Albert (ed). *The PL Yearbook of Jazz* (London: Hutchison & Co., 1946)

McCarthy, Albert. 'Lonnie Johnson,' *Jazz Journal*, June 1952, 5/6, pp. 1–2

McCarthy, Albert. 'Blues Recording Fund,' *Jazz Monthly*, 6/1, March 1960, p. 3

Mezzrow, Mezz with Wolfe, B. *Really the Blues* (London: Corgi, 1961 [sic]1946)

Middleton, Richard. *Studying Popular Music* (Milton Keynes: Open University Press, 1990)

Millichap, Joseph. 'James Agee, Walker Evans, and the Dialectic of Documentary: Representation in *Let Us Now Praise Famous Men*' in *Southern Quarterly*, Fall 2010, 48/1, pp. 81–99

Mitchell, Gillian. *The North American Folk Music Revival: Nation and Identity in United States and Canada, 1945–1980* (Aldesrhot: Ashgate, 2007)

Moglen, Seth. *Mourning Modernity: Literary Modernism and the Injuries of American Capitalism* (Stanford: Stanford University Press, 2007)

Muir, Peter. *Long Lost Blues: Popular Music in America, 1850–1920* (Chicago: University of Illinois Press, 2009)

Munslow, Alun. *Deconstructing History* (London: Routledge, 1997)

Murray, Albert. *Stomping the Blues* (London: Quartet Books, 1975)

Myrdal, Gunnar. *An American Dilemma: the Negro Problem and Modern Democracy* (London: Harper & Row, 1962 [sic]1944)

Myrdal, Gunnar. *Black and African-American Studies: American Dilemma, the Negro Problem and Modern Democracy* (Transaction, 1995)

Napier, Simon. 'Review of 'The Story of the Blues,'' *Blues Unlimited,* September 1969, No. 65, p. 20

Natanson, Nicholas. *The Black Image in the New Deal: The Politics of FSA Photography* (University of Tennessee Press, 1992)

Newton, Francis. *The Jazz Scene* (Harmondsworth: Penguin, 1961 [sic]1958)

Nicholls, David G. *Conjuring the Folk: Forms of Modernity in African America* (Ann Arbor: University of Michigan Press, 2000)

Oakley, Giles. *The Devil's Music: a History of the Blues* (Da Capo, 1976)

Olderman, Raymond M. 'Ralph Ellison's Blues and "Invisible Man,"' *Wisconsin Studies in Contemporary Literature,* (Summer 1966), Vol. 6 No. 2, p. 11

Palmer, Robert. *Deep Blues: A Musical and Cultural History, from the Mississippi Delta to Chicago's South Side to the World* (Harmondsworth: Penguin, 1981)

Panassie, Hugues. 'A Date with the Blues,' *Melody Maker,* 27/939, September 1951, pp. 9

Parsonage, Catherine. 'Fascination and Fear: Responses to Early Jazz in Britain,' in Neil A. Wynn (ed), *Cross the Water Blues: African American Music in Europe* (Jackson: University Press of Mississippi, 2007) pp. 89–105

Patterson, Anita. 'Jazz, Realism and the Modernist Lyric: The Poetry of Langston Hughes' in *Modern Language Quarterly,* Dec 2000, 61/ 4, pp. 651–82

Pearson, Barry Lee. *'Sounds Good To Me'—The Bluesman's Story* (Philadelphia, University of Pennsylvania Press, 1984)

Perks, A. & Thompson, A. (eds), *The Oral History Reader* (London: Routledge, 1998)

Peterson, Richard A. *Creating Country Music: Fabricating Authenticity* (Chicago: University of Chicago Press, 1999)

Portelli, 'What Makes Oral History Different,' in R. Perks & A. Thompson (eds), *The Oral History Reader* (London: Routledge, 1998), pp. 63–74

Price, Derrick. 'Surveyors and Surveyed: Photography out and about' in Liz Wells (ed), *Photography: A Critical Introduction*. 4th Edition (London: Routledge, 2009)

Ramsey, Frederic Jr. *Been Here and Gone* (New Jersey: Rutgers University Press, 1960)

Ramsey, Frederic & Smith, Charles E. (eds), *Jazzmen* (London: Harcourt Brace Jovanovich, 1939)

Raphael Fernandez, Heike (ed). *Blackening Europe: the African American Presence* (Routledge, 2003)

'Review of National Blues Convention,' *Blues Unlimited*, November 1968, No. 57, p. 16

'Review of 'The 2nd National Blues Convention, 1969, Conway Hall, 21st/22nd September,' *Blues Unlimited*, November 1969, No. 67, p. 16

Richards, Keith. *Life: Keith Richards* (W&N, 2010)

Riesman, Bob. *I Feel So Good: The Life and Times of Big Bill Broonzy* (Chicago: University of Chicago Press, 2011)

Rosengarten, Theodore. *All God's Dangers: The Life of Nate Shaw* (University of Chicago Press, 2000)

Roy, W. G. *Reds, Whites, and Blues: Social Movements, Folk Music, and Race in the United States* (Princeton: Princeton University Press, 2010)

Schmeisser, Iris. '"Un Saxophone en Mouvement"? Josephine Baker and the Primitivist Reception of Jazz in Paris in the 1920s,' in Neil Wynn (ed), *Cross the Water Blues: African American Music in Europe* (Jackson: University Press of Mississippi, 2007), pp. 106–24

Schwartz, Roberta Freund. *How Britain Got the Blues: the Transmission and Reception of American Style Blues in the United Kingdom* (Aldershot: Ashgate, 2007)

Schwartz, Roberta Freund. 'Preaching the Gospel of the Blues: Blues Evangelists in Britain' in Neil A. Wynn (ed), *Cross the Water Blues: African American Music in Europe* (Jackson: University Press of Mississippi, 2007), pp. 145–166

Shapiro, Harry. *Alexis Korner: The Biography* (London: Bloomsbury, 1996)

Shapiro, Nat and Hentoff, Nat. *Hear Me Talkin' To Ya: The Story of Jazz as Told by the Men Who Made it* (New York: Dover Publications, 1966 [sic]1955)

Sharpless, Rebecca. "The History of Oral History," in Thomas L. Charlton, Lois E. Myers, Rebecca Sharpless, Leslie Roy Ballard (eds). *The History of Oral History: Foundations and Methodology* (Altamira, 2007), pp. 9–32

Sitkoff, Harvard. *A New Deal for Blacks: the emergence of Civil Rights as a National Issue: the Depression Decade, 30th Anniversary Ed.* (Oxford University Press: Oxford, 2009)

Skoog, Lawrence. 'The Negro in America: His Life and Times,' *Blues Unlimited*, June 1969, No. 63, pp. 4–7

Smith, Graham. *When Jim Crow Met John Bull: Black American Soldiers in World War II* (London: IB Taurus & Co. Ltd, 1987)

Smith, Jeff. 'Folk Music Branches Out,' *Melody Maker*, November 21, 1959, p. 13

Sontag, Susan. *On Photography* (London: Penguin, 1977)

Spencer, Jon Michael. *Blues and Evil* (Knoxville: University of Tennessee Press, 1993)

Spencer, Jon Michael. 'Blues and Evil: Theomusicology and Afrocentricity' in Robert Sacre' (ed), *Saints and Sinners: Religion, Blues and (D)evil in African-American Music and Literature* (Liege: Belgium, 1996), pp. 37–51

Standish, Tony. 'Muddy Waters in London—Part II,' *Jazz Journal*, Feb 1959, 12/2, pp. 3–6
Stewart-Baxter, Derrick. 'A Date with the Blues,' *Melody Maker*, Sep 15, 1951, 27/939, p.9
Stewart-Baxter, Derrick. 'Preachin' the Blues,' *Jazz Journal*, January 1952, 5/1, pp.6–7
Stewart-Baxter, Derrick. 'Preachin' the Blues,' *Jazz Journal*, April 1952 5/4, pp. 6–7
Stewart-Baxter, Derrick. 'Blues in the Country,' *Jazz Journal*, April 1959, 12/4, pp.3–4
Stewart-Baxter, Derrick. 'Curtis Jones,' *Jazz Journal*, 13/ 3, March 1960, pp.3–4
Stewart-Baxter, Derrick. 'Blues Fell This Morning,' *Jazz Journal*, April 1960, 13/4, pp. 18–9
Stott, William. *Documentary Expression and Thirties America* (Oxford University Press, 1973)
Street, John. 'Shock Waves: the Authoritative Response to Popular Music' in Dominic Strinati and Stephen Wagg (eds), *Come On Down? Popular Media Culture in Post-war Britain* (London: Routledge, 1992), pp. 302–24
Szwed, John. *The Man Who Recorded the World: a biography of Alan Lomax* (London: William Heinemann, 2010)
Szwed, John. 'Review of *Conversation with the Blues* by Paul Oliver,' *Western Folklore,* Vol. 25, No. 3, (Jul. 1966), pp. 202–203
Thompson, Paul. 'The Voice of the Past: Oral History' in R. Perks & A. Thompson (eds), *The Oral History Reader* (London: Routledge, 1998), pp. 21–8
Titon, Jeff Todd. 'Reconstructing the Blues: Reflections on the 1960s Blues Revival' in N. V. Rosenberg (ed), *Transforming Tradition: Folk Music Revivals Examined* (Chicago: University of Illinois Press, 1993), pp. 220–40
Titon, Jeff Todd. 'The Life Story,' *Journal of American Folklore*, July- September 1980, Vol. 93 No. 369, pp. 276- 92
Tracy, Stephen C. (ed). *Write Me a Few of Your Lines: A Blues Reader* (Amherst: University of Massachusetts Press, 1999)
Tratchenberg, Alan. *Reading American Photographs: Images as History—Matthew Brady to Walker Evans* (New York: Hill & Wang, 1989)
Trotter, Joe William Jr. *The African American Experience: Volume II, from Reconstruction* (Houghton Mifflin: Boston, 2001), pp. 373–401
Tuck, Stephen. *We Ain't What We Ought to Be: The Black Freedom Struggle from Emancipation to Obama* (Belknap Harvard; London, 2010)
Von Eschen, Penny Marie. *Satchmo Blows Up the World: Jazz Ambassadors Play the Cold War* (Harvard University Press, 2004)
Wald, Elijah. *Escaping the Delta: Robert Johnson and the Invention of the Blues* (Amistad: New York, 2004)
Wald, Elijah. *Josh White: Society Blues* (University of Massachusetts Press: Amherst, 2000)
Ward, Brian. *Just My Soul Responding: Rhythm & Blues, black consciousness and race relations* (Berkeley: University of California Press, 1998)
White, Hayden. *Metahistory: the Historical Imagination in Nineteenth-Century Europe* (Baltimore: John Hopkins Press, 1973)
White, Hayden. 'Historical Text as Literary Artifact' in Hayden White, *Tropics of Discourse: Essays in Cultural Criticism* (London: John Hopkins University Press, 1978), pp. 81–100
Wright, Richard. *Black Boy: A Record of Childhood and Youth* (London: Longman, 1945)
Wright, Richard. *Native Son* (Harmondsworth: Penguin, 1940)
Wright, Richard. *12 Million Black Voices* (New York: Basic Books, 2008, c1941)

Wyman , Bill and Havers, Richard. *Bill Wyman's Blues Odyssey* (DK Publishing, 2001)
Wynn, Neil A. (ed), *Cross the Water Blues: African American Music in Europe* (Jackson: University Press of Mississippi, 2007)
Wynn, Neil A. & Terry, Jill (eds). *Transatlantic Roots Music: Folk, Blues, and National Identities* (Jackson: University Press of Mississippi, 2012)

Sound Recordings

Blues Fell This Morning: Rare Recordings of Southern Blues Singers, LP, (1960)
The Groundhogs, *Blues Obituary*, Arkama LP5271 LP (1969)

Television & Radio Programs

Black Wax: Gil Scott-Heron, Robert Mugge (1982), Sky Arts 1, 10pm, 9/7/2012
Blues Britannia: Can Blue Men Sing the Whites? Chris Rodley (2009), BBC4, 11pm, 9/12/2011

Websites & Podcasts

'Black and White Minstrel Creator Dies,' www.guardian.co.uk, 29/8/2002, http://www.guardian.co.uk/media/2002/aug/29/broadcasting2 retrieved 23/07/2012 at 16:28
'Conversation with Big Bill Broonzy, Memphis Slim and Sonny Boy Williamson,' Cultural Equity Research Center, http://research.culturalequity.org/get-audio-detailed recording.do?recordingId=11941 retrieved 27/6/2011 at 15:45
European Blues Asssociation, 'Michael Roach interview with Paul Oliver,' http://www.euroblues.org/members/podcast, retrieved 1/7/2011
Fox, Charles. 'Book & Disc Review: Blues Fell This Morning, Paul Oliver,' *Gramophone*, August 1960, p. 91 http://www.gramophone.net/Issue/Page/August%201960/91/853199/ Retrieved 20/6/2012 at 17:15
Seasick Steve's appearance on British TV in October 2009. http://news.bbc.co.uk/1/hi/entertainment/8310377.stm Retrieved 5/4/2011 at 12:30pm
Rolling Stone, *The 500 Greatest Songs of All Time*, http://www.rollingstone.com/music/lists/the-500-greatest-songs-of-all-time20110407/james-brown-say-it-loud-im-black-and-im-proud-19691231 Retrieved 30/04/2012 at 10:51
The Paul Oliver 70th Birthday Tribute, www.bluesworld.com/PAULOLIVER.HTML retrieved 22/8/2009 at 8:02
The Year of the Blues 2003 http://www.yearoftheblues.org/about.asp Retrieved 19/04/2012 at 14:09

Index

House, Eddie "Son," 5, 138, 143, 175–76, 184